STRATEGIC STUDIES INSTITUTE

The Strategic Studies Institute (SSI) is part of the U.S. Army War College and is the strategic-level study agent for issues related to national security and military strategy with emphasis on geostrategic analysis.

The mission of SSI is to use independent analysis to conduct strategic studies that develop policy recommendations on:

- Strategy, planning, and policy for joint and combined employment of military forces;

- Regional strategic appraisals;

- The nature of land warfare;

- Matters affecting the Army's future;

- The concepts, philosophy, and theory of strategy; and,

- Other issues of importance to the leadership of the Army.

Studies produced by civilian and military analysts concern topics having strategic implications for the Army, the Department of Defense, and the larger national security community.

In addition to its studies, SSI publishes special reports on topics of special or immediate interest. These include edited proceedings of conferences and topically oriented roundtables, expanded trip reports, and quick-reaction responses to senior Army leaders.

The Institute provides a valuable analytical capability within the Army to address strategic and other issues in support of Army participation in national security policy formulation.

i

Strategic Studies Institute
and
U.S. Army War College Press

THE CHINESE PEOPLE'S LIBERATION ARMY IN 2025

Roy Kamphausen
David Lai
Editors

July 2015

The views expressed in this report are those of the authors and do not necessarily reflect the official policy or position of the Department of the Army, the Department of Defense, or the U.S. Government. Authors of Strategic Studies Institute (SSI) and U.S. Army War College (USAWC) Press publications enjoy full academic freedom, provided they do not disclose classified information, jeopardize operations security, or misrepresent official U.S. policy. Such academic freedom empowers them to offer new and sometimes controversial perspectives in the interest of furthering debate on key issues. This report is cleared for public release; distribution is unlimited.

*****

*****

Comments pertaining to this report are invited and should be forwarded to: Director, Strategic Studies Institute and U.S. Army War College Press, U.S. Army War College, 47 Ashburn Drive, Carlisle, PA 17013-5010.

*****

All Strategic Studies Institute (SSI) and U.S. Army War College (USAWC) Press publications may be downloaded free of charge from the SSI website. Hard copies of this report may also be obtained free of charge while supplies last by placing an order on the SSI website. SSI publications may be quoted or reprinted in part or in full with permission and appropriate credit given to the U.S. Army Strategic Studies Institute and U.S. Army War College Press, U.S. Army War College, Carlisle, PA. Contact SSI by visiting our website at the following address: *www.StrategicStudiesInstitute.army.mil.*

*****

The Strategic Studies Institute and U.S. Army War College Press publishes a monthly email newsletter to update the national security community on the research of our analysts, recent and forthcoming publications, and upcoming conferences sponsored by the Institute. Each newsletter also provides a strategic commentary by one of our research analysts. If you are interested in receiving this newsletter, please subscribe on the SSI website at *www.StrategicStudiesInstitute.army.mil/newsletter.*

ISBN 1-58487-688-3

CONTENTS

FOREWORD

I am pleased to introduce The Chinese People's Liberation Army of 2025 which is the 2014 edition of an ongoing series on the People's Liberation Army (PLA) co-published by the Strategic Studies Institute (SSI), the National Bureau of Asian Research (NBR), and the United States Pacific Command (USPACOM). This volume builds on previous volumes and identifies potential trajectories for PLA force modernization and mission focus, and how these potential changes could impact external actors.

This volume is of special relevance today in light of the profound changes occurring within the PLA. I have spent a considerable amount of my professional career in the Western Pacific and, during that time, I have witnessed first-hand the rapid expansion of the size and capability of the PLA as it pursues a long-term, comprehensive military modernization program. China's desire to develop a military commensurate with its diverse interests is both legitimate and understandable. The challenge for USPACOM, and the reason why this volume is timely and important, is to understand how China will employ this growing military capability in support of its interests.

The scholarship presented in this edition addresses the uncertainty surrounding the potential direction of the PLA by examining three distinct focus areas: Domestic, External, and Technological Drivers of PLA Modernization; Alternative Futures for the PLA; and, Implications for the Region, World, and U.S.-China Relations. The analysis provides an insightful perspective into the factors shaping and propelling the PLA's modernization, its potential future orientation ranging from internally focused to globally focused, and how the PLA's choices may impact China's relations with its neighbors and the world.

NBR and SSI have, once again, provided an outstanding contribution to the growing body of research and analysis on the PLA. The Chinese People's Liberation Army of 2025 is a timely and important volume that will increase our understanding of the PLA at a time in history that requires a well-informed approach to the expanding role of China.

HARRY B. HARRIS, JR
Admiral, USN
Commander, U.S. Pacific Command

OVERVIEW

CHAPTER 1

INTRODUCTION

Roy Kamphausen
R. Lincoln Hines

The 2014 Chinese People's Liberation Army (PLA) conference occurred during a time of flaring regional tensions in the East and South China Seas, increasing military modernization by China and its neighbors, and a potentially changing Chinese approach to its regional security environment. In light of these continuing developments, the topic of this conference and this volume—*The Chinese People's Liberation Army in 2025*—is both timely and prescient. China's increasing military capabilities are creating complex shifts in regional security calculations. To understand the trends in China's military modernization and its implications for regional and global security, conference participants assessed: 1) the various domestic, international, and technological drivers of China's military modernization; 2) potential trajectories for PLA modernization; 3) and the implications of PLA modernization for the Asia-Pacific, the international order, and U.S.-China relations.

The bulk of this volume presents the papers that resulted from the 2014 Conference. This chapter discusses key contemporary developments that are pertinent to the topic of this volume. These developments include China's President Xi Jinping's relationship with the PLA, China's changing approach to regional security challenges, and developments in the Asia-Pacific and international security environments. After reviewing these developments, this chapter discusses the methodological framework for this volume, and provides a chapter-by-chapter summary of each of the papers included in this volume. This chapter concludes with a discussion of key themes that emerge from this analysis.

XI JINPING AND THE PLA

China's President Xi Jinping has quickly consolidated power during his first 2 years in office, despite both internal and external challenges to his leadership. Economically, Xi has stated that the market should play the "decisive" role in China's economy to support his so-called "China Dream," but still sees an important role for the state as an economic actor. Xi has also moved quickly to make reforms in domestic policy areas, such as banking and social policy (one-child policy and the *hukou* (户口) system). Xi also became Chairman of the Central Military Commission (CMC) at the same time as he became General Secretary of the Chinese Communist Party (CCP) in November 2012, unlike his predecessor, Hu Jintao, whose assumption of the CMC chairmanship was delayed for 2 years. Likewise, Xi has taken charge of the two new structures brought into being by the Fall 2013 Third Plenum of the 18th Party Congress: the National Security Commission and the Central Leading Group for Comprehensive Deepening of Reforms (CLGCDR).

But it is Xi's relentless implementation of a sweeping anti-corruption campaign that is perhaps the strongest indicator of his consolidation of power. Staking the Chinese Communist Party's future—as well as his own personal survival—on the campaign's success, Xi has provided top-level support for an anti-corruption campaign that has ensnared high-ranking civilian and military officials and potential rivals, such as Bo Xilai (薄熙来) and Zhou Yongkang (周永康). This anti-corruption campaign has also targeted top leaders of the PLA. Most recently, former CMC Vice Chairman General Xu Caihou (徐才厚) was expelled from the CCP and charged by prosecutors with accepting bribes in exchange for promotions. Xu is the highest-ranking PLA officer to be charged in court, and his retired status afforded no protection against prosecution, as had previously been the norm in Chinese politics. (Although Zhou Yongkang, a more senior but also already-retired Politburo Standing Committee Member, has also now been expelled by the Party and charged by prosecutors.) Whereas some observers have judged that taking on a "big tiger" of the PLA was part of an effort to gain control of the PLA, it seems more likely that Xi took his anti-corruption campaign to the top ranks of the PLA precisely because he had consolidated sufficient power to do so.

Xi's record of military service, albeit limited, and his status as a "princeling" or offspring of a top leader (His father, Xi Zhongxun (习仲勋), was a first generation CCP leader who served in several Party and People's Republic of China (PRC) government roles, ultimately ending up as the Party Secretary and Governor of Guangdong Province) are often offered as evidence Xi has a special relationship with the PLA. But these facts, important as they may be, are not sufficient to explain how Xi was able to take charge so rapidly. Additional rationales are also required; perhaps Xi has taken charge of a PLA that already wants to be led in the direction he seems inclined to be heading. For instance, it certainly appears that at least some sectors of the PLA seem anxious to try out the newer enhanced capabilities now resident in the

PLA. Because these new capabilities create new and different policy options, they might be of interest to the leadership, which might be inclined to see their use. A second instance in which Xi's goals might be in consonance with broader PLA desires concerns anti-corruption efforts. There are frequent reports of PLA officer discontent with rampant corruption, as well as a desire to more rapidly professionalize, despite official enjoinders that the PLA will always remain a "Party Army." Xi may be tapping into that impulse to some extent.

There remain some concerns, however, as to exactly how much control over the PLA Xi actually has. During his trip to India and visit with India's Prime Minister (PM) Narendra Modi in September 2014, there was a simultaneous incursion by PLA troops into the Ladakh region along the Line of Control (LOC), reportedly resulting in PM Modi taking Xi to task for the action. Following the trip, Xi reportedly demanded "absolute loyalty" from top-ranking PLA leadership and stated that PLA forces could "improve their combat readiness and sharpen their ability to win a regional war in the age of information technology." A potential second example occurred some months later. In November 2014, the PLA Air Force (PLAAF) rolled out the new J-31 stealth aircraft, reportedly with some specifications very similar to the U.S. Air Force's F-35, precisely during the Asia Pacific Economic Cooperation (APEC) summit in Beijing, which was attended by U.S. President Barack Obama.

In light of these developments, it is important for policymakers to focus on the evolving civil-military relationship, and especially Xi Jinping's interaction with the PLA. As Chairman of the CMC, Xi will continue the PLA's refocus from being a ground force centric military to a more balanced joint force with much stronger naval and air force capabilities. He will also oversee implementation of the Third Plenum's guidance on institutional and structural reform of the PLA, some which have obvious regional security implications. Xi almost certainly wants to have a more effective PLA, but not at the cost of raising regional security concerns.

CHANGING CHINESE APPROACHES TO THE ASIA-PACIFIC REGION

These reforms within the PLA take place as China seems intent to more assertively pursue its interests and claims in disputed maritime domains. Despite long-standing efforts to mitigate regional perceptions of a "China threat," Chinese actions in the East and South China Seas have alarmed both China's neighbors and the United States, as in the last several years China has become increasingly more assertive in staking its territorial claims in its near periphery. Increasingly alarmed by Chinese actions, regional actors have protested on the one hand and sought more active intervention by the United States on the other.

However, the PRC's pursuit of its aims in its "near abroad" have neither broached American "redlines" nor have they escalated confrontations to the point where military conflict seems likely. This approach — often referred to as a "salami slicing" approach — to attaining Chinese national security objectives has taken place in the gray area between normal peacetime and military conflict, albeit with the looming specter of an increasingly more capable Chinese military.

China's declaration of an Air Defense Identification Zone (ADIZ), which covered the airspace over the

Senkaku Islands in the East China Sea, prompted an equally assertive American response including a flight of B-52 bombers through the ADIZ and a presidential statement that the Senkaku Islands were covered under Article 5 of the U.S.-Japan Security Treaty, since they are under the administrative control of Japan. China also placed an oil rig near the disputed Paracel Islands in May 2014, an oddly timed act considering that the PRC and Vietnam had agreed to discussions about joint development in mid-2013. The Philippines, on the other hand, has attempted to settle its dispute with China through international arbitration—a legal effort in which China refuses to participate.

China's gradual or creeping assertiveness begs the question: what is driving China's new assertiveness? Certainly new capabilities and domestic pressure on the CCP to act like a great power (especially since a more restrained approach to conflicting claims in maritime dimensions has often been met with active occupation and/or reinforcement efforts by other claimants) are part of the story. Furthermore, more domestic actors—including state-owned enterprises, provincial and city governments, think tanks, netizens, among others—are engaged in the foreign policy process than previously, often arguing for different sorts of assertiveness. With these various pressures on Chinese foreign policy, it is important to ask: has there been a change in PRC strategy? Two key developments in 2013-14 suggest that subtle shift is underway. In October 2013, the PRC convened a conference on peripheral foreign policy, and Xi Jinping gave a major speech emphasizing the importance of regional relations. While great power relations were still judged to be important, a relative shift in importance toward regional security actors seemed clear.

Then President Xi Jinping gave a keynote speech at the 4th Summit of the Conference on Interaction and Confidence Building Measures in Asia (CICA) in May 2014 CICA Summit in Shanghai. In the speech, Xi argued vigorously for a system in which Asian nations take responsibility for Asia's issues, emphasizing that regional security challenges should be solved by Asian nations themselves. While in later speeches, State Councilor Yang Jiechi (杨洁篪) notably stated that all countries contributions were welcome in the building of a regional security order, the "Asia for Asians" theme is likely to be repeated. These rhetorical changes suggest that China is refocusing on Asia as a principal objective of PRC security policy.

REGIONAL AND INTERNATIONAL SECURITY ENVIRONMENTS

China's broad-based military modernization program and evolving posture toward the Asia-Pacific regional security environment take place within the context of a changing international security context. The stability of the international security system has relied, to a great extent, on the security that U.S. power has often provided to not only maintain its security commitments to allies and security partners, but to also discourage actions that threaten the norms that underpin the international system. However, though the United States remains an indispensable power, its monopoly on power, and thus to some extent the stability of the international system, is being challenged at the margins.

The years 2013-14 were turbulent internationally. Prominent challenges to the global order and the U.S.

capacity to sustain it have arisen in Eastern Europe and the Middle East. In Eastern Europe, Russian President Vladimir Putin's annexation of Crimea represented a flagrant disregard for international norms against territorial annexation, and altered regional security calculations and energy security dynamics. Large parts of the Middle East remain unstable, as Syria's ongoing civil war has reached its third year. The extremist group, the Islamic State of Iraq and the Levant (ISIL), has expanded its area of controlled territory and influence, and has executed American citizens. In light of these developments, the U.S. military has reengaged in Iraq and is now conducting airstrikes inside Syria. This is all occurring as the U.S. military experiencing severe spending cuts that constrain U.S. power projection and military response capabilities.

U.S. budget cuts and emerging crises thus call into question the U.S. capacity to sustain its security commitments in the Asia-Pacific, even holding Chinese activity constant. When an evolving set of capabilities and new apparent focus on the Asia-Pacific region by the PRC are added into the mix, dramatic changes seem possible. The key to determining the sustainability of this system will be determining, in this context, China's capacity for challenging the international system and regional components of this system.

The future-orientation of China's military will depend heavily on factors such as the leadership of President Xi Jinping, the consequences of China's actions in its near region, and continuing developments affecting the regional and global international order. As China continues its rise on world stage, the intentions and the strength of the PLA will become increasingly consequential for the regional and global security. Though it is not possible to predict China's future intentions or capabilities, it is possible to begin thinking about which areas are most likely to drive PLA modernization, possible vectors for PLA modernization, and how regional and global security might look for the PLA in a variety of future scenarios.

OVERVIEW

This volume and the conference that preceded it are deeply indebted to Mr. Lonnie Henley for crafting the conference précis that was provided to authors in the research and writing stage. The précis is essential reading for understanding the background of this effort and for the common frame of reference it provided to chapter authors, and has been included in Chapter 2 in this volume. In the précis, Henley notes the relative lack of clarity from PLA sources as to what PLA modernization objectives are through 2020, much less further into the future, complicating efforts to understand future trajectories. He makes clear, however, that the PLA's main strategic direction continues to be to prepare for a conflict with Taiwan and to deal with U.S. intervention in such a scenario. In developing three potential future scenarios, Henley first lists important variables that shape the futures, including Taiwan's status, U.S. military capabilities in the Asia-Pacific, and internal Chinese stability, among others. He further notes two important constants: China's view of its own history and a deep aversion to political fragmentation of the Chinese state. Henley asserts that some factors are "non-drivers," otherwise important factors that nonetheless will not have much impact on military modernization. Somewhat controversially, Henley includes that the fate of the CCP is a "non-driver" in that it does not rule out, or in, any particular future.

After considering these factors, Henley concludes that three potential futures for the PLA might be usefully explored. The first future is of a PLA that is regionally focused. The second future sees the PLA as having global expeditionary capabilities. The final future is of a PLA that is significantly weakened in reach and scope. Henley states the many permutations that could exist, but argues that these futures cover sufficient breadth to be useful to chapter authors. It is important to note that Phillip Saunders provided a very helpful set of assumptions about the future which participants urged be included in the précis, to which Henley readily agreed.

The remainder of the volume is dedicated to "looking over the horizon" at these alternative futures for the Chinese military in 2025. Chapters 3 to 5 examine the various and likely domestic, external, and technological drivers of China's military modernization. Chapters 6 to 8 discuss the potential alternative futures that could result from the interaction of the aforementioned drivers—a regionally focused PLA, a global expeditionary PLA, and a weakened PLA. Chapters 9 to 11 explore the implications of these alternative vectors of PLA modernization for East Asian regional dynamics, U.S.-China relations, and the global system.

Domestic, External, and Technological Drivers of PLA Modernization.

China's military modernization is and will continue to be driven by a number of variables. The authors in Chapters 3 to 5 assess the most plausible of these drivers. These three inputs can broadly be described as domestic, international, and technological drivers. It is important to note that none of these drivers should be viewed as occurring in isolation from one another. Instead, these variables should be viewed as dynamic and interconnected.

In Chapter 3, Joseph Fewsmith explores the main domestic drivers of PLA modernization. Fewsmith discusses the various domestic drivers that have led China to alter its policy of "avoiding the limelight and keeping a low profile" (*taoguang yanghui* 韬光养晦) introduced by Deng Xiaoping to an approach of "proactively getting some things done" (积极地有所作为) practiced since 2009, when Hu Jintao was in office. Though Fewsmith contends that part of this increasing assertiveness is a natural outgrowth of China's growing economic and military clout, he argues that the timing of China's policy actions suggests that the drivers of China's recent assertive foreign policy are largely domestic.

Fewsmith assesses several domestic factors influencing China's security calculus. These factors include domestic social stability, the role of nationalism, concerns over legitimacy issues, a sense of crisis among the CCP, and the leadership of Xi Jinping and China's new generation of leaders. China's local cadres are often incentivized to pursue interests contrary to the people over whom they govern; consequently, China has seen an uptick in the number of "mass incidents." In addition to these challenges, Fewsmith examines China's growing nationalism and the implications this could have for elite decisionmaking. A further source of domestic pressure discussed by Fewsmith is the increasing discontent among Chinese intellectuals regarding the pace of political reform in China, which have created a "sense of crisis" among China's political elites.

According to Fewsmith, Chinese President Xi Jinping has been quickly consolidating power and has adopted a more assertive foreign policy. This more assertive foreign policy serves to facilitate centralization, as opposition to these efforts can be framed as unpatriotic. Yet, how durable are these factors driving China's assertive foreign policy? Fewsmith contends that, although these trends may reinforce China's assertive posture in the near future, China will be challenged by several socio-economic problems (e.g., an aging population) that may necessitate the Chinese policymakers refocus their attention inward. Fewsmith concludes that these domestic inputs might drive a more regionally oriented force, however these factors would be unlikely to sustain the type of effort required to develop a global expeditionary force.

In addition to these internal drivers, PLA modernization will also be driven by a number of interconnected external variables. In Chapter 4, Eric Heginbotham and Jacob Heim analyze how regional actors, U.S.-China relations, and China's growing overseas interests are likely to affect China's perceived national security interests and the weapons systems that it seeks to procure.

To establish an operational context for parsing the impact of different scenarios on Chinese military requirements, the authors begin with a discussion of East Asian geography and the types of forces China would need to act at three distances from its borders: the immediate periphery (defined as within 1,000 kilometers [km] of China); the broader region (roughly 1,000 to 3,000-km); or areas outside region. Heginbotham and Heim also suggest that, although Chinese force development was optimized for operations in the country's immediate periphery through the early-2000s, it has, for the last decade, placed greater emphasis on adapting its military for broader regional contingencies.

The authors look at how relations with regional and global actors and China's expanding overseas interests could serve to reinforce current trends toward limited power projection and broader regional capabilities. They also discuss current trends that deviate from that trajectory — either toward a force optimized to operate in China's immediate periphery, a global expeditionary force, or a weakened PLA.

According to Heginbotham and Heim, there are a limited range of specific circumstances that could lead the PLA to refocus its military to its immediate periphery. A strong United States with a more adversarial relationship with China could potentially threaten China, spurring Beijing to focus more on short-range capabilities designed for defensive purposes in China's immediate periphery. Similarly, the authors contend that if China views a conflict with Taiwan as likely or if Taiwan appears to be pursuing de jure independence, the PLA may refocus on the periphery.

There are several scenarios that could drive China to accelerate the development of capabilities relevant to wider regional scenarios. Heginbotham and Heim contend this could occur if PRC-Republic of China (ROC) relations remain stable, but China's relationships with other regional neighbors worsen. A military conflict with one or more regional states or attacks on Chinese citizens in these states would provide particularly strong motivation. Heginbotham and Heim also contend that military-industrial cooperation and the formation of meaningful strategic partnerships with regional states could also provide incentives for China to develop certain types of regional military capabilities.

Chapter 4 also discusses scenarios that could make the PLA a more global expeditionary force. A more benign regional environment could provide a more permissive environment for diverting PLA resources to the development of extra-regional expeditionary capabilities. This could occur if China were able to resolve or, more likely, shelve its regional territorial disputes, or if its relations with the United States significantly improved. Threats to overseas Chinese citizens or investments in distant regions could spark domestic political demands for China to develop the forces necessary to protect its interests in those areas. China could also form deeper military-industrial ties with states beyond Asia and might then have added incentives for developing the military capacity to sustain those ties.

Finally, Heginbotham and Heim discuss the various external factors that could result in a weakened PLA. Though the authors note that internal factors are more likely to produce this outcome than external ones, they explore various external drivers that could weaken the PLA. If the PLA were to engage in a protracted and unsuccessful military conflict, public support for military modernization could diminish or resources could be drained more directly by the conflict itself. Diminished access to technology and components from Russia could affect the Chinese ability to produce or maintain certain types of systems. Or support from an outside power for domestic insurgency or terrorism could plausibly contribute to weakening the PLA's ability to fight conventional wars by diverting resources and attention toward domestic counterinsurgency.

In addition to these external drivers, in Chapter 5, Richard Bitzinger and Michael Raska examine the technological drivers of the PLA's military modernization. Bitzinger and Raska explore the PLA's approach to and capacity for innovation, and how these technological factors would serve a weakened, regionally oriented, or a global expeditionary PLA. Overall, this chapter examines China's approach to military modernization, initiatives aimed at reforming China's defense industry, and evaluates these efforts.

Bitzinger and Raska first review literature on the role of innovation in military affairs, defining the parameters by which they evaluate the PLA's innovative capacity. From these parameters, the authors assess the PLA's capabilities for making "disruptive" innovations, and the PLA's capacity for making more incremental innovations. According to the authors, China has been trying to "catch up" with Western powers in terms of defense for the past 150 years with varied levels of success. In the mid-1990s, China instituted reforms to make its defense industry more efficient and responsive to its customer base. As part of its reform efforts, China has attempted to unify, standardize, and legalize its weapons procurement process. China is also making efforts to leverage civil military and dual-use technologies better.

Although China's military innovation lagged behind that of Western powers, China's "latecomer advantage" has enabled it to skip various phases of development. As a latecomer, the PLA has been able to identify and absorb key foreign civil and military technologies. China's military has benefitted from dramatically expanding defense budgets and increased funding for research and development. China has been working on 16 mega projects, with three classified projects. Bitzinger and Raska discuss the likely candidates for these three classified projects: 1) the Shenguang (Divine Light) laser program; 2) the Second Generation Beidou-2 Satellite System; and, 3) a hypersonic vehicle technology project.

Overall, Bitzinger and Raska contend that China's military has benefitted from investing heavily in military modernization, yet the PLA technological modernization still faces several obstacles in terms of innovation. The PLA's indigenous innovative capabilities remain limited and the PLA's technological innovation is still being outpaced by foreign competitors. Furthermore, few Chinese companies have the knowledge, experience, or capacity required for high-level production.

Bitzinger and Raska conclude that China's military might have the capacity for gaining niche asymmetric advantages that may increase its capability as a regionally oriented force, because regionally oriented forces, such as so-called anti-access/area-denial (A2/AD) capabilities may only require incremental innovations. However, Bitzinger and Raska contend that China's current defense industry does not appear set to have the capacity for the type of disruptive innovations necessary for developing a robust global expeditionary force. As for a weakened PLA, the authors contend that China could continue its process of incremental innovations and would likely focus more on developing its defensive capabilities.

Alternative Futures for the PLA.

The aforementioned domestic, external, and technological drivers will produce a wide range of possible alternative futures for the future composition and orientation of the PLA. Authors in Chapters 6 to 8 considered three plausible and distinct, though not necessarily mutually exclusive, futures for the PLA: 1) a regionally focused PLA; 2) a global expeditionary PLA; and, 3) a weakened PLA.

In Chapter 6, Bernard Cole discusses the potential makeup of a PLA focused on regional issues. According to Cole, in such a scenario, Taiwan would still remain a top contingency, but that the PLA's most immediate maritime concern would be establishing sea control in "near seas" or "three seas."

Cole discusses the various changes that might occur in the PLA's orientation and structure to become a regionally oriented force. To meet regional challenges, the PLA's personnel and budget prioritization would likely shift away from the PLA and move toward the PLA Navy (PLAN) and the PLAAF. As the ballistic missile capabilities of these forces continue to increase, the responsibility for controlling China's nuclear forces will likely be divided among the Second Artillery Force (SAF), the PLAN, and PLAAF, with the SAF playing the leading role. Furthermore, Cole contends that the PLA will also likely continue efforts at reforming its personnel management and Professional Military Education (PME). Much of the PLA's reforms will hinge upon the PLA's ability to rid the PLA of corrupt promotion practices and develop a professional, career non-commissioned officer corps.

According to Cole, a regionally oriented China would likely have greater power projection capabilities, such as improved amphibious assault capabilities. With these growing capabilities, the PLA will likely increase the frequency of interregional port calls, and increase its involvement in nontraditional missions, such as counterpiracy and Humanitarian and Disaster Relief (HADR) operations.

The PLA could also become a force with a more global reach. In Chapter 7, Oriana Skylar Mastro explores the potential makeup of a global expeditionary PLA. According to Mastro, the PLA will have to overcome significant hurdles and make several changes to its doctrinal, strategic, and force posture to become a global expeditionary force.

Specifically, Mastro posits a series of changes China would need to make to its doctrine, strategic guidelines, and operational concepts to be able to conduct global expeditionary operations on a limited scale. The PLA would likely move beyond its current doctrinal formulation of "local war under informationized conditions," and seek to develop greater power projection capabilities to carry out "win-win operations." The PLA would also reprioritize certain operational concepts, emphasizing joint island landing campaigns and strategic air raids, thus leveraging the PLA's asymmetric advantages. Furthermore, Mastro contends that the PLA would likely seek to form more institutionalized strategic partnerships necessary for expeditionary concepts.

According to Mastro, the PLA would need to develop the relevant air, naval, and ground forces required to ensure that the PLA could not be denied air and sea space access in areas far from Chinese territory. Additionally, China will need to make significant technological progress in terms of space, cyber, and electronic warfare capabilities. Throughout Chapter 6, Mastro discusses the types of developments in air, sea, and ground power, as well as changes to organization, training, and logistics that the PLA will need to support global expeditionary forces.

From these observations, Mastro discusses what a global expeditionary PLA could mean for China's propensity to use force, as well as regional and global stability. If China gains global capabilities it may alter its grand strategy and move beyond its current regional aims. This could be a positive development if a global PLA becomes enmeshed in the global order and contributes more to global public goods. On the other hand, a global PLA could also interfere in areas around the world where the United States may prefer China to adopt a more "hands-off" approach. Even if China's focus remains regional as it becomes more active globally, newfound capabilities could create a backlash among regional powers and the United States, resulting in regional instability or even armed conflict.

After examining the potential makeup of a regionally focused, as well as a global expeditionary PLA, in Chapter 8, Erin Richter and Daniel Gearin discuss the potential makeup of a weakened PLA. Richter and Gearin explore some of the variables that could lead to a weakened PLA, and how these could reorient China's security concerns, and the new challenges this would present for China.

According to Richter and Gearin, there are several factors that could potentially result in a weakened PLA, but the most probable cause would be domestic — either from social instability or an economic downturn. In the case of social instability or a sharp economic decline, the PLA would likely have to divert resources away from PLA modernization and reallocate these resources toward internal security and self-defense.

A weakened PLA will have to be more selective in how it invests its resources. Richter and Gearin contend that though the PLA would like to have a reformed organizational structure and a more modern order of battle, a weakened PLA would have to refocus its training and make unplanned force reductions. The PLA would also have to slow the development and production of new combat systems and extend maintenance cycles. As a result, the PLA would have declined troop proficiency and combat readiness. The PLA would likely be able to carry out limited defensive military operations in its immediate periphery, but would be unable to meet challenges outside its immediate periphery. Richter and Gearin assess how these changes would affect various branches of the PLA, such as the PLA, PLAN, PLAAF, and the Second Artillery Force. Overall, a weakened PLA could have broader implications for regional security. A weak PLA could potentially encourage China's neighbors to exploit China's weakness. On the other hand, the PLA could also potentially seek to resolve territorial disputes before its military capabilities further deteriorate.

Implications for the Region, World, and U.S.-China Relations.

There are various potential trajectories for the PLA's modernization. Whether the PLA is significantly weakened, anchored regionally, or is a robust global expeditionary force, these futures will have profound implications for East Asian regional security dynamics, U.S.-China relations, and the global system. Authors in Chapters 9 to 11 examine how the aforementioned alternative futures will affect relationships with, and factor into the security calculations of, regional actors and the United States, and ultimately the implications of this for the global system.

In Chapter 9, Michael McDevitt examines the implications of PLA modernization for countries in the Asia-Pacific region. According to McDevitt, China's military modernization is not a new phenomenon, and that China can already "reach out and touch" many countries in its near region. Therefore, for some countries in China's immediate neighborhood, China's military modernization will be threatening regardless of whether it increases, or if the pace begins to slow. For other countries, however, China can use various elements of its "smile diplomacy" to reassure them of China's benign intentions, and allay regional anxieties.

According to McDevitt, China's military modernization, regardless of which vector it takes, will have the same impact on certain countries in China's near periphery. For example, South Korea, Japan, Taiwan, and Vietnam will likely continue their military modernization programs regardless of the vector of China's military modernization. South Korea's primary security threat will likely continue to come from North Korea, and South Korea has ambitious naval modernization plans underway. Japan, Taiwan, and Vietnam are close enough in China's periphery to be highly concerned about China's military modernization program, even if its pace begins to slow.

Further outside the region, countries in Southeast Asia can be divided as follows: countries that are likely to be threatened immediately by China's military modernization efforts; countries that are affected by how China handles its maritime disputes; and countries that are more likely to accommodate China. Countries such as Australia and India are most likely to be concerned about China's naval modernization efforts, particularly its efforts at obtaining global expeditionary capabilities. Nevertheless, McDevitt believes that China can allay regional anxiety through its political, economic, and diplomatic efforts. As for the future composition of the PLA, McDevitt envisions a PLA that is primarily a regional force, with some global expeditionary elements, as these capabilities are not mutually exclusive.

Beyond its implications for regional dynamics, the PLA's modernization will have significant implications for the international system. In Chapter 10, Phillip Saunders explores the implications of the PLA's modernization for the international system. After examining Chinese debates regarding international norms, Saunders argues that China appears to be a "moderate revisionist power." The factors likely to determine China's approach to international norms include China's aversion to a military conflict with the United States, China's global economic ties, its domestic stability, regional stability, and China's power relative to the United States. Overall, Chapter 10 explores how a regionally focused PLA, a global expeditionary PLA, and a weakened PLA could impact the international system.

The first scenario considered by Saunders is that of a China and a PLA that remain focused on regional challenges. This implies a more competitive U.S.-China relationship within Asia. Saunders suggests Beijing would likely seek to moderate competitive tensions with bilateral cooperation on issues of mutual concern and adopt an incrementalist approach to altering the international system. Globally, China would likely pursue strategic partnerships to promote trade and finance rules more amenable to Chinese interests, and to promote the yuan as a global reserve currency. China would remain opposed to any U.S. intervention. Saunders also contends that China could become more active internationally in combating transnational concerns such as terrorism. However, one concern for U.S. policymakers would be that China could develop closer relations with countries hostile to the West when it has concrete interests at stake.

Saunders also examines the implications of a global expeditionary PLA for the international system. According to Saunders, a PLA focused on global power projection implies that China has peacefully resolved its regional disputes and that the United States is comparatively weaker. In such a circumstance, the United States may encourage China to take on greater global responsibilities, and the two could achieve peaceful coexistence. Yet, if China's new position of power is a result of failed U.S. policy, U.S. policymakers may approach Beijing with more suspicion. A global expeditionary PLA may also be motivated to meet security challenges in alternative security institutions outside the purview of the United Nations. It is likely, however, that the PLA would be selective in its use of force, considering that Chinese elites view U.S. interventions in Iraq and Afghanistan as eroding U.S. power.

Lastly, Saunders discusses the implications of a weakened PLA for the international system. This would likely be the result of domestic problems that cause Chinese leaders to redirect resources away from PLA modernization to address internal security, requiring the PLA to assume a more defensive posture. A weakened PLA would likely allay U.S. and global concerns about China, but would not preclude China from conducting demonstrations or limited use of force when major interests are at stake. In international institutions, China would likely continue to oppose interventionist policies, and Beijing would likely seek closer bilateral relationships with other countries dealing with separatist issues such as Turkey, Russia, and Central Asian states.

In Chapter 11, Robert Sutter examines how the alternative futures discussed in previous chapters will affect U.S.-China strategic dynamics. Sutter discusses various aspects of U.S.-China strategic dynamics, such as the state of strategic equilibrium, China's tougher approach in the Asia-Pacific, China's domestic occupations, the high degree of economic interdependence between the United States and China, and U.S. leadership in the region.

Sutter contends that if the PLA becomes a regional force, although it would challenge U.S.-China relations, relations between the two would likely remain manageable. If China is a regionally oriented force and the United States maintains its leadership role in the region, China would likely be very cautious to enter into a military conflict with the United States. There are, however, "wild card" factors that could provoke conflict. For example, belligerent regional neighbors in Taiwan or Southeast could adopt policies that bring the United States and China into greater tension.

As for a global expeditionary PLA, Sutter contends that the implications of such a development would depend significantly on the reasons why China became a global expeditionary force. If China becomes a globally oriented force because it has resolved its territorial disputes peacefully and has reassured its neighbors, Chinese expeditionary forces may be welcomed and may be coordinated with the United States. If, however, China attains its position of power through coercive measures or by forcing the United States out of the region, the United States may check Chinese expansion outside of Asia. On the other hand, the two powers could possibly form a more pragmatic and cooperative relationship.

Lastly, Sutter examines the implications of a weak CCP for U.S.-China relations. According to Sutter, U.S.-China relations in this scenario would depend largely upon whether or not China was still ruled by the CCP. If the CCP still ruled over China, it would be reasonable to expect greater U.S. interference. However, it is not in U.S. interests for the CCP to experience a sudden collapse. Thus, one of the key themes in future U.S.-China relations will be how the United States approaches its relations with the CCP.

THE PLA IN 2025

This volume is an effort to assess some of the most plausible drivers and trajectories for the PLA's modernization and the potential ramifications this could have for regional, international, and U.S.-China relations. From these chapters several themes emerge. First, the futures are not mutually exclusive. While there will be differences in terms of magnitude, none of these futures rule out all elements of the other futures. For example, though a robust regional PLA may not possess or require forces to project power globally, this does not preclude the PLA from having an increased presence in international operations. Similarly, a weakened PLA, with fewer resources and thus more limited capabilities, could still maintain forces with considerable potential impact on regional neighbors.

Second, this volume somewhat considers the domestic political context in which PLA modernization will occur over the next decade, but it inevitably makes judgments about the future based on what has already occurred. It does not, and indeed cannot, anticipate all future possibilities. Consider for example, the case of General Xu Caihou, discussed at the beginning of this chapter. Setting aside the relative merits of the charges against him, or even what the charges say about how endemic corruption might be within the PLA, it is the case that the PLA has not prosecuted a retired CMC Vice Chairman in the past; it was a wholly new development. Going forward, there may well be future scenarios that lack historical precedent, and which will clearly have uncertain and unanticipated effects on the PLA.

Third, as is concluded in several of the chapters in this volume, and was evident during the broader conference discussion at Carlisle, *The Chinese PLA in 2025* is anticipated still to have a regional orientation. In one scenario, these capabilities will be limited, in another much more robust, and in a third scenario, a regionally-capable PLA would be part of a larger global expeditionary force. Indeed, many of the technologies procured by a future PLA will have dual functions, making them useful for regional contingencies or limited power projection. That participants foresaw a PLA largely maintaining a regional orientation for a decade hence is certainly consistent with the shift in prominence to regional foreign affairs that has emerged in 2013-14.

Fourth, a PLA that it is largely regionally oriented would have important policy implications for the United States. Would such a PLA be less likely to strive for global competitor status with the United States, thereby avoiding the fundamental system struggle experienced by the United States and the Union of Soviet Socialist Republics during the Cold War? If so, a certain level of security tension might be avoided. But it becomes also necessary to assess whether a regionally focused PLA will be less welcoming of U.S. posture and presence, especially if an "Asia for Asians" motif gains strength. If this proves true, we can expect higher levels of security contestation since the United States would likely continue pursuing its freedom of navigation aims and support for regional allies.

Fifth, even though the PLA must overcome many obstacles in its modernization efforts, if the PRC continues to invest heavily in PLA modernization, the PLA could very well develop the types of capabilities that could supplant a regional focus with a more global orientation. Yet, as the PLA continues to modernize policymakers must accord these developments their proper weight, and assess whether technological developments address important tactical goals or more strategic aims. Moreover, the degree to which the PLA is a technological innovator will shape how much the PLA is able to fundamentally reshape the regional security landscape and potentially challenge U.S. interests and sustained focus on the Asia-Pacific region, thus on the part raising important policy implications for the United States.

Sixth, the process of transition to alternative futures—how they come to pass—will likewise have important ramifications for regional security. For instance, a strong and regionally focused PLA does not necessarily harm U.S. interests if disputes are resolved peacefully and if China is able to successfully reassure the United States and its regional neighbors. Likewise, a PLA that is weakened is not necessarily a future that should be welcomed if it invites aggression from China's neighbors or if it leads China to behave more belligerently in an effort to resolve territorial disputes before its capabilities go into further decline.

Last, any future-oriented assessments must be approached with caution. There are numerous, unexpected "wild card" events that could potentially undermine the trajectories discussed in this volume. These wild cards include both domestic and external developments. Similarly, though PLA capabilities will be a significant component of China's comprehensive national power, future-oriented projections of China's role in the world must take into account other factors such as economic interdependence and diplomacy. Additionally, the future of China's political leadership likely matters as well. While conference participants were not predisposed to imagine a China without the CCP in charge, such a huge change would almost necessarily have an impact on PLA futures as well.

Overall, the trajectory China's military follows will be of significant consequence for security dynamics in the Asia-Pacific region and for global security and international norms. This volume represents an effort to examine the drivers, potential vectors, and implications of China's military modernization for the near-to-medium future. The authors in this volume are among the foremost experts on China's military. Their unique insights and perspectives illuminate some of the most pressing concerns for policymakers in the near future. We hope readers find this book to be informative and that it illuminates their own work regarding China.

CHAPTER 2

WHITHER CHINA?
ALTERNATIVE MILITARY FUTURES, 2020-30

Lonnie D. Henley

The views expressed in this chapter are the author's alone, and do not necessarily reflect the views of the Department of Defense or any other element of the U.S. Government.

Projections of China's future are hardy perennials in the garden of punditry, so this chapter does not pretend to any earth-shaking new insights.[1] Its purpose is to frame the discussion for other authors in this volume. The focus is on alternative visions of Chinese military posture in the decade between 2020 and 2030, dates chosen because of the Chinese People's Liberation Army's (PLA) continued reliance on 5- and 10-year planning cycles. Although Chinese public statements are not very transparent about the goals set for the PLA between now and 2020, it is reasonably clear that there are such goals and that barring a major change in strategic objectives, the PLA's course through 2020 is already determined. We will examine what those goals might be, and what kind of developments might lead them to change between now and then. The main focus of this chapter, however, is on what might happen afterwards if the PLA achieves its 2020 goals and what direction PLA force development might take in the following decade through 2030.

ASSUMPTIONS

To assess potential PLA development toward 2020-30, we must first establish a baseline understanding about the future of the global order. Dr. Phillip Saunders wrote the chapter in this volume entitled "Implications: China in the International System," in which he explores the impacts on China's participation in the global order under the three future scenarios detailed later in this discussion. In his original conference draft, Saunders listed a range of assumptions about the international system and global technology in 2025 that should be taken into consideration when considering the future. As Saunders' list was the most comprehensive and captured all of the various inputs discussed in the conference, participants urged that the assumptions be incorporated into an enlarged conference précis, which served as the starting point for each individual chapter as authors undertook their assigned tasks. Assumptions about the international system and global technology and assumptions about China in 2025 will be discussed.

Assumptions about the International System and Global Technology in 2025.

- Today's global governance (United Nations [UN] General Assembly; UN Security Council; nonproliferation regime) and economic (International Monetary Fund, World Bank, and World Trade Organization) institutions still exist and perform their basic functions. Their effectiveness is a function of the degree of major power consensus on particular issues, with less U.S. ability to shape consensus and determine outcomes.

- Globalization and a liberal global trade regime continue, but major economies and major regional powers are more willing to carve out exceptions to global rules when it suits their particular economic interests. Regional trade mechanisms have become more widespread and cover a significant percentage of global trade. Enforcement of global trade, finance, and intellectual property rules and norms has become more difficult.
- Continued growth in major regional powers means that the U.S. share of the global economy has declined somewhat relative to others. The United States is still the most powerful country, and one of only a handful of states able to wield all the elements of national power (diplomatic, information technology, military, and economic) on a global level.
- The United States still plays an active global role and is involved in most other regions of the world. The United States depends even less on Middle East oil, but its economy is still affected by fluctuations in global oil and natural gas prices.[2] The Asia-Pacific is the region of most importance to the U.S. economy.
- The United States has significant military power projection capabilities, but is less willing to intervene militarily in other regions. The United States will provide military training; advisors; intelligence, surveillance, and reconnaissance (ISR) support; and logistics and airlift to help allies and partners deal with regional instability on a case-by-case basis.
- Other major powers have only limited extra-regional power projection capabilities (less than

today in case of European Union members; somewhat more than today in case of Russia and major regional powers such as India and Brazil).

- The world includes a diverse range of democratic, semi-democratic, and authoritarian regimes.
- Most countries remain dependent on fossil fuels for most of their energy; renewable forms of energy and nuclear power have a somewhat expanded share.[3]
- No fundamental improvements in the speed and cost of land, water, and air transportation, although the Northern passage will provide a shorter route from Asia to Europe during summer months.
- The speed and distribution of telecommunications and internet access continue to increase in both developed and developing countries; satellites play a more important role in global communications.
- Only a few countries and companies produce state-of-the-art weapons (e.g., fifth generation fighters), which are sold to select customers at high cost and in limited quantities.
- Weapons that incorporate 1980s-1990s technology are widespread in medium-sized developed countries and major regional powers; some countries have militaries equipped with somewhat more advanced technologies, including some anti-access/area-denial (A2/AD) capabilities.
- Major regional powers and some medium-sized developed countries have deployed better sensors (radars, drones, and satellites) and Com-

34

mand, Control, Communications, Computers, Intelligence, Surveillance and Reconnaissance (C4ISR) capabilities to improve their situational awareness and military effectiveness.

Dr. Saunders' assumptions provide critical context for the individual chapter authors' analysis in this volume. Beyond the context these assumptions have provided authors, they also serve to demonstrate the expected developments, in a global context, to which the PLA will need to adapt its goals and capabilities in the coming decades.

2020 DEVELOPMENT GOALS

It is clear that the PLA relies heavily on 5- and 10-year plans to guide long-term force development. It is much less clear what those plans contain. The 2020 goal is frequently stated in terms of "basically accomplishing mechanization" and "making substantial progress in informationization" to "lay a solid foundation for the building of fully informatized military forces."[4] Even more vaguely, the 2006 defense white paper articulated PLA modernization goals as "lay[ing] a solid foundation by 2010," "mak[ing] major progress around 2020," and "basically reach[ing] the strategic goal of building informatized armed forces and being capable of winning informatized wars by the mid-21st century."[5] The 2020 part of that formula appeared again in the 2010 defense white paper, with no more definition.[6]

Public statements about 5-year plan objectives are equally opaque. Press articles about the General Staff Department's "Plan for Reform of Military Training during the 12th Five-Year Plan"[7] ("十二五"时期军事

训练改革总体方案) are full of PLA-speak platitudes about advancing from training under conditions of mechanization to training under conditions of informationization, accelerating the change in PLA modes of training to respond to the rapidly changing requirements for generating combat power, etc.[8]

The Hong Kong journal *Wen Wei Po* asserted in 2011 that the PLA will enjoy a major upgrade in military hardware during the 12th Five-Year Plan (FYP).[9] The article quoted then Chief of General Staff Chen Bingde speaking at the end of the 2011 National People's Congress, saying the PLA will:

> make accelerating the transformation of the modes for generating combat power the main battle lines of national defense and armed forces development, and carry out the entire process of armed forces development and reform and military combat preparations in every realm.[10]

After decades of studying the PLA, I still cannot decide whether the reams of boilerplate issued on such occasions convey any useful information to PLA insiders. I certainly get little out of them.

Since the PLA will not tell us what its development goals for 2020 consist of, we are left to infer them from logic and our basic understanding of Chinese security objectives. The goals seem to fall into two major categories. The first, and most challenging, is completing preparations for potential conflict around China's periphery. These "strategic directions," the Chinese equivalent of U.S. Defense Planning Scenarios, were articulated in the 2004 iteration of the *Military Strategic Guidelines for the New Era* (新时期军事战略方针), issued by the Central Military Commission on behalf of the collective political leadership.[11] Authoritative

PLA documents make clear that the "primary strategic direction" (主要战略方向) serves as the driver of military force development, or "army building" (军队建设) in the PLA lexicon:

> Planning for the national defense and modernization of army building, and planning for military combat preparations requires a prominent primary strategic direction. While paying attention to other strategic directions, the primary strategic direction is the impetus for army building in other strategic directions.[12]

A 2013 text for masters' degree candidates at the Academy of Military Science says that there should be only one primary strategic direction at any given time, providing the foundation for strategic decisionmaking, combat preparations, strategic disposition, and the employment of forces.[13]

Although the PLA tries not to discuss openly what scenario constitutes the primary strategic direction, many sources make clear that it is the "southeast coast" (东南沿海); that is, a conflict with Taiwan and the United States over Taiwan's status.[14] The secondary strategic directions are harder to identify. One source specifies the South China Sea and the Indian border;[15] other obvious candidates include the East China Sea (that is, conflict with Japan over the Senkaku/Diaoyu Islands), the Korean border, and possibly the Central Asian frontier.

It is also clear that the PLA does not yet have all the capabilities it requires for those missions. I will not rehash the arguments developed very well in many other sources — the U.S. Department of Defense annual report to Congress,[16] previous volumes from this conference series,[17] monographs and edited volumes by my many esteemed colleagues.[18] It therefore seems likely that one major focus of PLA force development through 2020 is on the hardware, doctrine, organizational structure, tactics, techniques, and procedures, and support structures required for the Taiwan mission, including counterintervention operations against U.S. forces and any third party that joins in defending Taiwan, and training the force to execute such operations. With only a few exceptions, the capabilities required for the other strategic directions are a lesser included set of those required for Taiwan.

The other candidate for 2020 force development objectives is the out-of-area power projection capabilities required for the "Historic Mission of Our Armed Forces in the New Century and New Era" (新世纪新阶段我军历史使命) articulated by Hu Jintao in 2004.[19] Again, my colleagues have examined in depth the associated missions, the capabilities required, and where the PLA stands in pursuit of those objectives, and there is no need to repeat that excellent work here.[20]

That leaves the question of the relative balance between those two objectives, between getting ready for potential fights around China's periphery versus developing capabilities to defend China's interest outside the immediate East Asia region and to conduct other "military operations other than war" (非战争军事行动, MOOTW). It seems to me that the former must take priority until such a time as the PLA can assure political leaders that it is fully capable of defending China's territory and sovereignty, including compelling Taiwan's unification with mainland China by military force if called upon to do so. This is not to the exclusion of building other capabilities, as highlighted by the focus of China's 2012 defense white paper on "diversified missions" for the PLA.[21] But the Taiwan mission will take priority, in my view.

If nothing changes, the most likely course of events for the PLA is to stay focused through 2020 on developing whatever capabilities the PLA and Chinese leaders have decided are necessary to fight and win a war with Taiwan and to thwart U.S. military intervention in that conflict. But something will change sooner or later, if only that the PLA achieves its Taiwan-related force development goals and is able to give more attention to other issues. The heart of this chapter, therefore, addresses the range of possible outcomes for Chinese military force posture, starting with a set of assumptions by Dr. Saunders about China through 2025, leading to an examination of the factors likely to have the greatest impact on the outcome. The concluding section aggregates these drivers into several representative cases illustrating the range of alternative futures of interest for this conference.

Assumptions about China in 2025.

- China will remain dependent on imports (food, energy, and raw materials) and foreign markets and thus must be engaged internationally. Higher economic growth rates will likely increase Chinese demand for imports (and likely increase exports as well). China will continue to be the world's largest oil importer and its demand for imported oil, natural gas, and coal will increase significantly through 2025.[22]
- The pattern of Chinese trade will determine the relative economic priority Chinese leaders place on different regions.
- Chinese interests outside Asia will likely follow this pattern, with highest priority countries and regions listed first:

— Internal Security: Beijing will focus on countries that might support terrorist or separatist groups operating in China and seek to obtain cooperation in suppressing the activities of those groups. Priorities: South Asia (Pakistan, Afghanistan, India), Central Asia (bordering countries), and the Middle East (Turkey, Saudi Arabia, Iran, and Yemen).

— Energy: Beijing will focus on countries able to export oil and natural gas to meet China's energy needs. Priorities: Middle East, Africa, Central Asia, Latin America, and North America.[23]

— Raw Materials: Beijing will focus on countries able to export minerals, metals, and food to meet China's economic needs. Priorities: Africa, Latin America, and Central Asia.

— Markets: Beijing will focus on markets for Chinese exports, with developing countries gradually playing a more important role. Priorities: Europe, North America, Middle East, Latin America, and Africa.

• China's military posture will have only a limited direct impact in shaping the international security environment outside Asia. That impact will depend primarily on China's ability and willingness to project power outside Asia or to sell significant quantities or types of advanced weapons that change local military balances. However, Chinese actions in Asia (e.g., using coercion to assert control over disputed territory, ignoring rulings by international courts, or enforcing restrictive rules on military operations in exclusive economic zones) may set precedents that affect other regions.

- The approach Chinese leaders adopt toward regions outside Asia will remain focused on obtaining concrete benefits (or forestalling specific harms) for China and Chinese citizens.
- China will have neither an ideology with global appeal nor an attractive vision of a new world order; as a result China's "soft power" will remain limited.[24] The partial exception is potential support for Chinese calls for an international economic order more favorable to developing countries, although concerns about competition from Chinese companies will complicate Chinese efforts to build coalitions on this issue.

Drivers Part 1: Variables.

Most of the factors likely to drive the course of Chinese military development are variables, in that there are a number of possible paths to consider in each category. The variables that seem most likely to have an impact include:

- Status of Taiwan. If Chinese leaders are able to achieve a reconciliation with Taiwan that satisfies their political and nationalist objectives, and that they can be confident will endure, this may eventually lead them to relieve the PLA of the requirement to be able to intimidate and coerce Taiwan or compel its unification with China with military force. It probably would not have that effect immediately, as it would take some time to gain confidence that whatever compromise they had achieved would not be reversed by future leaders in Taipei or Washington. So a reconciliation in the next year or two probably would not change China's military posture until 2020 or so, while a much later reconciliation might not have military effect until closer to 2030. Conversely, if Chinese leaders lose confidence in the long-term viability of political and economic approaches to Taiwan, becoming convinced that time is not on China's side and that developments on Taiwan are foreclosing the possibility of peaceful unification, then it is likely they would accelerate military modernization beyond the pace currently intended, and that out-of-area missions would drop to a much lower priority. Finally, if neither of those extremes comes to pass, but the Taiwan issue remains unresolved, then achieving and maintaining the capabilities required for a Taiwan conflict will remain the central focus of Chinese military modernization, at roughly the same development pace as today.

- U.S. Military Capabilities. The PLA's modernization trajectory is shaped in large part by Chinese perceptions of current and future U.S. military capabilities relevant to a potential conflict in China's "near seas."[25] If they reach their 2020 force development objectives only to find that U.S. capabilities are progressing faster than they anticipated in an environment where the Taiwan mission remains their primary focus—if U.S. military modernization has moved the goalposts, so to speak—then the subsequent decade of PLA modernization through 2030 probably also will center on countering U.S. military intervention in a Taiwan conflict. Conversely, if they achieve their goals and consider themselves ready for whatever the United States might bring to the fight, then their 2020-

30 force development may exhibit more balance between staying ready for a conflict near China and projecting power elsewhere in the world.

- Military Conflict. If China is involved in a military conflict with any of its neighbors or with the United States (probably in support of a neighbor), that will radically change Chinese perceptions of the international security environment, and not for the better. Even if China is successful militarily, the conflict is likely to so inflame patriotic sentiment among elites and the general public that Chinese leaders perceive the need for more rapid military development to prepare for the next fight.
- Status of Territorial Disputes. Closely related to possible conflict is how well China and its neighbors deal with festering disputes in the East China Sea, South China Sea, and along the Indian border. If Beijing were able to reach some kind of accommodation with rival claimants, either a final settlement or a durable *modus vivendi*, then depending on the status of the Taiwan issue discussed earlier, it might not perceive any near-term issue that would be likely to spark a conflict with the United States. It is likely Chinese leaders still would perceive a long-term U.S. intention to contain China's rise to world power, and perceive that military pressure would always form a central part of that containment scheme. So preparing for a potential conflict with the United States would still shape Chinese military modernization, but the perceived arena for that contest might be broader than China's maritime periphery. At the other extreme, a potential war

with the United States in the Senkaku/Diaoyus or Spratlys could replace Taiwan as the focus of PLA modernization.

- Internal Stability. How Beijing views the outside world depends heavily on how well they are coping with their many internal challenges. "Internal strife and external calamity" (内乱外患) will always be linked in the Chinese mind, but as Chiang Kai-shek famously said, the external threat is a disease of the limbs, but the internal threat is a disease of the heart. A Chinese regime that was overwhelmed with internal crises might welcome a relatively benign external environment, to the extent that it cut spending on warfighting capabilities in order to concentrate resources on internal political, economic, environmental, and security concerns (to include, of course, the military's ability to crush opponents inside China). A severe and prolonged economic downturn would probably accompany such strife, if it did not cause it in the first place, further reducing the resources available for military modernization. Alternatively, beleaguered officials could stir up external trouble to divert their internal opponents. Such events are rarer in actual world affairs than in political prognostications, but they do occur.

- Progress toward China's Strategic Goals. By the mid-2020s, China could have made enough progress toward being a respected great power to begin defusing the deep-seated sense of historical victimization and national grievance against the outside world. A more satisfied China could take a more relaxed and nuanced approach to relations with its neighbors, to Taiwan affairs, and to the United States and other great powers. Alternatively, the growth of Chinese power could fuel greater national arrogance, a determination to impose China's will on others using all the components of comprehensive national power, including military might. Similarly, at the other extreme, a China that was visibly failing to achieve its goals of economic prosperity, military strength, and international influence could seethe with resentment at those deemed responsible for frustrating its rightful ambitions. Least likely, but still possible, is a national acceptance that such ambitions were overly grandiose to begin with, and that China needs to be less confrontational abroad in order to focus on its own internal problems.

Drivers Part 2: Constants.

There are several factors likely to influence the course of Chinese military modernization that do not seem likely to vary over the coming 15 years, at least in the opinion of this observer.

- Chinese Views of China's History. The narrative that dominates Chinese views of their own modern history pivots around China's unjust treatment at the hands of rapacious foreign powers, China's "century of humiliation" from the Opium War to the reunification in 1949, and of the "sacred mission" to complete China's return to national power and international respect. The Communist Party-dominated regime has assiduously fanned the flames of

wounded nationalism, but they did not invent
this narrative, and it will not fade soon from
public consciousness, regardless of any other
developments. As a result, any future China,
however consumed with internal problems or
however satisfied with progress toward its strategic goals, will remain distrustful of foreign
intentions and feel the need for a significant capability to defend against the world's leading
military powers for considerably longer than
the 2030 time frame of this projection.

- Aversion to Political Fragmentation. Closely
related to the historical narrative is the perception that China must, at all costs, remain politically unified and remain committed in the
long term to regaining lost territories such as
Taiwan. Political fragmentation was one of
the main tools China's enemies used to drag
it down from the world's richest nation in the
high Qing dynasty to one of its poorest in the
mid-20th century, according to the narrative,
and no patriotic Chinese of any political per-
suasion could countenance dividing the country. Of course, some ethnic minority groups
disagree on whether Tibet and Xinjiang should
rightly be part of China, but the majority Han
Chinese opinion on such issues is not likely to
evolve very far in the next decade or two. As
a result, if there is no acceptable political resolution of the Taiwan, the Senkaku/Diaoyu, or
South China Sea issues, those will continue to
shape Chinese military modernization for the
foreseeable future.

Drivers Part 3: Non-Drivers.

Finally, a few issues that will not have much effect on the course of military modernization, in this author's opinion, even though others might vigorously disagree.

- Fate of the Chinese Communist Party. It matters a great deal whether the Chinese government is able to maintain stability, address the legitimate demands of the people, and sustain economic development while ameliorating its adverse effects. For the purposes of projecting military modernization trends, however, I am convinced that it does not much matter whether that government is the Chinese Communist Party or a post-Communist regime of some sort. Of course, it matters how traumatic the transition was, whether the successor regime was hostile to the United States, whether they blamed us or praised us for whatever sequence of events led to the end of the former regime. But with regards to the effect on China's military posture, whether the Party retains power is a dependent variable driven by the independent variables outlined earlier. Any of the alternative futures assembled below could come to pass under Communist leadership or under any of various possible post-Communist governments. Or so it seems to me.
- Party-Army Relations. Similarly, for the purposes of this analysis, it does not matter much whether the PLA remains the army of the Communist Party or becomes a nonpolitical national army. The issue at hand is what kind of missions the Chinese armed forces are

prepared to undertake, what national aspirations and economic resources underpin military modernization, and what kinds of issues might lead to military conflict between China and other states. Whether the Chinese armed forces develop such capabilities in the name of the Party or the state has little effect on those questions. So in the remainder of this chapter, we will continue referring to "the PLA" for convenience sake, but the reader should interpret that to mean "China's military forces" in general, whatever their future name or political orientation.

ALTERNATIVE FUTURES

This list of drivers is far from exhaustive, although a motivated pundit probably could stuff whatever other factors one wanted to raise into one of the broad categories listed previously. Nonetheless, there are far more permutations of those variables and constants than we can examine here, and each construct is a perfectly plausible alternative for how China might develop over the coming decade and a half. Our purpose here is not to predict the single most likely outcome, but we also should not get lost in an endless thicket of possible futures. In order to set the stage for useful analysis by the other contributors to this volume, we will group the hundreds of possible futures into three major bins.

**Alternative Future 1: A PLA Focused
on Regional Issues.**

In this future, the PLA's primary mission remains
to prepare for conflict on China's periphery, particularly its maritime frontier along the southeast coast,
and in particular to fight a high-intensity war against
U.S. military forces intervening on behalf of Taiwan,
Japan, Vietnam, or whoever else China is fighting.
The Taiwan issue has not been resolved to China's
satisfaction, or some other issue has loomed as large
as Taiwan was before. The Chinese government has
its internal issues well enough in hand to continue
prioritizing and funding military modernization. The
PLA is not confident that its modernization through
2020 was sufficient to meet the U.S. threat, and out-
of-region missions continue to take a back seat as
the PLA responds to the previously-unexpected increase in U.S. military capabilities. Regional conflict
remains the central focus of PLA military modernization through 2030, and its ability to project power to
other regions of the world increases only as an adjunct
to developing combat capabilities out to the second
island chain.

Alternative Future 2: A Global Expeditionary PLA.

The PLA's primary focus has shifted to military
power projection beyond China's maritime periphery, whether because regional tensions have faded,
because the PLA has satisfied Chinese leaders that
it has achieved what needs to win regional conflicts,
or because unexpected events elsewhere in the world
have raised Beijing's sense of urgency about protecting Chinese interests farther afield. The government

has internal issues under control and can afford the required new military capabilities. For most of the decade between 2020 and 2030, the PLA focuses on power projection, the details of which we leave to other contributors to explore.

Alternative Future 3: A Weakened PLA.

Chinese leaders are overwhelmed with China's internal problems, and the resources available for military modernization have dropped sharply. The PLA failed to achieve the development it intended, and the decade through 2030 is consumed in a protracted effort to achieve capabilities relative to the United States that it intended to achieve by 2020. Internal missions including disaster relief, internal security, and assistance to civil authorities consume a great deal of the PLA's time. The external situation remains tense, the possibility of conflict has not diminished, and Chinese interests remain threatened in other parts of the world, but the PLA does not have the time or resources to address those challenges as well as it would wish.

POSTSCRIPT

The arbitrary choice of three alternatives is not intended to constrain further analysis, but just to provide a framework for discussion. The other contributors to this volume will do the heavy lifting, examining their assigned topics in light of these three alternatives, then pointing out any other important possibilities which this overly-simplistic schema omits. I hope this exercise has at least provided a good starting point for their analysis.

ENDNOTES - CHAPTER 2

1. See, for example, Michael D. Swaine *et al.*, *China's Military & The U.S.-Japan Alliance In 2030*, Washington, DC: Carnegie Endowment for International Peace, 2013.

2. Daniel Yergin, "The global impact of US shale," *China Daily*, February 12, 2014.

3. See *World Energy Outlook 2013*, Paris, France: International Energy Agency, 2013.

4. Liu Yazhou (刘亚洲), "Implement the Strategic Arrangements Made by the 18th CPC National Congress, Promote the In-depth Development of the Revolution in Military Affairs With Chinese Characteristics" ("贯彻落实党的十八大战略部署；推动中国特色军事变革深入发展"), *Qiushi, Seeking Truth* (求是) online, July 2013, available from available from *www.qstheory.cn/zxdk/2013/201313/201306/t20130628_244172.htm*.

5. People's Republic of China, State Council Information Office, "China's National Defense in 2006," December 2006, available from *www.china.org.cn/english/features/book/194421.htm*.

6. People's Republic of China, State Council Information Office, "China's National Defense in 2010," March 2011, available from *english.gov.cn/official/2011-03/31/content_1835499.htm*.

7. The 12th Five-Year Plan (FYP) runs 2011-15, the 13th FYP will run 2016-20.

8. Liu Feng'an (刘逢安) and Hu Junhua, (胡君华), "High-level Interview: How Will Military Training be Reformed during the PLA 12th Five-Year Plan?" (高端访谈：解放军 十二五 时期军事训练如何改革?"), *PLA Daily* online, September 23, 2011, available from *news.mod.gov.cn/headlines/2011-09/23/content_4300202.htm*. See also Hu Junhua (胡君华) and Liu Feng'an (刘逢安), "GSD Issues 'Plan for Reform of Military Training during the 12th Five-Year Plan'," *PLA Daily* online, September 23, 2011, available from *www.mod.gov.cn/auth/2011-09/23/content_4300347.htm*.

9. "Armed Forces Development will Greatly Raise the Level of Weapons and Equipment in the Armed Forces in the 12th Five-Year Plan" ("「十二五」军队建设武器装备大提升"), *Wen Wei Po* (文汇报 online, Hong Kong), March 10, 2011, available from *trans. wenweipo.com/gb/paper.wenweipo.com/2011/03/10/YO1103100004. htm*.

10. *Ibid.*

11. David M. Finkelstein, "China's National Military Strategy: An Overview of the 'Military Strategic Guidelines'," in Roy Kamphausen and Andrew Scobell, eds., *Right Sizing the People's Liberation Army: Exploring the Contours of China's Military*, Carlisle, PA: U.S. Army War College, Strategic Studies Institute, 2007.

12. Chapter 5, "Using the Military Strategic Guidelines for the New Period to Maintain the Overall Situation of Army Building," in PLA General Political Department, *Outline for Studying Jiang Zemin Thought on National Defense and Army Building*, 2003, cited in Finkelstein, 2007. Thanks to David Finkelstein for finding this source and citing it in his 2007 article.

13. Shou Xiaosong, (寿晓松), chief editor, Science of Strategy (战略学教程), Beijing, China: Military Science Press, 2013, p. 168.

14. "The Dialectical Relationship between the Primary Strategic Direction and Other Strategic Directions" ("主要战略方向与其他战略方向的辩证关系"), April 4, 2006, available from *www.chinamil.com.cn/site1/ztpd/2006-04/04/content_448207.htm*. See also Zhangpu County (Fujian) county government, "Views on Chihu Township Militia Political Work in 2010" ("赤湖镇二０一０年年民兵整组政治工作意见"), March 20, 2010, available from *chz.zhangpu.gov.cn/admin/manage/news/news_show.asp?id=610*.

15. Chen Yongjian (惬永建), ed., *Army Tactical Modules: Research on Employment of Integrated Operations* (陆军战术模块 一体化作战运用研究), Beijing, China: Military Science Press, 2006, p. 19.

> The Military Strategic Guidelines for the New Era . . . shifted the primary strategic direction from southeast coast to focus on the Taiwan Strait, and the important strategic directions are the South Sea and the Sino-Indian border.

16. U.S. Office of the Secretary of Defense, *Annual Report to Congress: Military and Security Developments Involving the People's Republic of China 2013*, Washington, DC: U.S. Department of Defense, available from *www.defense.gov/pubs/2013_china_report_final.pdf*.

17. Roy Kamphausen, David Lai, and Travis Tanner, eds., *Learning By Doing: The PLA Trains at Home and Abroad*, Carlisle PA: Strategic Studies Institute, U.S. Army War College, 2012.

18. Ashley J. Tellis and Travis Tanner, eds., *Strategic Asia 2012-13: China's Military Challenge*, Seattle WA, and Washington, DC: National Bureau of Asian Research, 2012. Richard P. Hallion, Roger Cliff, and Phillip Saunders, eds., *The Chinese Air Force: Evolving Concepts, Roles, and Capabilities*, Washington, DC: National Defense University Press, 2012. Phillip C. Saunders *et al.*, ed., *The Chinese Navy: Expanding Capabilities, Evolving Roles*, Washington, DC: National Defense University Press, 2011. Dennis J. Blasko, *The Chinese Army Today: Tradition and Transformation for the 21st Century*, 2nd Ed., London, UK, and New York: Routledge, 2011.

19. Daniel M. Hartnett, *Towards a Globally Focused Chinese Military: The Historic Missions of the Chinese Armed Forces*, CNA document number CME D0018304.A1, Alexandria VA: The CNA Corporation, June 2008.

20. Roy Kamphausen, David Lai, and Andrew Scobell, eds., *Beyond the Strait: PLA Missions Other than Taiwan*, Carlisle PA: U.S. Army War College, Strategic Studies Institute, 2009.

21. People's Republic of China, State Council Information Office, "The Diversified Employment of China's Armed Forces," Beijing, China, April 2013.

22. See International Energy Agency, *World Energy Outlook 2013*.

23. *Ibid.*

24. David Shambaugh makes this argument persuasively in *China Goes Global: The Partial Power*, New York: Oxford University Press, 2013.

25. Defined as the East China Sea, Taiwan Strait, South China Sea, and the waters east of Taiwan. Chinese People's Liberation Army Military Terminology (中国人民解放军军语), Beijing, China: Military Science Press, 1997.

DOMESTIC, EXTERNAL, AND TECHNOLOGICAL DRIVERS OF PEOPLE'S LIBERATION ARMY MODERNIZATION

CHAPTER 3

DOMESTIC DRIVERS OF
CHINA'S FUTURE MILITARY MODERNIZATION

Joseph Fewsmith

If there is any tenet of Chinese foreign policy that seems to have held over the decades, it is that foreign policy serves the needs of domestic politics. Thus, the whole policy of "reform and opening" adopted by the Dengist leadership beginning in 1978 was designed to support China's economic development by opening up markets, bringing in new technologies, and encouraging large-scale foreign investment. Deng Xiaoping undertook three major foreign trips—to Japan in October 1978, to Southeast Asia in November 1978, and to the United States in January-February 1979—to help create a peaceful international environment to support his reform program.[1] Throughout the 1980s, "peace and development," a theme officially endorsed in 1984, dominated China's approach to foreign policy. In 1989 and in the years immediately following, China adopted the policy of "avoiding the limelight and keeping a low profile" (*taoguang yanghui* 韬光养晦). Evolving over the 1990s to include such phrases as "get some things done" (有所作为) and "never take the lead" (决不当头), this policy was expressed differently at different times, but it always undergirded a policy of caution.[2]

Over the first decade of the new century, however, China's *taoguang yanghui* policy came under increasing criticism for being too weak. Finally, in 2009, Hu Jintao said China should adopt a strategy of "upholding avoiding the limelight and keeping a low profile and **proactively** (积极的) getting some things done."[3] That more pro-active approach to foreign policy has continued to the present.

What needs to be explained is why China would move beyond a foreign policy that had been so successful for it and adopt a more active or assertive foreign policy that seems, at least from the outside, to have many negative consequences for China itself. The most obvious factor is that China is simply a much stronger actor than it was either coming out of the Cultural Revolution when its economy and polity were in shambles or in 1989 and the early-1990s when its economy was still not strong, its military not yet well-modernized, the Soviet Union—the strategic basis for Sino-U.S. relations—had broken up, when the Chinese Communist Party (CCP) itself had been badly shaken by the events of Tiananmen, and when socialism around the world seemed headed quickly for the dust bin. Twenty-five years later, China has emerged as the second largest economy in the world, its military is vastly improved, and the world, if not quite multipolar, is certainly less unipolar than it has been any time since the fall of the Soviet Union. Basic international relations theory suggests that countries that are stronger economically and militarily are simply going to pursue their interests more vigorously on the world stage.

Yet, the stronger economy and military still does not explain why, **in this particular period**, China has adopted a more activist foreign policy, especially when its previous policy, which employed a healthy dose of reassurance to offset concerns aroused by China's rapid economic growth and military modernization, seemed to serve China's interests so well. It seems that one needs to turn to domestic factors, including issues of social stability, legitimacy, nationalism, and generational change to have a more nuanced understanding of why China's foreign policy stance has evolved and where the country may go in the future.

SOCIAL ORDER

It has been evident for some time that China faces challenges of governance and legitimacy, and these challenges appear to be growing over time. As is well known, the Public Security Bureau reported that there were 8,700 "mass incidents" in 1993 and that by 2005, the last year the Public Security Bureau reported such figures, the number of mass incidents had increased to 87,000. Later, there was a widely reported figure of 180,000 mass incidents for the year 2010. The definition of a "mass incident" has generally been more than five people engaged in public protest, but that definition has varied enough over time that there can be no confidence that these figures are accurate or consistent in terms of what is being reported. Moreover, there are obvious reasons why some authorities might want to minimize the numbers, while others might want to exaggerate. Whatever the accuracy of the numbers, there is widespread agreement that the number of mass incidents has been increasing, the number of people involved is growing, and the level of violence is increasing.

As early as 1993, Wan Li, the head of the National People's Congress (NPC) reported that when the peasants in Renshou County (仁寿县, the location of a particularly large mass incident that year) were asked what they needed, they said, "We need nothing but Chen Sheng and Wu Guang (陈胜and吴广)," the legendary leaders of the peasant rebellion who brought down the Qin dynasty in 209 BCE.[4] In 2003, more than 3.1 million people participated in mass incidents (Chung, Lai, and Xia, 2006), and there were at least 248 mass incidents involving more than 500 participants between 2003 and 2009.[5]

Increasing concern with social stability was reflected in a new policy of "social management" ("社会管理"), which was introduced at a collective study session of the Politburo in September 2010. As Hu Jintao would later explain, social management would include "supporting people's organizations"; forming "scientific and effective mechanisms" for coordinating interests, expressing demands, and mediating contradictions; and improving the "management of and services for" the transient population and special groups. There was also a coercive aspect of social management that revolved around "stability maintenance" ("维稳").[6]

Perhaps the most direct evidence of growing concerns with social order comes from the creation and growth of new organs assigned to deal with the issue. In 1991, the party created the Central Commission on Comprehensive Social Order (中央社会治安综合治理委员会) to better coordinate among departments of the State Council. The new commission was headed concurrently by the head of the Political and Legal Commission, giving the two organs a largely overlapping leadership, but the latter organ had a broader mandate. In 1993, nine new ministries became members of the Commission on Comprehensive Social Order, including Post and Telecommunications, Communications, People's Bank of China, and the Ministry of Personnel. In 1995, the scope of the commission was expanded yet again to include the Central Discipline Inspection Commission, the Ministry of Supervision, the Family Planning Commission, and others.[7] In 2003, the 610 office, whose duties are to handle "heterodox religions" ("邪教"), was added, and in 2011, the Commission was expanded yet again, adding 11 new departments and changing its name to the Central Commission on Comprehensive Social Management (中央社会管理综合治理委员会), reflecting the new focus on "social management."

As the commission expanded, its budget rose accordingly. It should be noted that figures are difficult to obtain, in part because so much of security expenditures are off-budget—they come from funds obtained through fines and penalties. For instance, in 1996, the budget expenditures for public security in Guangdong province were only 30 percent of their total spending. In Qinghai and Gansu, 40 percent of county-level expenditures were financed through fines and penalties. Overall, according to official figures, spending on public security increased more than 10-fold from 28 billion yuan in 1995 to 390 billion yuan in 2009. By 2013, the public security budget had risen to 769 billion yuan ($123 billion), exceeding China's announced defense budget of 720 billion yuan.[8]

Despite the increase in the amount of money and personnel devoted to maintaining social stability, as noted previously, the number of mass incidents has increased. This is surprising not only because protest is a high-risk activity, but also because the state made a serious effort to respond to a major cause of unrest, namely overtaxation. Although not the only cause of unrest, the 1994 tax reform, which recentralized much of China's fiscal system, left local government—counties and townships—largely bereft of funds. Local party cadres, under a mandate to continue economic growth, responded by overtaxing local residents.

Whereas rural taxes were not supposed to exceed 5 percent of income, local governments often taxed 30-40 percent. No wonder mass incidents increased.

In 2006, however, the government responded by abolishing agricultural and miscellaneous taxes, cutting off this revenue source for local governments. Local governments, ever resourceful, responded by turning to land sales, and in order to sell land, they had to requisition it first. Although land is collectively owned, it is farmed by individual households through the contract system. One would think that overtaxation would affect everyone, generating widespread discontent, but that requisitioning land would only affect those unfortunate enough to have their land taken from them (compensation varied but was widely viewed as inadequate). Although the local state has continued to do things, whether to pay civil servants or collect funds for necessary projects, in general peasants have had their financial burdens reduced. Nevertheless, the number of mass incidents continued to increase, suggesting widespread discontent with local government.

It has often been noted that the concepts "state" and "society" are not so neatly divided in China (and Asia in general) as they are in the West. There can often be a dynamic interaction in which contesting interests negotiate with each other, reaching accommodations that do not threaten the authoritarian government on the one hand or legitimize societal actors on the other. Indeed, protest can provide information to the regime and provide a safety valve for societal frustration. Moreover, as Ching Kwan Lee has recently suggested, there seems to be an increasingly salient "market nexus" between state and protest in which the state buys off protestors and protestors seem to be willing to monetarize their citizenship rights. Nevertheless, the continued increase in the number of mass incidents suggests a gradual undermining of state authority. Although the sort of cash nexus that Lee discusses could extend the life of the regime, she also sees it as introducing a "creeping erosion of state authority" that may "subject the regime to a deep-seated vulnerability. . . ."

When one looks at public opinion polls, there are two results that suggest that such an erosion of state authority has already set in. First, citizens routinely rate the effectiveness of the central government more highly than they do their own local government—the one they come into contact with more often. Moreover, the more citizens come into contact with government, the less satisfied they are with it. Second, the group that citizens see as benefiting the most from reform and opening are cadres.[9] Such survey results suggest that the state is right to spend more money on "stability maintenance" even though such expenditures are likely to feed further dissatisfaction.

When one looks closely at the causes of mass incidents, it is apparent that the fundamental cause is structural—the cadre management system forces cadres to fulfill mandates given by their superiors, not to respond to the needs or desires of their constituents.[10] This suggests that the problems of governance are likely to get worse over time even if specific issues are addressed.

NATIONALISM

It is difficult to discuss nationalism in contemporary China because nationalism has been the leitmotif of 20th century China. Yet, China's policy of reform

and opening was accompanied—for the most part—
by a new wave of cosmopolitan thinking, epitomized
if not limited to the 1988 television series "River
Elergy" (河殇).[11] Part of the backlash against such cosmopolitan trends came in the early-1990s as the government sponsored a "patriotic education campaign,"
as populist nationalism spread with the publication
of such books as *China Can Say No* (中国可以说不)
and *Looking at China through a Third Eye* (第三支眼睛
看中国), and the development of the so-called "New
Left," which built on neo-Marxist thought to critique
China's policy of reform and opening.[12] This "new
nationalism," as it is sometimes called, was certainly
rooted in previous nationalist traditions but was new
in its juxtaposition to the intellectual trends of the
previous decade.

There were several incidents that fed into and exacerbated such trends in the 1990s. First, there was
China's bid to host the Olympics in the year 2000.
When that bid failed, the United States was widely
blamed; indeed, the Congress had passed nonbinding
resolutions opposing the Chinese bid, thus fanning
the flames. It was after that event that one often heard
statements such as the United States was not opposed
to the Chinese government for human rights violations but rather was opposed to China. This was an
early expression of the popular belief that the United
States is trying to "contain" China, a narrative that
seems quite wide spread in recent years. Second, there
was the 1995-96 Taiwan Straits crisis, an event that not
only kicked People's Liberation Army (PLA) modernization into high gear but also generated expressions
of popular nationalism, such as *China Can Say No*. It is
useful to recall that there had been no popular discussion of Chinese foreign policy in the years before that.

Such expressions certainly had support from some official quarters, but they also appealed to many people. Third, there was the *Milky Way* incident, in which a ship thought to be carrying precursor chemicals for the making of chemical weapons was stopped and searched before entering the Straits of Hormuz. No chemicals were found; and no apology was issued. The popular impression of the United States as the "world's policeman" spread. Finally, there was the U.S. bombing of the Chinese embassy in Belgrade, which touched off days of demonstrations against the United States.[13]

The question is: How widespread is such nationalism? How intense is it? Does it affect Chinese foreign policy, and, if so, how? These questions are not easy to answer. There are questions about how to measure nationalism, about how widespread nationalism needs to be to have an effect on foreign policy, and how such nationalism is perceived by policy elites. For instance, it is apparent that strong nationalistic opinions are expressed on the Internet, but it is far less clear how representative of the Chinese people such expressions are.

Although many scholars, including myself, have subscribed to the belief that nationalism is widespread and rising, Alastair Iain Johnston has used survey results to argue that nationalism is not particularly widespread, not particularly intense, and, moreover, tends to decrease as people become more affluent and travel more. Assuming that Chinese citizens are likely to become more affluent and travel more, perhaps the issue of nationalism is a passing one.[14]

But even assuming that Johnston's survey research has accurately measured nationalist feelings in China, officials may still be right to focus on the sorts of people who post highly nationalistic rants on the Web after all; such people are more likely to take to the streets over some incident. In other words, even if the "echo chamber" of Chinese nationalism is smaller than many presume, it may still be large enough for Chinese officials to be wary of it.[15]

The really interesting question, however, is how policy elites interact with public opinion. Before trying to answer this question, however, it is necessary to look at issues of legitimacy and the sense of crisis that seems to be prevailing.

LEGITIMACY ISSUES

Evidence has mounted in recent years that many intellectuals are clearly unhappy with the pace of political reform. Intellectuals may not have the social status and impact that they once did, but they can still mobilize significant public opinion—which is why the government keeps such a close eye on them. About a decade ago, a group of intellectuals tried to bring about political reform by focusing on the law. The catalyzing event was the Sun Zhigang case (孙志刚事件). Sun Zhigang was an unemployed college graduate who travelled to Guangzhou in search of employment. Mistaking him for a migrant laborer, police asked to see his identification. Unfortunately for Sun, he had forgotten to carry his, and he was quickly detained under China's custody and repatriation (收容遣送) system whereby unemployed migrants are detained before being sent back to their villages. What happened next is not clear, but for some reason, he was badly beaten and died.

In response, three recent Ph.D.s in law—Xu Zhiyong (许志永), Teng Biao (滕彪), and Yu Jiang (俞江)—

66

wrote an appeal to the NPC Standing Committee, the body charged with interpreting China's constitution, arguing that the custody and repatriation system violated the constitution. The system had long been controversial, and the Standing Committee took the opportunity of the legal appeal to rule the system illegal. This fascinating case seemed to open up a path to political reform not by confronting the government but by pressuring it to enforce its own laws. Quickly dubbed the "rights protection movement" (维权运动), the Sun case quickly spawned a group of public interest lawyers.[16]

Unfortunately, the so-called "color revolutions" broke out the following year, and before long the growing ranks of "stability maintenance" police began to look at the rights protection movement as a problem for social stability. This contest between popular rights and social stability has continued through to the present, not only derailing an effort to build law but also resulting in the recent arrest and conviction of Xu Zhiyong, one of the founders of the movement.

The issue was rejoined shortly after China's President Xi Jinping took office at the Eighteenth Party Congress in November 2012. Like Presidents Jiang Zemin and Hu Jintao before him, Xi Jinping gave a major speech on the 10th anniversary of the promulgation of China's 1982 constitution, declaring, "protecting the authority of the constitution means protecting the authority of the common will of the party and the people." He went on to assert:

> To manage state affairs according to law, first we must run the country in accordance with the Constitution. The key to holding power in accordance with the law is to first rule in accordance with the Constitution. The party leadership formulates the Constitution and the

law, and the party itself must act within the scope of the Constitution and the law to truly achieve the party leadership's establishment of the law, ensuring the enforcement of the law, and taking the lead in abiding by the law.[17]

Xi's strong comments seem to have led liberal-minded reformers to push ahead, either believing that Xi was inclined to support them or that circumstances would convince the new party chief that he should support them. In December 2012, 70 scholars signed a petition calling for political reform, particularly constitutional government.[18] The Guangzhou-based paper, *Southern Weekend* (南方周末), picking up on Xi's theme of a "China dream," wrote a New Year's editorial for the paper—"China's Dream is the Dream of Constitutional Government"—that was rewritten by Guangdong provincial propaganda chief Tuo Zhen as a paean to the party. Journalists at *Southern Weekend* objected and petitioned provincial authorities; soon they went on strike, only to have the editor removed. The *Global Times* then ran an article, republished throughout China, saying with unusual bluntness that "anyone with common sense knows that in China there is no room for a 'free press,' and that the media should not harbor the unrealistic hope of becoming a 'political special zone'."[19]

This incident was particularly important because the new Xi administration reacted particularly strongly in asserting ideological control. In April 2013, the General Office promulgated "Document No. 9" denouncing seven trends it found pernicious. The first one was propagating the idea of "constitutional government," which it denounced as a way to negate the leadership of the party and "import the Western political system into China." Document No. 9 set off a wide-ranging debate as conservative publications supported the government's position and liberal intellectuals took to the Internet to support constitutional government.

The important point was that it became evident in the course of the debate that both sides had significant support within the party. Such a politically charged argument about China's direction suggested deep division within the party, sharp division among politically active intellectuals, and a very weak middle position that might potentially restrain debate.[25]

SENSE OF CRISIS

During the Jiang Zemin era, China made significant progress in extricating itself from the diplomatic isolation in which it found itself following Tiananmen. Perhaps ironically, given today's tensions between China and Japan, it was Tokyo that took the lead in breaking ranks with the Western nations that had imposed economic sanctions following Beijing's crackdown. Before long, China established diplomatic relations with Indonesia, Singapore, South Korea, Saudi Arabia, and South Africa, stealing diplomatic partners from Taiwan and breaking out of the near pariah state that China had been in only 3 years before. Economically China's gross domestic product (GDP) moved ahead rapidly, growing from about 1.7 trillion yuan in 1989 to about 12 trillion yuan in 2002 when Jiang Zemin left office.[26] Jiang's doctrine of the "Three Represents" was much lampooned, but it dealt with a critical issue in China's political economy, namely the political status of entrepreneurs. As Jiang advisor Li Junru (李君如) wrote at the time, if China did not absorb the most dynamic sector of the economy—entrepreneurs and young intellectuals—it would inevitably push them into opposition.[27]

In his first term, Hu Jintao was rather active. He effectively reinterpreted the "Three Represents" by emphasizing the third principle (representing the interests of the vast majority of the people) rather than the first principle (representing the advanced productive forces), by introducing the "scientific development concept," talking about the need to create a "harmonious society," and launching China onto the path of a welfare state by emphasizing a "service-oriented" government. Although spending on welfare (health care, education, pensions, and so forth) continued to grow in Hu's second term, it is difficult to point to any major initiatives in those 5 years. Whether this slowdown was due to Hu's weak personality, the size of the Politburo Standing Committee (which stood at nine members), interference from retired leaders, or the growth of so-called "vested interests," there was a sense that stagnation had set in.

This sense that the Hu Jintao administration, particularly the second term, had been a period of stagnation was put pointedly by Deng Yuwen (邓聿文), deputy editor of *Study Times* (学习时报), the weekly publication of the Central Party School, in a famous article. As Deng said, "It cannot be denied that this decade has seen the festering or creation of immense problems" and "the decade of the Hu and Wen has seen no progress, or perhaps even a loss of ground" with regard to several issues, including the economic structure, environment, "ideological bankruptcy," and political reform.[28]

Although Deng expressed his frustration from the "right" side of the political spectrum, the "left" felt equal frustration. These were the years in which leftists looked to Mao Zedong for political inspiration and when, politically, Bo Xilai (薄熙来) promoted the

70

Chongqing model, which drew on Maoist populism to go after organized crime, implement new land exchange schemes, build new housing for the disadvantaged, and—most famous of all—re-emphasize socialism through the signing of "red" songs.[29]

There was also a sense of vulnerability—that China's political system might follow those of other socialist nations onto the dustbin of history. For instance, a debate on the cause of the failure of the Soviet Union heated up around the 20th anniversary of that event. The orthodox view that Russian President Mikhail Gorbachev was the cause that was countered by more liberal commentators who blamed the demise of the Soviet Union on structural problems.[30] This concern with the fate of the Soviet Union, which has been even stronger in the period of Chinese President Xi Jinping reflects the continued debate about the appropriate course for China to follow and the sense that, unless appropriate measures are taken, China could go the same way.

XI JINPING AND THE EMERGENCE OF A NEW GENERATION

When popular nationalism emerged in the mid-1990s, despite support from some quarters in the political system, it was still very much on the periphery. Two decades later, however, following impressive economic growth that is nonetheless accompanied by inequality, social instability, legitimacy issues, and growing populism, a new generation of leaders has emerged on the scene. As the children of revolutionary leaders, they are "to the manor born." This is not to say that all "second generation revolutionaries" ("红二代") are united; on the contrary, there have been some very obvious divisions and, no doubt, there are others that are not as visible. However, Xi Jinping and his close associates are quite different than Jiang Zemin, who was promoted to general secretary unexpectedly in a crisis situation, or Hu Jintao, whose father was a small entrepreneur (小业主). Although the dynamics of leadership succession are not well understood, Xi Jinping has certainly been able to move much faster than his predecessors to consolidate power and set an agenda. His family background and network among the political elite account for at least some of this. As suggested earlier, there is a sense of urgency stemming from a sense of vulnerability derived from legitimacy issues and a sense that the party pursues departmental interests more than national interests.

Some of what we have seen from Xi in the first year and more of his administration reflects, in part, what all new leaders need to do—consolidate power (by prosecuting rivals), carrying out campaigns, and adopting new ideological slogans. But what Xi and the new leadership have been doing, both domestically and in terms of foreign policy, exceeds a new leadership's need to set an agenda. The strong reaction to the Japanese arrest of a fishing captain who rammed two Japanese Coast Guard ships, the reaction to the Philippine fishing in Scarborough Shoal, the extremely strong reaction to the Japanese purchase of three of the Senkaku/Diaoyu islands, the sudden declaration of an air defense identification zone (ADIZ), the apparent effort to take control of Second Thomas Reef, and the movement of an oil-drilling rig into waters claimed by both China and Vietnam suggest a pattern of behavior that is more provocative than China's past behavior.

The question is why, when China is facing enormous domestic challenges, would it pursue a seemingly provocative foreign policy? Why has China's policy moved from the cautious "avoid the limelight and keep a low profile" stance of the 1990s to emphasize the more "proactively get some things done." As suggested earlier, this evolution was largely the result of a debate carried out by policy elites in the first years of this century, but behind that evolution lies a volatile combination of a sense of stagnation (in the Hu-Wen years) and vulnerability (legitimacy remains uncertain), the seeming self-confidence of a particular group of "princelings," and nationalistic emotions among parts of the public and the policy elite. Moreover, a certain degree of assertiveness in China's foreign policy, particularly combined as it is with the articulation of ideals of greatness (the China Dream), depictions of victimhood (the exhibit on China's "Road to Renaissance" in the Revolutionary History Museum), the campaign against corruption, and the revival of certain revolutionary traditions (the mass line, criticism and self-criticism), appears to have certain benefits for the new leadership: nationalism and assertive policy appear to facilitate centralization (resistance appears unpatriotic), it builds off of and co-opts the populist neo-Maoist ideas of Bo Xilai, and it appears to allow the new leadership to confront—to some still unknown extent—some of the factions and vested interests that might otherwise be expected to resist the leadership's initiatives.

It must be noted that the concern of the new leadership with the fate of the former Soviet Union, a concern never far from the surface in any leadership, seems to have become a near obsession. There was Xi's internal but widely reported remarks in Guangdong in December 2012 when he reportedly asked:

Why did the Soviet Union disintegrate? Why did the Soviet Communist Party collapse? An important reason was that their ideals and convictions wavered. . . . Finally, all it took was one quiet word from Gorbachev to declare the dissolution of the Soviet Communist Party, and a great party was gone. In the end nobody was a real man, nobody came out to resist.[31]

Since then there have been many similar, if less colorful, warnings. For instance:

- In October 2013 a "Ren Zhongping" ("任仲平") (short for "Important Commentary from *People's Daily*" ["人民日报重要评论"]) commentary said unusually bluntly:

    Today, the Soviet Union, with its history of 74 years, has been gone for 22 years. For more than 2 decades, China has never stopped reflecting on how the communist party and nation were lost by the Soviet Communists.

- In September 2013, National Defense University produced a film called "Silent Contest" ("较量无声"), which warned of Western attempts to subvert China through propaganda and spreading ideas like constitutional government.[32]
- In October or November 2013, the Central Discipline Inspection Commission, the Chinese Academy of Social Sciences, and the Research Center on World Socialism jointly produced a four-part documentary called, "In Memory of the Collapse of the Communist Party and the Soviet Union" ("苏联亡党亡国20年祭").[33]
- In November 2013, the party's theoretical journal, *Qiushi* (求是), published an article by its

commentator that warned, "The collapse of a government usually starts in the field of ideology. . . . What caused the dissolution of the Soviet Union?" the journal asked, "An important reason was the wavering of ideals and beliefs."

- In November 2013, Li Zhanshu (栗战书), the head of the General Office and reportedly a close friend of Xi Jinping, wrote an article in *People's Daily* in which he said that the Soviet Union and the countries of Eastern Europe had undertaken "reform" (it was in ironic quotation marks in the original), but it had gone array, leading to the "burying of the socialist enterprise. The lesson is extremely deep," Li declared.[34]

As long as this strategy is not over played, i.e., does not lead to real conflict or set loose uncontrollable populism, and is put in the service of attaining the economic reform objectives put forward by the Third Plenum in November 2013, it could prove to be a relatively effective strategy, albeit one that inevitably kicks the most difficult issues down the road.

DURABILITY

At the moment, it seems that domestic political factors and the dynamics of the new leadership are aligned to support, if not drive, a continued assertive security policy. Whether one considers the current more proactive policy as a matter of responding to significant domestic issues, including social issues, weak legitimacy, and a sense of vulnerability, or more a matter of competition among elite actors, any which of whom could face criticism if a "weak" policy was adopted, the current dynamic supports a more assertive policy. One caveat is in order, and that is that tension seems to serve the leadership well, but conflict, with its much greater consequences, does not. Thus, we may see some ratcheting down of tensions if the costs rise significantly.

Would domestic issues and/or pressures permit or drive a yet more assertive policy and the degree of investment in military modernization that would be necessary to support it? To the extent that the military pursues institutional interests, it seems likely to continue to pursue military modernization, which may, to a greater or lesser extent, conflict with broader political goals. But defense spending as a percentage of central government revenues (which is different than GDP growth) has remained quite consistent in recent years, suggesting that there are real limits that domestic expenditures are not likely to exceed. These trends suggest that a PLA focused on more than regional issues is unlikely, despite nationalistic trends.

The social and economic challenges China faces in the not so distant future—a slower growth rate, an aging population, a more expensive labor force, environmental challenges, a shrinking labor force, and the loss of a demographic dividend in terms of a young work force—all suggest that there are real limits to China's ability to support the development of the PLA as a global expeditionary force. The possibility that defense expenditures could compete with social expenditures—health care, education, environmental control, pensions, and so forth—seems real. This is something that has not happened over the 3 decades of reform and opening, so it would take something of a political upheaval to imagine a significant reduction in military expenditures.

CONCLUSION

The emergence of the new nationalism, however widespread or narrow it might be, certainly supports China's turn toward a more assertive foreign policy, but it does not, in and of itself, propel China in such a direction. However, the migration of nationalism from the periphery toward the policymaking elite is a new and significant trend. But however nationalistic China's new leadership is, it appears that it is more their concern with issues of social stability, legitimacy, and systemic vulnerability that drive their more assertive nationalism. Public opinion, aided by the power of social media, makes it more difficult to back down—and disaffected elites seem ready to turn to social media to suggest that the leadership is too "weak." Elite competition, the institutional interests of the PLA, concerns with social and regime stability all seem to bias the system toward a more assertive policy, and 3 decades of economic development and military modernization support such inclinations.

Although the emergence of a more assertive foreign policy predates the Eighteenth Party Congress (remember Hu Jintao's vow to "proactively get some things done"), the new leadership seems better positioned to use nationalistic appeals to quell elite divisions, centralize power, and possibly to carry out an economic reform agenda.

To the extent that such strategies are successful, they will reinforce more assertive policies. But, so far at least, there is a caution underlying China's policies. There is no indication that China welcomes armed conflict, much less that it would initiate such conflict. Given the socio-economic issues likely to dominate

Chinese politics over the next decade or more, it seems likely both that a degree of nationalistic assertiveness will continue, but that it is unlikely to undergird the sort of national effort that would be required to support a global expeditionary force.

ENDNOTES - CHAPTER 3

1. Ezra Vogel, *Deng Xiaoping and the Transformation of China*, Cambridge, MA: Harvard University Press, 2011, pp. 280-293, 297-308, and 333-345.

2. On the evolution of this policy, see Dingding Chen and Jianwei Wang, "Lying Low No More? China's New Thinking on the *Tao Guang Yang Hui* Strategy," *China: An International Journal*, Vol. 9, No. 2, September 2011, pp. 195-216.

3. *Ibid.*, p. 212. See Zhu Weilie (朱威烈), "韬光养晦：世界主流文明的共有观念" ("Avoiding the limelight and keeping a low profile: An idea shared by mainstream civilization throughout the world"), originally published in *Wenhuibao* (文汇报), August 14, 2010, available from *www.news365.com.cn/jy/201008/t20100814_2798784.htm.*

4. Thomas P. Bernstein, "Farmer Discontent and Regime Responses," Merle Goldman and Roderick MacFarquhar, eds., *The Paradox of China's Post-Mao Reforms*, Cambridge, MA: Harvard University Press, 1999, pp. 197-219.

5. Tong, Tanqi and Shaohua Lei, ""Large-Scale Mass Incidents and Government Responses in China," *International Journal of China Studies*, Vol. 1, No. 2, pp. 487-508.

6. Joseph Fewsmith "'Social Management' as a Way of Coping with Heightened Social Tensions," *China Leadership Monitor*, No. 36, Winter 2012.

7. *Ibid.*

8. Xie Yue (谢岳), 维稳的政治逻辑, *(The Political Logic of Stability Maintenance)*, Hong Kong: Tsinghua Publishing (清华书局), 2013, pp. 141-142.

9. Xie Yue (谢岳), "Rising Central Spending on Public Security and the Dilemmas Facing Grassroots Officials in China," *Journal of Current Chinese Affairs*, Vol. 2, 2013, p. 83.

10. *Ibid.*, p. 88.

11. Andrew Jacobs and Chris Buckley, "China's Wen Warns of Inequality and Vows to Continue Military Buildup," *The New York Times*, March 5, 2013.

12. Ching Kwan Lee, "State & Social Protest," *Daedalus*, Spring 2014, pp. 124-134.

13. Wang Junxiu (王俊秀), Yang Yiyin (杨宜音), and Chen Wuqing (陈午晴), "2006 年中国居民生活质量调查报告" ("Survey Report on China's Social Mood, 2006"), in Ru Xin (汝信), Lu Xueyi (陆学艺), and Li Peilin (李培林), eds., 2007 年：中国社会形势分析与预测, *(China's Social Circumstances, Analysis and Prediction: 2007)*, Beijing, China: Social Sciences Archive Press (社会科学文献出版社), 2007, p. 66.

14. Wang Junxiu *et al.*, "Survey Report on China's Social Mood, 2006," p. 68.

15. Joseph Fewsmith, *The Logic and Limits of Political Reform in China*, New York: Cambridge University Press, 2013.

16. If the thrust of the 1980s was toward more cosmopolitan thinking, there was also sharp resistance, including the 1983 campaign against "spiritual pollution" and the 1987 campaign against "bourgeois liberalization."

17. Suisheng Zhao, "Chinese Intellectuals' Quest for National Greatness and Nationalist Writings of the 1990s," *The China Quarterly*, No. 152, December 1997, pp. 725-745; and Suisheng Zhao, "State-Led Nationalism: The Patriotic Education Campaign in Post-Tianamen China," *Communist and Post-Communist Studies*, Vol. 31, No. 3, September 1998, p. 287-302.

18. Joseph Fewsmith, *China Since Tiananmen*, 2nd Ed., Cambridge, MA: Cambridge University Press, 2008.

19. Alastair Iain Johnston, "Chinese Middle-Class Attitudes Toward International Affairs: Nascent Liberalization?" *The China Quarterly*, No. 179, September 2004, pp. 603-628; and Alastair Ian Johnston, "The Correlates of Beijing Public Opinion Toward the United States, 1998-2004," Alastair Iain Johnston and Robert S. Ross, eds., *New Directions in the Study of China's Foreign Policy*, Stanford, CA: Stanford University Press, 2006, pp. 340-378.

20. I borrow the term "echo chamber" from Susan Shirk, *China: Fragile Superpower*, Oxford, UK: Oxford University Press, 2007.

21. Keith Hand, "Using Law for a Righteous Purpose: The Sun Zhigang Incident and the Evolving forms of Citizen Action in the People's Republic of China," *Columbia Journal of Transnational Law*, No. 114, 2006-07.

22. 人民日报, *People's Daily*, December 5, 2012.

23. Zhang Qianfang, "Proposal for Consensus on Reform," *Caijing Online*, December 26, 2012.

24. Ching Cheong, "Xi Faces the Test of His Reform Image," *Straits Times Online,* January 11, 2013; David Bandurski, "Inside the Southern Weekly Incident," *China Media Project*, January 8, 2013.

25. See Joseph Fewsmith, "Debating Constitutional Government," *China Leadership Monitor*, No. 42, Fall 2013.

26. These are official figures drawn from the *China Statistical Yearbook, 2011*, Bejing, China: China Statistics Press, 2011.

27. Li Junru (李君如), "正确理解和坚持党的阶级性" ("Correctly Understand and Uphold the Party's Class Nature"), *Lilun dongtai* (理论动态), July 20, 2001.

28. Deng Yuwen, "The Hu-Wen Legacy," originally posted to *Caijing wang.*

29. For a review of the Chongqing model from a supporter, see Cui Zhiyuan, "Partial Intimations of the Coming Whole: The Chongqing Experiment in Light of the Theories of Henry George, James Meade, and Antonio Gramsci," *Modern China*, No. 37, No. 6, 2011, pp. 646-660.

30. Contrast Zhou Xincheng (周新城), "历史在这里沉思—苏联解体近 20 年的思考" ("History Here Pondered—Reflections on the Breakup of the Soviet Union Nearly 20 Years on"), and Xu Yuangong (徐元宫), "揭秘挡安对苏联阶梯原因研究的意义" ("The Significance of Declassified Files for Research of the Causes of the Dissolution of the Soviet Union"), *Xuexi shibao* (学习时报), December 26, 2011.

31. Christopher Buckley, "Vows of Change Belie Private Warning," *The New York Times*, February 15, 2013.

32. The film can be watched at *www.youtube.com/watch?v=M_81SjcoSw8*.

33. The film can be watched at *v.youku.com/v_show/id_XNDEOMjI4NDEy.html*.

34. Li Zhanshu (栗战书), "遵循四个坚持的改革经验" ("Follow the Reform Experience of the 'Four Persistents'"), *People's Daily* (人民日报), November 26, 2013.

CHAPTER 4

PEOPLE'S LIBERATION ARMY TRAJECTORIES: INTERNATIONAL DRIVERS

Eric Heginbotham
Jacob Heim

INTRODUCTION

It takes only modest imagination and a cursory look at the historical record to understand that external events, even those that do not directly involve a given country, can profoundly shape its military trajectory. The Franco-Prussian War, a war in which Britain did not participate, sparked the most fundamental army reforms there since Oliver Cromwell's day, as well as a reevaluation of England's long-standing antipathy toward peacetime continental commitments. The Great Depression not only facilitated the rise of fascist and fascist-leaning regimes, but also caused strains within the community of democratic nations that made confronting Germany and Japan far more difficult. As a rapidly rising state, China's strategic direction may be as subject to redirection or redefinition as America's or Germany's was during the late-19th or early-20th centuries, as both of those countries assumed the mantles of great power.

This chapter assesses the impact of external variables on four potential futures: (1) a People's Liberation Army (PLA) focused on its immediate periphery; (2) a regionally oriented PLA with some power projection capability; (3) a globally expeditionary PLA; and (4) a weakened PLA. The Chinese military, once focused overwhelmingly on its immediate periphery, is already set on a path to acquire capabilities relevant to wider regional and, to a very limited extent, global missions. The discussion of variables and their impact assesses movement off of the current trajectory. In other words, the question is not what could prompt the PLA to develop power projection capabilities, but rather what could cause the PLA to accelerate the acquisition of power projection capabilities or, alternatively, to refocus on forces optimized for conflict in its immediate periphery?

Following is a discussion of the differences between a PLA optimized for combat in China's immediate periphery from one with a wider regional orientation — a distinction that results in a slight modification of the trajectories discussed by Lonnie Henley in his excellent introduction to this volume. We then move on to discuss a range of external variables. The first three groups of variables primarily affect the geographic focus of the Chinese military. These include: (1) the degree of conflict with China's regional neighbors, including Taiwan, Japan, India, Vietnam, and the Philippines; (2) U.S. power, strategy, and Sino-American relations; and, (3) the development of Chinese interests or challenges outside the region. We also examine a set of possible developments that could produce a weakened PLA: military failure that could discredit the military, foreign overcommitment that could strain resources, a loss of external sources of technology, and external support for domestic Chinese insurgency or terrorism.

PERIPHERAL VS. WIDER REGIONAL CAPABILITIES

Discussion of a "regional" military capability in Asia can be somewhat misleading for those who may not fully appreciate the distances involved. With a bit of rearranging, the combined 37 countries of Western Europe, Southern Europe, and Northern Europe would fit more than twice into mainland China; they would fit almost two more times in Australia; and, if placed in the South China Sea, they would spill just a bit outside the sea's maritime exits. Flying a mission from China's Hainan Island to Bali (3,000 kilometers [km]) would be roughly the same distance as flying from Madrid to the Crimea; and even the distance from Hainan to the Spratly Islands (1,700-km) would be equivalent to that of Madrid to the Czech border.

Military and Operational Distinctions.

Given the great area encompassed by Asia, we differentiate a PLA optimized for operations along the immediate periphery (operationalized as roughly 1,000-km from the Chinese mainland) from a PLA optimized for fighting in the wider regional space (between 1,000 and 3,000-km). The ability to project power can always be evaluated on a continuum, and from one perspective, this parsing of regional distances simply adds an intermediate distance into the equation. However, the military distinctions between capabilities required for a close fight in China's immediate periphery and one at more distant locations in the region are important. The types of anti-access/ area denial (A2/AD) capabilities developed by China in recent years are most relevant to its immediate periphery, and, while it could develop another, longer-range layer to its A2/AD capabilities, the costs would be higher—making the trade-offs involved more questionable.

The 1,000-km distinction made here is useful for several reasons. It corresponds to the 1,000-km range definition of short range ballistic missiles (SRBM), which are generally one-stage systems and therefore cheaper than generally two-stage medium range ballistic missiles (MRBM) and intermediate range ballistic missiles (IRBM).[1] The distinction also roughly matches the unrefueled combat radius of fighters and strike aircraft (which are somewhat less than 1,000-km for single-engine fighters and roughly 50 percent more than this for larger, twin-engine aircraft). Just as important is the relative ability to use ground-based or air-breathing (as opposed to space-based) communications and intelligence surveillance and reconnaissance (ISR) systems.[2] Although range limitations may be less clear cut, the relative utility of diesel submarines, green water surface craft, and even lighter frigates and destroyers, would be more in scenarios within 1,000-km of China than in contingencies farther from home. Finally, the distinction also has political significance within Asia, roughly corresponding to those areas inside the first island chain and those outside of it.

Mapping Strategic Depth: Taiwan vs. the Rest.

The PLA's focus on Taiwan during the 1990s and early-2000s drove it toward short range forces with limited power projection capabilities. As China's focus has shifted beyond Taiwan since the mid-2000s, the PLA has begun to place greater emphasis on limited regional power projection capabilities. While an escalation in tensions with Taiwan could encourage the PLA to redouble its attention to peripheral capabilities, the same would not necessarily be true of tensions with other neighbors. Taiwan is unique among China's potential military targets in terms of its lack of strategic depth—i.e., in terms of the size of territory across which forces opposing China could be deployed and in terms of the most distant militarily usable territory from China.

Taiwan is the only major neighboring "state" (using the term to denote territory controlled by an independently functioning government) in East or West Asia that falls entirely within range of Chinese short-range combat systems. Measured by the distance from the closest part of mainland China (including Hainan) to the most distant point of each neighboring state, Taiwan's depth runs to roughly 380-km, while the other neighboring countries with which combat is most thinkable (including Japan, the Philippines, Vietnam, and India) range between 1,170-km and 2,160 or 2,500-km in depth (depending on how distances against Japan are measured). Taiwan is also far smaller than the others in its total land area and in length of coastline.

	Max distance from PRC Mainland (in km)	Total land area (in km2)	Length of Coastline (in km)
Taiwan	380	32,300	1,600
Vietnam	1,170	310,100	3,400
Japan	1,260/2,500*	364,500	29,800
Philippines	2,160	298,200	36,300
India	2,380	2,973,193	7,000

* If measured across the Korean Peninsula, the shorter distance applies. The longer distance applies to distances measured around third party airspace.

Table 4-1. Indicators of Strategic Depth vis-à-vis China.

Using SRBMs and ground-launched cruise missiles, China could strike all air and naval bases on Taiwan.[3] If the PLA could suppress Taiwanese air-defenses, most of China's 4th generation strike fighters could range over the entire country without refueling. PLA naval forces, including diesel submarines, could move to positions off all ports and harbors relatively quickly or easily.[4] To be sure, major Taiwan scenarios (including either blockade or invasion) would be extremely demanding for the PLA, and an invasion could fail even without U.S. intervention. Power projection capabilities would be useful for the PLA in Taiwan scenarios for a variety of purposes. But the trade-offs between "tooth" (combat capabilities) and power projection "tail" (support capabilities) would be different against Taiwan than against virtually all other plausible opponents.

U.S. participation in a Taiwan scenario would vastly complicate the PLA task and could potentially expand the potential battle area. But the impact of this new depth would be limited unless significant adjustments were made to U.S. force posture. (See the upcoming section on U.S. military force posture and strategy for more on this topic.) U.S. forces are overwhelmingly concentrated in a few bases in Northeast Asia, almost all well within range of Chinese MRBMs.[5] The United States operates a single U.S. Air Force Base (Kadena) and a single Marine Corps Air Station (Futemna) within unrefueled fighter range of Taiwan—against roughly 40 for China, as shown in Figure 4-1.[6] Under some circumstances, Chinese leaders might believe that they could either deter the United States from entering a conflict by holding even a handful of bases hostage, or, potentially, hold off U.S. attacks long enough to achieve their objects with regard to Taiwan.

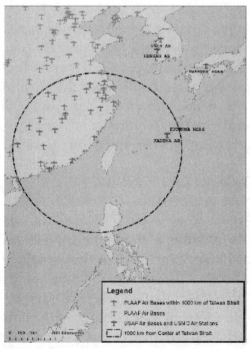

Figure 4-1. PLAAF, USAF, and USMC Air Bases within 1,000-km of Taiwan Strait.

In contrast, other regional states that have conflicts with China have significantly greater strategic depth than Taiwan and would require a greater mix of at least regional power projection capabilities. As Table 4-1 indicates, all have areas that would constitute sanctuaries against a Chinese adversary armed exclusively with short range systems. In reality, China already has the capability to launch limited punitive operations against any of these states. Nevertheless, if PLA leaders anticipate the possibility that an adversary could extend the campaign in time or space, they would have significant incentives to invest further in at least some types of limited power projection capabilities. Vietnam, Japan, the Philippines, and India all have the strategic depth to support and continue a fight from positions beyond the range of Chinese short range air and missile systems. Hence, even if a conflict began over a flashpoint in China's immediate periphery, such as the Senkaku/Daioyu Islands, it may need to engage forces significantly further away. In the Senkaku case, the PLA would presumably want to be able to strike Yokota Air Base (the U.S. Air Force Base near Tokyo) or even more distant locations even if it would prefer to keep the conflicted limited.

IMPACT OF RELATIONS WITH REGIONAL ACTORS

China's relations with neighboring states will be an important driver of PLA direction. In addition to geography, political factors and the military capabilities of regional states will also affect the degree and manner in which tensions or conflict with regional states will influence future PLA trajectories. This section provides a very brief country-by-country overview of political and military issues related to each actor. It begins with Taiwan, which represents the only case where, if the relationship sours and military conflict becomes more likely, the PLA will refocus relatively greater efforts on peripheral capabilities. It then goes on to address other potential competitors in Asia: Japan, India, Vietnam, and the Philippines. Increased conflict with all of these would push China, on balance, toward the acquisition of a regional power projection capability. Given limited space, Indonesia and Malaysia are not discussed, though they each have at least minor territorial disputes with China and could potentially come into sharper conflict with it.

Taiwan.

In addition to Taiwan's unique geographic position (discussed earlier), Taiwan is also a special case from the political dimension. Under Beijing's one-China policy, Taiwan is an inseparable part of China. When Chinese senior leaders deliver formal remarks on the state's "core national interests," sovereignty over Taiwan and Tibet are often the only examples they provide.[7] Indeed, some sources suggest that the language of "core national interests" was created by Beijing in order to better control the discussion of Taiwan.[8] Preventing Taiwan's de jure independence is central to the Chinese government's legitimacy.[9] Should China feel that Taiwan is moving toward de jure independence, the military requirements for Taiwan contingencies will likely take precedence over those of other contingencies even if the latter scenarios also become more likely.

Although Taiwan's defense capabilities have suffered a prolonged decline relative to China's, they remain potent. This is especially true in the context of an amphibious invasion; capability against a blockade campaign would be somewhat more questionable. Taiwan operates 192 4th generation fighters (a combination of F-16s and Mirage 2000s) and 26 surface combatants (including three classes of U.S. ships and six La Fayette class frigates), in addition to substantial ground forces. If it felt an invasion might be necessary, China would probably seek to acquire more modern amphibious ships, and given the possibility of U.S. intervention, would also probably seek to reinforce its A2/AD capability and fighter forces. While it could accomplish many tasks using short range capabilities, it would nevertheless benefit from tankers, airborne early warning and control aircraft (AWACS), and conventionally armed MRBMs and IRBMs.

Japan.

After Taiwan, China's security position vis-à-vis Japan is probably the second most important to the legitimacy of the government in Beijing. Against a backdrop of distrust dating from Japan's imperial era (and fed by Chinese propaganda and Japanese nationalist rhetoric), territorial disputes over the sovereignty of the Senkaku/Diaoyu Islands, the economic exclusion zone boundary in the East China Sea, and the oil and gas deposits under the East China Sea serve as potential flashpoints.[10] Both sides are extraordinarily sensitive to perceived unilateral changes in the status quo affecting these interests.

Among regional states, Japan stands out as having the largest defense budget after China's. Japan's 47 principal surface combatants include two *Hyuga* class helicopter destroyers, each carrying up to 11 helicopters and designed primarily for anti-submarine warfare (ASW) and amphibious landing functions. (They could also potentially support short take-off and vertical landing aircraft.) Japan operates 18 submarines, all commissioned post-1990. The five most modern are Soryu class boats with air independent propulsion (AIP). The Japan Air Self-Defense Force operates almost 300 modern fighter aircraft (the F-2 and the F-15J), supported by a small fleet of AWACS and aerial tankers.

Given the political importance of Japan issues, the country's strategic depth, and its potent military capabilities, significantly increased tensions with Japan could encourage the PLA to increase regional power projection capabilities and acquire a sizable number of tankers and AWACS, MRBMs, large surface combatants, and nuclear and conventionally powered submarines.[11] Liu Yazhou, a PLA Air Force (PLAAF) General at the Chinese National Defense University, has cited the failure to reform military institutions prior to the Sino-Japanese War of 1894-95 as a key factor in China's loss.[12] The reference comes in the context of a contemporary discussion military reforms today that would likely enhance the status of the PLA Navy (PLAN) and PLAAF and better support power projection.[13]

India.

India is the only neighbor with which China has significant continental territorial disputes (centered on Aksai Chin and Arunachal Pradesh). Having decisively bested India in the 1962 border war, China looms far larger in the minds of Indian strategists than India does in Chinese thinking.[14] However, media reforms in China have produced increased reporting on Indian perceptions of rivalry and opened the door to negative feedback dynamics between the two. The Indian acquisition of additional power projection, missile, and nuclear capabilities, often justified by the Chinese threat, has caught the attention of the Chinese strategic community.[15]

India's defense budget is large and, unlike Japan's, has grown rapidly over the last decade. Administrative and organizational problems endow it with capabilities that are not necessarily equal to the funds spent, but it does have pockets of strength. India's 25 principle surface combatants include two aircraft carriers (one acquired from the Unitd Kingdom (UK) and one from Russia), and it is building two additional carriers at home. The Indian navy also operates 14 modern submarines. The Indian air force has roughly 300 modern fighters (including the MiG-29, Su-30 variants, and the *Mirage* 2000), supported by small numbers of AWACS and tankers. Increased tensions or crises with India would, on balance, push China toward acquiring more regional power projection capabilities, including conventionally armed MRBMs and IRBMs, AWACS and tanker capabilities, nuclear and conventional submarines, and, possibly, more aircraft carriers. They would also justify continued modernization of the ground forces, perhaps especially army aviation.

Vietnam.

Similar to the Indian case, China looms larger in Vietnamese strategic thinking than Vietnam does in China's, but maritime disputes between the two keep Vietnam in the Chinese news. Recent collisions between vessels, protests, and riots over China's deployment of an oil rig in Vietnam's claimed waters led China to evacuate thousands of Chinese citizens from Vietnam and provided a sharp reminder of China's sensitivity to the stability of its relations with its southern neighbor.

Despite its limited resources and small defense budget, Vietnam has taken steps to modernize its military such that it could offer some resistance to China in the air and at sea, and mount a more serious challenge on the ground. Vietnam has begun to acquire a small but capable force of modern fighter aircraft and submarines. As of late-2013, it had a total of 34 Su-27s and Su-30s in service with another 14 on order. As of April 2014, it had taken delivery of two Kilo-class submarines, and has four more on order. Its two Russian-built frigates (the *Dinh Tien Hoang* class) have reduced radar signatures and field modern anti-ship cruise missiles and air defenses. Continued friction between China and Vietnam could encourage the PLA to further modernize its land forces, as well as further develop its fleet of large surface combatants, MRBMs, and modern fighter aircraft, and AWACS. Aircraft carriers and tankers would be relatively less important in this case, given the proximity of Vietnam to Chinese bases.

Philippines.

Like Vietnam, ongoing maritime disputes between China and the Philippines provide an ongoing source of concern for Beijing. The Philippines lacks any modern air or naval power, but unlike India, Japan, and Vietnam, military operations against even the closest Philippines territory would require considerable reach. (The nearest point on Luzon is some 650-km from the mainland.) While it is starting essentially from scratch, the Philippines has begun the process of modernizing its forces by acquiring jet training aircraft from South Korea.[16] A recently concluded agreement with the United States to expand access to Philippine bases could also facilitate the modernization of Philippines' military capabilities.[17] Anticipated military conflict with the Philippines could encourage the PLA to increase its power projection capabilities including large surface combatants, flat-deck amphibious ships, aircraft carriers, MRBMs, IRBMs, tankers, and AWACS. The quantity of forces required, however, would be less than in the case of India, due to the much smaller scale of the Philippines military.

Lastly, for completeness, a quick survey of the PLA serves to highlight the military balance between it and the other selected regional powers. (See Table 4-2.) The PLA Air Force's roughly 600 modern fighters are a mix of J-10s, J-11s, and Su-27/Su-30 variants. These are supported by a handful of tankers (converted H-6 bombers) and a growing inventory of AWACS. Its 70 surface combatants include its first aircraft carrier, 15 modern destroyers, and 54 frigates. Its modern submarines include Shang SSNs, as well as Kilo, Song, and Yuan SSKs.

	2013 Defense Budget (in billions$)	Modern Fighter Aircraft	Principle Surface Combatants	Modern Submarines	Active Duty Military Personnel
Taiwan	10.3	192	26	0	290,000
Japan	51.0	277	47	16	247,150
India	36.3	312	25	14	1,325,000
Philippines	2.2	0	0	0	125,000
Vietnam	3.8	34	2	2	482,000
PRC	112.0	~600	70	35	2,333,000

Sources: *The Military Balance*, Vol. 114, No. 1, London, UK: International Institute for Strategic Studies, 2014; "Vietnam Navy Receives 2 Russia-Made Project 636 Kilo Class Diesel Electric Submarines," April 6, 2014, accessed on May 8, 2014, available from *www.navyrecognition.com/index.php/news/defence-news/year-2014-news/april-2014-navy-naval-forces-maritime-industry-technology-security-global-news/1725-vietnam-navy-receives-2-russia-made-project-636-kilo-class-diesel-electric-submarines.html.*

Table 4-2. Key Military Capabilities of Selected Regional Powers.

IMPACT OF U.S. POWER, POSITION, AND MILITARY STRATEGY

Despite periodic Chinese debates about the potential decline of American power—and assertions about the continued advance of multipolarity—the United States remains by far the most significant factor in Chinese foreign and security policy. The United States receives singular treatment in successive editions of Chinese national defense white papers, whether by name or clear implication. Article searches in *PLA Daily* suggest that discussions of disputes involving the United States and those involving other neighbors have generally co-varied over time (see Table 4-3). This stands to reason, as the United States is generally drawn into disputes with China's neighbors and is often seen as the instigator by Beijing. In other words, the degree of disputation with neighbors and that with the United States is not zero-sum—an increase in the former will not diminish the importance of the United States in Chinese security planning.

Year	U.S. Disputes	Other Neighbors' Disputes*	Ratio US:Others
1984-1988	14	10	1.4
1989-1993	18	14	1.3
1994-1998	51	34	1.5
1999-2003	72	57	1.3
2004-2008	64	50	1.3
2009-2013	103	70	1.5
Total	322	235	1.4

*Neighbors included Japan, India, Vietnam, the Philippines, and Taiwan.

Source: 解放军报 full text database, *The China National Knowledge Infrastructure*, Bejing, China.

Table 4-3. Articles in JFJB Discussing U.S. Disputes and Selected PRC Neighbors' Disputes.*

*Article searches included country name (e.g., 美国) in title and "dispute" (分歧 or 争端) anywhere in the article text. Note that not all of the disputes mentioned were necessarily with China. Thus, the data should only be taken as a very aggregate indicator of threat perception in the context of other, qualitative evidence.

By almost any measure, U.S. power relative to China's has declined over the last 20 years, and Chinese official publications see a continuing trend toward multipolarity in the international system. In the military realm, China has increased its military spending faster than the United States, and, in part because of its low starting position and the availability of military technology from international sources, China has been able to narrow (but not close) the technology gap. Nevertheless, U.S. comprehensive national power remains superior to that of China, and a number of Chinese specialists predict that the United States will remain the world's premier power for at least the next 20 or 30 years.[18] In the military realm, the readjustment of U.S. military assets toward the Pacific and the pursuit of entirely new types of technologies have mitigated the impact of Chinese modernization. Even if U.S. dominance has waned somewhat, the United States remains the only military in Asia with clearly superior military capabilities.

Several U.S.-related developments could shift Chinese calculations and produce incentives to adjust the balance of capabilities toward one of the trajectories discussed earlier: (1) distracted or diminished U.S. power; (2) changes to U.S. military strategy or posture; (3) Sino-American crises that highlighted the danger of war between the two; or, (4) a more cooperative relationship that was more welcoming of a significant Chinese role in global security.

Distracted or Weakened U.S. Power.

A United States that was seriously distracted by events elsewhere, or a significant weakening of relative U.S. military power such that continuing "rebalancing" would no longer significantly mitigate the impact, could produce uncertain results. The United States has been the great equalizer of Asian military power, especially around China's immediate periphery. Potential U.S. involvement in a Taiwan conflict, for example, has maintained the standoff between a country of 1,300 million people and one of 20 million. Viewed from one perspective, then, the weakening of U.S. commitment might free Chinese military planners to focus on other, more distant tasks, if they believed their capabilities were sufficient for security in the immediate periphery.

There is, however, another equally plausible outcome. Balancing by regional states — and in particular, a strong lean toward the United States — has sometimes led Beijing to moderate its international approach lest it push neighbors further into the U.S. camp. A diminished U.S. commitment might lead Chinese leaders to take more forceful positions with regard to local disputes, leading to more crises and worse relations with neighbors. This, in turn, could lead the PLA to focus on capabilities maximized for peripheral or wider regional warfighting. Even in this latter case, however, the withdrawal of the U.S power would reduce the requirement for some types of A2/AD capabilities, such as the DF-21D ASBM, and increase the incentives to acquire systems that might allow it to control air or sea areas against regional foes.

U.S. Military Force Posture and Strategy.

The impact of the United States on Chinese military strategy will not simply rest on the maintenance of U.S. composite or military power or its degree of commitment to Asia. It will also depend on the U.S.

military strategy and force posture. Since the end of the Cold War, the United States has pursued operationally offensively oriented doctrines and operational practices.[19] Although these practices have developed partly as a function of America's dominant military position, they may have become an enduring habit. In recent wars, the United States has had the initiative and been able to launch early and intensive attacks, leading with airpower and missile strikes.[20] The U.S. forward-leaning posture in Asia, its permanent rotational deployment of bombers to the region, and the AirSea Battle concept all suggest that the United States might rely heavily on offensive action from the outset of a conflict in Asia, even if it did not initiate hostilities.[21]

However, with the diminution of U.S. all-aspects dominance in Asia and increased pressure on the defense budget, there is some debate about whether the United States should rethink its forward-leaning strategy. There has, for example, been some discussion about whether a blockade strategy could either complement or replace a strategy that relies on early and intensive strikes.[22] Less noted but potentially as consequential is the discussion about improving operational resiliency through a combination of measures that might include: operating from more bases, in smaller packages, with greater mobility and flexibility, and with improvements to active and passive defenses.[23] Unlike a blockade strategy, which faces strong resistance from within the military (especially the navy), the concept of resiliency has strong support (at least in principle), and some funds have already been allocated. Key elements to improve operational resilience, including new techniques for rapid runway repair, hardening of critical infrastructure, and operating aircraft in an expeditionary manner, have already begun.[24] This strategy could include the dispersion of assets to bases or locations at greater distances from China, followed by phased operations taking the force closer as Chinese A2/AD capabilities were degraded.

If the United States moves more concertedly toward an approach that capitalizes on strategic depth within Asia (either as part of a blockade strategy or phased entry strategy or both), it will likely accelerate the Chinese development of power projection forces. The distinction between a center of gravity in the first island chain and one spread over the first and second island chains and extending into southern Southeast Asia and the Indian Ocean may appear one of degrees. But for Chinese military planners, the differences would be important.

If U.S. forces are able to operate from hundreds of miles away from the Chinese coast and still threaten the People's Republic of China (PRC) values in the event of war, Chinese planners would have more incentives to develop longer range strike systems, and, especially, a far more robust support structure for regional power projection. Assuming that they wished to challenge U.S. operations near their source of operations, or at least interdict attacks coming from distant locations, greater U.S. depth would place a premium on Chinese space-based communications and ISR. Aircraft would require a large number of tankers to extend the PLAAF's range beyond the first island chain. Operating beyond the range of land-based air surveillance and C2 sites would create a greater need for airborne early warning and command and control aircraft. Naval platforms would require more at-sea replenishment capacity, driving a requirement for a larger Chinese combat logistics fleet.

China might also seek, on balance, larger and longer-ranged systems. Longer-range bombers may be sought, as smaller strike aircraft may no longer have the range to strike key U.S. bases or command facilities. More and larger destroyers, especially air-defense destroyers, would be useful to provide enduring presence in operational areas. The PLA might also seek to increase the proportion of nuclear powered attack submarines in the submarine force, since submarines may be required to operate even beyond areas of U.S. presence in order to isolate U.S. basing areas and prevent the flow of reinforcements to them. To the extent that China wished to extend its TBM range to newly relevant operational areas, it would have to build multi-stage conventionally armed MRBMs and IRBMs — though given the expense, it might also shift to relatively greater reliance on cruise-missile armed bombers.

In the multistep game of positioning for advantage during peacetime, China will, like the United States, have many options, and it would not have to adopt the force structure discussed previously. The PLA could, for example, conceivably adopt a hedgehog strategy. It could continue to strengthen its shorter-range capabilities, allowing it to decisively influence events around its immediate periphery and then dig-in and ride-out more attacks into its operational periphery — much as Japan sought to do during World War II. However, this would cede initiative to the United States, and it is more likely that China would shift relatively greater resources toward an ability to influence events farther away.

The PLA forces designed to contest areas in more distant parts of Asia may not require the same kinds of very large lift aircraft or support ships that a more globally oriented strategy would. Nevertheless, these intermediary steps would move the PLA incrementally toward a more global power projection capability.

Intensified Sino-American Tensions or Clashes.

If U.S. military capabilities remained strong relative to those of China and Sino-American relations grew appreciably worse, punctuated by clashes or more frequent crises, the PLA would have greater incentives to maintain its high priority on defensive, A2/AD, and peripheral warfighting capabilities. Chinese leaders might rate the chance of being attacked at home (even as part of a war that the United States might be fighting defensively) more highly, and might therefore seek to continue improving defensive capabilities. While offensive and support systems could still be useful, they are expensive and the relative value of expenditures on them would lessen. Consequently, more might be spent on short range fighters, surface-to-air missiles, and improvements to basing infrastructure. On the naval front, there would be less incentive to build aircraft carriers, which would be vulnerable to U.S. submarine and air attack. Submarines might remain the naval weapon of choice.

U.S. Welcome for Larger Chinese Global Role.

When Chinese Foreign Minister Wang Yi spoke of the "new model of major-country relations" to a Brookings audience in September of 2013, he said:

> China is prepared to engage in all-dimensional cooperation with the United States at regional and global levels. . . . China is ready to shoulder international

responsibilities commensurate with its national strength and realities, and together with the United States, offer more quality public goods for the international community.[25]

China is already a major contributor to United Nations (UN)-sponsored international peacekeeping efforts, as well as to some ad hoc international efforts, such as anti-piracy operations in the Gulf of Aden. At a minimum, improved relations with the United States would, on balance, free up resources that might otherwise be devoted to defensive or peripheral tasks. A more enthusiastic or explicit welcome by Washington of global roles for China might further encourage it to engage in peacekeeping and other operations overseas. On balance, this should increase incentives to develop a range of support systems, such as long range air- and sea-lift and satellite communications and ISR, as well as "harder" power projection capabilities, such as aircraft carriers and, possibly, nuclear submarines.

IMPACT OF GLOBAL INTERESTS AND DISTANT CHALLENGES

The growth of Chinese material and human interests overseas, as well as the development of strategic military relationships with foreign states, could also prompt China to invest relatively greater resources in developing a globally oriented military.

Protecting Overseas Assets and People.

China's 2013 white paper on national defense included a section on "protecting overseas interests" — the first time the topic has been addressed in a Chinese defense white paper. The document observes the growth of Chinese interests overseas and stipulates, "vessel protection at sea, evacuation of Chinese nationals overseas, and emergency rescue have become important ways and means for the PLA to safeguard national interests."[26]

China's overseas trade has grown rapidly over a period of 30 years. However, its overseas investments, which may be a bigger driver of overseas residency, have only grown to significant levels in the last decade. In 2005, Chinese overseas investments and contracts totaled around $18 billion yuan, a figure that rose more than 600 percent to $132 billion yuan by 2013. While the first and second largest recipients of Chinese foreign direct investment (FDI) are the United States and Australia, Chinese investment in developing countries, including a number of unstable ones, is disproportionately large. For example, Africa accounts for around 2.5 percent of total global gross domestic product. Less than 4 percent of China's total trade between 2005 and 2013 was with African states. But fully 18 percent of China's outgoing FDI over that same period was in Africa, where it made investments in 30 different countries.[27]

The number of Chinese citizens overseas has risen as a function of both overseas investment and growing wealth. A total of 97 million Chinese traveled overseas for tourism in 2013, up from 29 million in 2004.[28] Some 9.3 million Chinese went abroad to work or study in 2013, up from 4 million in 1990.[29] The Chinese business presence has become a popular and political target in countries where local entrepreneurs or labor struggles, and anti-Chinese riots have been witnessed in Solomon Islands (2006), Tonga (2006), Lesotho (2007), Algeria (2009), Papua New Guinea (2009), and

Zambia (2012).[30] Riots in Vietnam, sparked primarily by the activities of Chinese energy companies in Vietnamese claimed exclusive economic zones, were also fed by dissatisfaction over labor conditions. In 2011, Thai soldiers were charged in the killing of 13 Chinese sailors in Thailand.[31] Kidnappers have also targeted overseas Chinese, taking 29 construction workers in Sudan and 25 workers in Egypt in 2012. Closer to home, ethnic Chinese have been targets of violence and discrimination for much longer. Ethnic Chinese were attacked in both the post-1965 anti-communist purges in Indonesia and in riots in May 1998 on the eve of Suharto's fall.[32]

Historically, China has not taken a forceful position with regard to the protection of overseas citizens or, especially, noncitizen ethnic Chinese. This may be changing. While the Chinese government was relatively passive as Indonesian Chinese came under attack in 1998, the Chinese government came under pressure from overseas ethnic Chinese to act, forcing it to condemn the violence and encourage restraint.[33] The increased flow of information to and within China since the 1998 riots, as well as higher expectations concerning national power, may make it even harder in future cases for the Chinese government to satisfy its public with statements of condemnation. Indeed, the recent production of a documentary in Indonesia depicting the post-1965 killings there triggered public calls in China for Beijing to write the massacre into history books and cease aid to Indonesia — all over a case that is now nearly 50 years past.[34]

As the 2013 white paper suggests and the 2011 Libyan case demonstrated, the PLA is ready and willing to participate in the evacuation of Chinese nationals. In the Libyan case, it diverted a destroyer from the Gulf of Aden to the Libyan coast and dispatched four Il-76s on 40 sorties to evacuate 1,655 people to Sudan.[35] Chinese pundits and netizens have begun to debate whether China should develop capabilities that would make more forceful measures possible. Of the killing of Chinese sailors in Thailand, an editorial posted on Tencent (腾讯网) said, "Many netizens feel that the appropriate authorities in this case were not tough enough" and asked "if the dead were American, would an aircraft carrier already have sailed to Thailand?"[36] In 2011, Wei Xudong, a professor at the Chinese National Defense University recommended considering the establishment of a special strike unit and conducting prior consultation with overseas governments so that action to assist Chinese nationals could be conducted with the cooperation of local authorities.[37]

A 2013 article by Yue Gang, a former colonel with the PLA general staff, offers perhaps the most ambitious proposal.[38] Gang writes:

> The PLA should protect Chinese people overseas. . . .
> The army should act as a deterrent against those who attempt to harm Chinese people. We will not allow any repeat of such tragedies as the May 1998 riots in Indonesia.[39]

He suggests the PLA should do four things to strengthen its ability to protect overseas assets. First, it should increase its transport capacity, to include large transport aircraft. Even when the Y-20 enters service, he notes, it will have less than half the lift capacity of a U.S. C-5 aircraft. Second, it should increase its "forward" presence. Third, it should deepen its international military-to-military cooperation. And fourth, it should build up its military capacity to show its "will and determination."

Two things could increase the relative emphasis on protecting assets and people overseas. The first would be the continued rapid increase of investment and travel overseas. This would increase the stakes for China overseas and increase the incentives for China to develop the kinds of global power projection capabilities that would enable it to protect its interests around the world. The second would be a large-scale attack on Chinese nationals or diaspora, or the nationalization or destruction of important material assets or investments overseas.[40] There are a number of different capabilities that could be considered. Most, however, would involve the acquisition of naval and air lift and long-range capabilities, as well as the development of special operations forces with functions similar to those of the U.S. Delta Force or SEALs.

One question is what sort of global economic and security environment would correlate with and help propel Chinese overseas investment. It stands to reason that a stable and prosperous global economy will make overseas investment relatively safe and lucrative. Notably, commodity prices would also rise, and much of China's current overseas investment is in these areas. A sharp global downturn or instability overseas could put Chinese investments at risk, increasing the incentives to develop the capability to defend or evacuate assets and people, but the interests themselves will grow faster during periods of growth.

Strategic Military Relationships.

Another set of interests that could push the PLA toward a global trajectory is the development of strategic military relationships with overseas partners. The further expansion of overseas trade and investment would provide some incentives for developing or deepening such strategic relationships, as the PLA might seek, for example, to protect an ever larger volume of shipping and might, therefore, look for dependable locations from which it could provision ships on escort duty.

However, other factors, some less well appreciated, could also work to promote overseas strategic relationships. One such driver would be a desire to consolidate and build on common geopolitical interests with states that share Chinese views on global governance or specific international problems. Sharper differences between the developed world and rising powers on such issues as trade, the environment, and, especially, sovereignty norms could cause Chinese leaders to cement ties with other like-minded states by increasing military cooperation or assistance.

Expanded military-industrial ties could also serve to cement new strategic relations. China's arms sales have a checkered history. Previous sales, such as Chinese sales of armored vehicles to Thailand during the 1980s, came with very little support, were of shoddy quality, and gained China a reputation as a poor supplier. However, the quality of and support for Chinese sales is improving. Chinese arms sales remain modest, but are increasing rapidly. In 2013 (the most recent year for which data are available), China is estimated to have exported roughly $3.3 billion worth of military equipment.[41] The total value of arms sales for the 5 years between and 2009 and 2013 were more than three times those of the period from 2004 to 2008. (See Figure 4-2.)

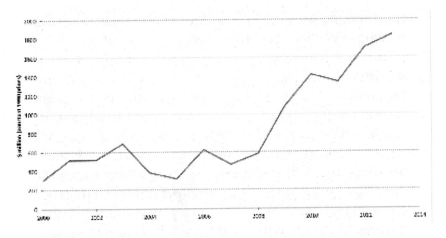

Source: *Arms Transfer Database*, Stockholm, Sweden, Stockholm International Peace Research Institute, 2013.[42]

Figure 4-2. Annual Chinese Arms Exports, 2000-13.

Although China is best known for the sale of small arms and other relatively light weapons, it is moving toward the export of larger and more complex platforms, such as fighters, frigates, and submarines.[43] A more significant departure (since it has exported some larger platforms in the past) is the increasing tendency to include licensed production or "joint" development as part of its deals. The JF-17, for example, was designed for Pakistan to be a low-cost 4th generation aircraft utilizing avionics and other features from the J-10, and Pakistan has committed to purchase 250 of the aircraft. JF-17 Block 2 production began in 2013, with Pakistan's share of the airframe production stipulated at 58 percent.[44] The fighter is currently being marketed in Latin America and the Middle East, with co-production being negotiated with Argentina.[45]

As the JF-17 example demonstrates, China is also marketing its weapons, with some success, to a wider range of clients. Turkey's announcement that it would purchase the FD-2000 (an export version of the HQ-9 long-range SAM system) surprised many — and elicited warnings from Turkey's U.S. North Atlantic Treaty Organization (NATO) ally — but Ankara, the Turkish capital, was drawn to the deal by both the low cost and the Chinese willingness to co-produce the systems.[46] Turkey is also interested in the FJ-17 for largely the same reasons. Indonesia is looking to license produce the Chinese C-705 anti-ship missile.[47] Thailand, a long-time partner, is deepening its military-industrial relationship with China by jointly developing a guided multiple rocket launcher system (the DTI-1G) as follow-on to earlier unguided systems imported from China.[48] It is also considering a range of portable Chinese SAM systems.[49]

Although China is currently the world's fifth largest arms exporter, it lags far behind the United States and Russia. However, the combination of low price, reasonable (and much improved) quality, good terms (often including co-production), few political conditions, and a growing range of available sub-systems and weapons could mean China is on the cusp of significant expansion in overseas arms sales. The consequences would likely be significant. Military-industrial ties bring senior military leaders into regular contact to discuss issues of common military interest. Arms sales are often accompanied by the dispatch of technicians and advisors to recipient nations, and licensed production and joint development may involve technology transfers greatly appreciated by the receiving nation.[50] The Chinese expansion of arms sales, licensed production, and joint development overseas will likely create interests that China will want to secure.

In general, closer strategic relations with more distant powers (to include those in southern Southeast Asia) will encourage the PLA to place greater emphasis on power projection capabilities. Transport aircraft, possibly supported by long range tankers, may be a desirable way of bringing equipment, units, and delegations to partner countries—even if commercial transportation would be just as practical. Similarly, replenishment ships could support an expanded schedule of fleet visits. Finally, a wider range of military and strategic partners could, at the margins, also increase the incentives to deploy and maintain aircraft carriers and other large surface ships that could carry the flag and increase Chinese prestige in distant locations.

INTERNATIONAL VARIABLES AND A WEAKER PLA

Many of the most important developments that would impinge on PLA strength are Chinese domestic factors, rather than international ones. At the most extreme, domestic variables would include serious domestic instability, such as that brought on by regime collapse or civil war, or an economic meltdown. Smaller, but nevertheless important developments would include unchecked or more widely publicized corruption within the military, a more pronounced economic slowdown than that currently being experienced, or significantly increased nonmilitary demands on the military budget. Although the most likely drivers of a weaker PLA would be domestic, there are several international developments that could also contribute to that outcome.

Military Failure and Misbehavior.

Military failure, especially failure that was accompanied by apparent incompetence, misbehavior, or civilian suffering, could undermine support for the PLA at home. For example, a sharp defeat in a conventional conflict against Japan might create pressure to find a military culprit for manifest humiliation at the hands of an old enemy. Should China become involved in a conflict farther afield, such as one that might grow out of a peacekeeping operation in Africa or elsewhere, widely publicized misbehavior by Chinese forces could similarly discredit or embarrass the military. Loss of support is not the only possible outcome of defeat, and a number of other intervening variables would come into play. Domestic economic and social maladies almost certainly exacerbated the U.S. reaction to the Vietnam War and even more significant domestic problems conditioned Soviet responses to losses in Afghanistan.

Imperial Overstretch.

Chinese leaders are likely to remain extraordinarily cautious about overseas military commitments. However, should this change and China find itself engaged in large scale, protracted operations to protect overseas interests, PLA modernization efforts could be undermined. China's military budget is far smaller than that of the United States, and although PLA units are unlikely to deploy with all the amenities that accompany U.S. forces, resources could be severely stretched and crowd out modernization priorities. Alternatively, the PLA might, like U.S. forces conducting stability operations in Iraq and Afghanistan, be forced to specialize in particular types of skills and structures that would not translate well to high-intensity operations against more capable foes. Weighed against these potential negative effects would be the accumulation of combat experience and a likely acceleration of lift acquisition.

Failure of Sino-Russian Military-Industrial Relationship.

With the continued development of China's own defense industries, foreign arms purchases and technology acquisition have become progressively less important to the PLA. Nevertheless, Russian military industry remains significantly ahead of China in a number of areas (e.g., aircraft engines, stealth technology, SAM systems, and systems integration more generally). A shift in Russian threat perception or a further deterioration in Russian confidence with regard to Chinese intellectual property rights protection could impinge on China's ability to leverage its relationship with Russia to acquire key capabilities. Alternatively, a major surge in Russian arms purchases for its own military might consume its industrial capacity and crowd out exports for a period. A similar result could obtain from a collapse of the Russian arms industry brought on, for example, by serious political or social instability, or by Western sanctions.

External Support for Domestic Chinese Terrorists.

Although the degree of internal threat faced by the regime will be determined largely by domestic variables, external support for domestic insurgencies or terrorists could increase the level and intensity of the threat. The most plausible scenarios would involve support to Uighur separatists from extremist groups. This would be particularly problematic for China if it included weapons, such as advanced explosives or portable surface-to-air missiles that could neutralize the Chinese military's mobility and firepower advantages. Intensified domestic threats could force the PLA to turn inwards, toward counterinsurgency missions. Although this could provide incentives for the acquisition of helicopters and other short range lift assets, it would generally detract from the PLA's ability to optimize its capabilities to counter more advanced opponents.

SUMMARY AND OUTCOMES: DESCRIBING FUTURE WORLDS

Having discussed a range of key variables, this section returns to the trajectories themselves and summarizes which combinations of variables might push China toward each outcome.

Trajectory 1: PLA Optimized for Operations in the Immediate Periphery.

The PLA is currently developing greater regional power projection capabilities. While a variety of factors may be leading the PLA in this direction, it is possible to imagine changes in the international environment that would threaten China in its immediate periphery and push it to refocus on short range systems. These would include a relatively strong United States with poor relations with China, perhaps brought on by international crises that led Washington to recommit itself to regional defense beyond the current pivot to Asia. The impact would be particularly pronounced if it were accompanied by additional U.S. investments in systems that could be used to strike targets in mainland China (such as prompt global strike or long range hypersonic missiles). Poor Chinese relations or crises with Taiwan, and anticipated military conflict with it, could have similar effects. Under these circumstances, Chinese political and military leaders might believe that anti-access capabilities and large numbers of short range platforms might be a cost effective way to maximize its ability to prevail in relevant areas.

Trajectory 2: A PLA Prepared for Regional Power Projection and Warfighting.

A different combination of factors could push China to accelerate its acquisition of regional power projection capabilities. If relations with Taiwan remained stable, while those with other states in Southeast, East, or South Asia worsened, the incentives to develop capabilities to influence events further from home will grow. Wildcards, such as naval or air clashes with regional states or large-scale attacks on the Chinese diaspora or citizens in these areas, would provide additional incentives to acquire such capabilities. Positive regional developments (from China's perspective) could also draw Chinese military farther from home. For example, were China to develop more robust strategic relations with regional states, perhaps cemented in part through military-industrial cooperation, Beijing might wish to develop the lift and other capabilities to support exchanges or the transportation of heavy equipment or units for combined training exercises. Needless to say, a region in which some countries are military or key strategic partners and some present challenges is entirely possible, and this combination could draw China powerfully toward a wider regional strategy.

Trajectory 3: Accelerated Investment in Global Power Projection.

A peaceful environment in Asia and the shelving or resolution of disputes with neighbors would provide the permissive environment in which the PLA could accelerate its acquisition of global capabilities. The growth of Chinese foreign investments, drawing more Chinese companies and workers farther afield, would provide the positive incentives for a globally oriented PLA. The development of close strategic ties with powers outside the region, underpinned in some cases by military-industrial cooperation, could create practical demands for the ability to deliver and sustain equipment and people to distant locations. An environment of global economic growth and prosperity is more likely to be associated with this outcomes than is one in which the world economy stagnates. A Washington that welcomed Beijing's cooperation in peacekeeping or stability operations overseas, while not necessary, would provide yet another boost for the development of small but high quality expeditionary forces.

Trajectory 4: A Weaker PLA.

The most plausible variables that might weaken the PLA are domestic. Less likely, but still important, external developments could contribute to a weaker PLA. A high-profile military failure overseas could undermine support for the PLA and PLA modernization at home. Alternatively, protracted overseas military operations could drain resources away from modernization. Although China's defense industries have become progressively less dependent upon foreign assistance, a loss of access to Russian technology might slow PLA's modernization in key areas. Finally, foreign support for domestic Chinese insurgency or terrorism, particularly in Xinjiang, could turn the PLA's focus inward and produce a military less well suited for operations against foreign states.

ENDNOTES - CHAPTER 4

1. By convention, MRBMs have ranges between 1,000 and 3,000-km, and IRBMs have ranges between 3,000 and 5,500-km. As an example of the cost of an MRBM, the average procurement cost of the two-stage Pershing II missile produced by the United States in the 1980s would be roughly $11 million per missile in 2014 dollars. See Sharman Stein, "Missile Makeup Pershing II's Path Typical in U.S. Defense Industry," *Orlando Sentinel*, May 27, 1985. Procurement spending for 254 Pershing II MRBMs was approximately $1.3 billion in 1985, which implies an average cost of 1,300/254 = $5.118 million per missile in 1985 dollars. the BLS inflation calculator was used to adjust to 2014 dollars.

2. By way of illustration, an aircraft flying at 40,000 feet has a line of sight of approximately 400-km. Thus, when preparing to project force beyond 1,000-km, beyond-line-of-sight communications, such as satellite-based communications, becomes critical in a way that it is not for shorter range operations.

3. David A. Shlapak, David T. Orleysky, Toy I. Reid, Burray Scot Tanner, and Barry Wilson, *A Question of Balance: Political Context and Military Aspects of the China-Taiwan Dispute*, MG-888, Santa Monica, CA: RAND, 2009, pp. 31-51.

4. For example, at an average cruising speed of 10 knots, Chinese submarines could move from the North Sea Fleet to the vicinity of Taiwan in under 4 days. Transit from the East and South Sea Fleets would take even less time.

5. The exception is Andersen AFB on Guam, which is currently only within range of the aging nuclear-armed DF-3 IRBM. China has announced that it will field a new conventionally-armed IRBM by 2015, which will pose a new threat to Guam. See Zhang Han and Huang Jingjing, "New Missile Ready by 2015," *People's Daily Online*, February 18, 2011; Doug Richardson, "China Plans 4,000-km Range Conventional Ballistic Missile," *Jane's Missiles and Rockets*, March 1, 2011.

6. Kadena is roughly 770-km from the center of the Taiwan Strait and about 650-km from the nearest point on Mainland China. It is well within range of the DF-21C, with a range of roughly 1,750-km. The new DF-16 is estimated to have a range between 800 and 1,000+-km. As a much smaller and lighter missile, it could potentially be produced in greater numbers than the DF-21 and potentially used against Kadena and other facilities on Okinawa. "DF-21 (CSS-5)," *Jane's Strategic Weapons Systems*, September 6, 2013; and "DF-16," *Jane's Strategic Weapons Systems*, December 4, 2013.

7. This was true, for example, of President Hu Jintao's comments on the subject when he visited Washington in January 2011. See Michael D. Swaine, "China's Assertive Behavior, Part One: On 'Core Interests,'" in *China Leadership Monitor*, No. 34, p. 11.

8. An Gang, "The Core of the Issue: China's Declaration of its Key Interests Misinterpreted by Many," *Beijing Review*, August 26, 2013.

9. Taiwan's importance to China stems from a host of factors, including its historical importance as a reminder of past perceived humiliations, the threat it poses to the legitimacy of the CCP, the strategic importance of Taiwan's geography, and its role as a key organizing mission for the PLA. See, for example, Drew Thompson and Zhu Feng, "Why Taiwan Really Matters to China," *Jamestown China Brief*, No. 4, Vol. 19, 2004; Alan M. Wachman, *Why Taiwan? Geostrategic Rationales for China's Territorial Integrity*, Redwood City, CA: Stanford University Press, 2007.

10. Jian Yang, "Of Interest and Distrust: Understanding China's Policy Towards Japan," *China: An International Journal*, Vol. 5, No. 2, 2007, pp. 250-275. Public opinion surveys indicate wide-

spread mistrust between the Japanese and Chinese populations; Voice of America, "Survey: Mistrust High between Japanese, Chinese Citizens," *VOA News*, January 7, 2013, available from *www.voanews.com/articleprintview/1579369.html*, accessed on May 20, 2014.

11. In order for MRBMs to range Japan's full strategic depth, China would need to launch them from northeastern China. The quickest way to achieve this would be by relocating some of its road-mobile MRBM units from the south. If China wished to make a more permanent threat to the full extent of Japan, then it could build a new home garrison for an MRBM brigade in North-eastern China.

12. "刘亚洲：甲午战争是日本制度的胜利" ("Liu Yazhou: The Sino-Japanese War was a Victory of the Japanese System"), 参考消息 (*Reference News*), April 12, 2014.

13. "Chinese Leader, Seeking to Build Its Muscle, Pushes Overhaul of the Military," *The New York Times*, May 24, 2014.

14. Tien-sze Fang, *Asymmetrical Threat Perceptions in India-China Relations*, New York: Oxford University Press, 2014; Lionel Martin, "Mistrust and Cooperation: Analyzing Sino-Indian Relations," *Jamestown China Brief*, No. 4, Vol. 21, 2004; Lora Saalman, "Divergence, Similarity, and Symmetry in Sino-Indian Threat Perceptions," *Journal of International Affairs*, Vol. 64, No. 2, 2011, pp. 169-194.

15. See, for example, 章节根 (Zhang Jiegen), "印度核战略对中国安全环境及南亚政策的影响" ("Impact of Indian Nuclear Strategy on China's Strategy Environment and South Asia"), 同济大学学报 (*Tongji University Journal*, Social Sciences Section), April 2011.

16. See Frances Mangosing, "PH Acquires P23.7B-Worth of Fighter Jets, Helicopters," *Inquirer.net*, March 28, 2014, available from *newsinfo.inquirer.net/589890/ph-acquires-p23-7b-worth-of-fighter-jets-helicopters*, accessed on May 8, 2014.

17. Mark Landler, "U.S. and Philippines Agree to a 10-Year Pact on the Use of Military Bases," *The New York Times*, April 27, 2014.

18. See, for example, "王缉思：20年内美国仍是唯一超级大国" ("Wang Jisi: For the Next 20 Years, the United States will Remain the Lone Superpower"), 环球时报 (Huanqiu Shibao), August 6, 2011; and《美国问题研究报告(2011)：美国的实力与地位评估》[*Research Report on U.S. Topics: Evaluation of U.S. Power and Position*], Bejing, China: Chinese Academy of Social Sciences, 2011.

19. To some extent, this was already true by the end of the Cold War. During the 1980s, the United States adopted the Air-Land Battle concept, which called for deep interdiction of the battle area, as well as high-intensity offensive action. However, despite some calls for attacks into Eastern Europe, it was generally understood that the United States and its NATO allies would be on the defensive in a strategic and operational sense, at least during the opening phases of conflict.

20. This approach has been on display in all of America's recent wars, including Operation DESERT STORM (1991), Operation ALLIED FORCE (1999), Operation ENDURING FREEDOM (2001), Operation IRAQI FREEDOM (2003), and (in modified form) Operation ODYSSEY DAWN (2011). Our colleague Alan Vick has argued that there were five key components to the American way of war in these conflicts: (1) rapid forward deployment of air, ground, and naval forces; (2) creation of rear area sanctuaries; (3) close monitoring of enemy forces; (4) denial of enemy forces' ability to monitor U.S. forces; and, (5) generation of large number of aircraft sorties essentially at will. See Alan Vick, "Challenges to the American Way of War," *Global Warfare Symposium*, Los Angeles, CA, November 11, 2011, available from *secure.afa.org/events/natlsymp/2011/scripts/AFA-111117-Vick.pdf*, accessed on May 19, 2014.

21. U.S. forces are overwhelmingly concentrated in Northeast Asia, well within range of Chinese systems, and the United States has maintained a rotational bomber deployment on Guam since 2004. The AirSea Battle is an operational concept rather than a strategy, but many of the examples of synergies that might be developed involve ISR and strike systems cooperating to "disrupt, destroy, and defeat" adversary A2/AD capabilities, which would be highly useful in offensive strategies. "Barksdale AFB: B-52's Deploying to Guam, Part of Routine Rotation of Continuous Bomber Presence on Guam," *Pacific News Center*, August 28, 2013;

Admiral Jonathan W. Greenert and General Norton A. Schwartz, "Air-Sea Battle," *The American Interest*, February 20, 2012; and Air-Sea Battle Office, *Air-Sea Battle: Service Collaboration to Address Anti-Access and Area Denial Challenges*, Washington, DC: Department of Defense, May 2013.

22. See, for example, Douglas C. Peifer, "China, the German Analogy, and the New Air-Sea Operational Concept," *Orbis*, Vol. 55, No. 1, Winter 2011; Sean Mirski, "Stranglehold: The Context, Conduct and Consquences of an American Naval Blockade of China," *The Journal of Strategic Studies*, Vol. 36, No. 3, 2013; Evan Branden Montgomery, "Reconsidering a Naval Blockade of China: A Response to Mirski," *The Journal of Strategic Studies*, Vol. 36, No. 4, 2013; T. X. Hammes, "Offshore Control: A Proposed Strategy for an Unlikely Conflict," Washington, DC, NDU Strategic Forum, June 2012.

23. Funding for some limited measures has already been allocated under the Pacific Airpower Resiliency (PAR) initiative. These measures include hardening key logistical facilities and improving the ability to recover runways and disperse aircraft after attack. See "Pacific Sites Named in Massive U.S. Military Construction Plan," *Pacific Islands Report*, Washington, DC: East-West Center, April 2013, available from *pidp.eastwestcenter.org/pireport/2013/April/04-16-01.htm*.

24. The USAF has been working to improve rapid runway repair with the Critical Runway Assessment and Repair (CRATR) capability, See R. Craig Mellerski, "Airfield Damage Repair — The Future Now," *The Civil Engineer*, August 2009. Efforts to protect critical infrastructure from current threats have been conducted under the Hardened Installation Protection for Persistent Operations (HIPPO) applied research and development effort. See U.S. Army Corps of Engineers, July 5, 2013, available from *www.erdc.usace.army.mil/Media/NewsStories/tabid/9219/Article/15844/two-year-hardened-installation-effort-ends-on-a-high-note.aspx*, accessed on August 13, 2013. Efforts to rapidly deploy fighter plans to austere bases and operate are underway. In 2013, the USAF tested a "Rapid Raptor" concept that uses a single C-17 transport aircraft to deploy four F-22s to a forward location and have them combat-ready within 24 hours. See Marc V. Schanz, "Rapid Raptor Package," *Air Force Magazine*, September 27, 2013, available

from *www.airforcemag.com/Features/Pages/2013/September%202013/box092613rapid.aspx*, accessed on May 8, 2014. The USMC has also exercised its ability to rapidly open and operate from an austere airfield, such as during the Geiger Fury exercise on Tinian in 2012. See Brett Kelman, "Marines head to Tinian for Exercise Geiger Fury," *Marine Corps Times*, May 15, 2012, available from *www.marinecorpstimes.com/article/20120515/NEWS/205150329/Marines-head-Tinian-Exercise-Geiger-Fury*, accessed on May 8, 2014.

25. Speech by Wang Yi to Brookings.

26. "The Diversified Employment of China's Armed Forces," Bejing, China: PRC, Information Office of the State Council, August 2013.

27. Trade statistics are from IMF Direction of Trade Statistics database. FDI figures are from the "China Global Investment Tracker" database, Washington, DC: The Heritage Foundation, available from *www.heritage.org/research/projects/china-global-investment-tracker-interactive-map*. FDI statistics are notoriously inconsistent, and the Heritage figures do not match with those of the Chinese Ministry of Commerce, which lists just over $90 billion in non-financial overseas investments in 2013 (as opposed to the $132 billion figure provided by Heritage).

28. "97 Million Chinese Tourists Went Abroad in 2013," *South China Morning Post*, February 10, 2014.

29. "Big Rise in Chinese Overseas," *China Daily*, January 22, 2014.

30. "Overseas and Under Siege: An Apparent Rise in Violence Against Chinese Labourers Working Overseas," *The Economist*, August 11, 2009; Mathieu Duchatel and Bates Gill, "Overseas Citizen Protection: A Growing Challenge for China," SIPRI Newsletter, February 12, 2012; and ZAMBIA.

31. "Thai Soldiers 'Murdered' Chinese sailors," *The Telegraph*, October 2011.

32. In the latter case, estimates of the number killed range between 1,000 and 1,500. Rape was also reportedly widespread,

though impossible to quantify due to the under reporting of sexual assaults.

33. With the Chinese government largely silent, Joe Tan, an ethnic Chinese living in New Zealand, organized protest through his website, Global Huaren. Demonstrations were organized near Chinese embassies around the world, and forceful statements by prominent Hong Kong and Taiwanese officials and politicians generated additional pressures. Sheng Ding, "Digital Diaspora and National Image Building: A New Perspective on Chinese Diaspora Study in the Age of China's Rise," *Pacific Affairs*, Winter 2007-08.

34. "Chinese Demand Apology as Indonesian Communist-Purge Film Gets Oscar Nod," *South China Morning Post*, January 21, 2014.

35. "The Diversified Employment of China's Armed Forces."

36. "If the 13 Dead Crewmembers were Americans," *Tengxunwang*, October 25, 2011. The editors ultimately caution against the use of force and suggest strengthening consular functions instead.

37.韩旭东 (Wei Xudong), "国防大学教授: 保护海外中国人 亟待我组建准军事力量介入" ("Chinese National Defense University Professor: We Must Urgently Establish Military Forces for Intervention in Order to Protect Overseas Chinese Citizens"), 环球时报 (*Global Times*), October 25, 2011.

38. 岳刚 (Yue Gang), "中国军力增长应捍卫海外利益" ("The PLA Must Protect China's Overseas Interests"), 中国新闻网 (*China News online*), April 18, 2013. The article identifies Yue as a former colonel with the General Staff Department.

39. *Ibid.*

40. The increasing Chinese stake in resource extraction from unstable regions increases the probability of threats. For example, China Metallurgical Group's 30-year lease of the Mes Aynak copper mine in Afghanistan could be threatened if instability in Pakistan or Afghanistan increases over the next few decades.

41. Estimates are from the SIPRI Arms Transfers Database and represent an estimate of the value of weapons actually transferred, rather than the actual price paid or the value of new contracts. SIPRI numbers are provided in constant U.S. 1990 dollars, with the figure on 2012 arms transfers cited in the previous text having been converted to 2012 dollars using the U.S. CPI, available from *www.sipri.org/databases/armstransfers*. Note that *IHS Jane's* reports a figure for 2012 of $2.2 billion, which may reflect different methodologies, for example, an estimate based on executed contracts or actual (reported) sales prices.

42. Estimates are from the SIPRI Arms Transfers Database and represent an estimate of the value of weapons actually transferred, rather than the actual price paid or the value of new contracts. SIPRI numbers are provided in constant U.S. 1990 dollars, available from *www.sipri.org/databases/armstransfers*, accessed on May 23, 2014.

43. "Chinese Arms Industry Makes Global Inroads," *The New York Times*, October 20, 2013. Pakistan took delivery of the last of four F22P (improved Jiangwei-class) frigates and is negotiating for six S20 (modified Yuan-class) submarines. It has long been a client for fighter aircraft, with quality and sophistication improving rapidly in recent years. "China-Pakistan Set for Submarine Deal by the End of the Year, Says Officials," *Jane's Defense Weekly*, February 3, 2014.

44. In all, Pakistan is expected to purchase 250 JF-17 aircraft. "PAC Announces Start of JF-17 Block 2 Construction," *Jane's Defense Weekly*, December 19, 2013.

45. "Argentina – Air Force," *Jane's World Air Forces*, January 27, 1914. In addition to the appeal of co-production and the low-price (estimated at roughly $20-$25 million), the ability to employ an increasingly wide range of highly capable air-to-air, air-to-ground, and anti-ship missiles provides significant appeal.

46. "Update: Turkey Remains Defiant About Co-Producing Missile Defense System with China," *Defense Update*, October 25, 2013.

47. "Indonesia and China Move Closer to Deal on C-705 Production Agreement," *Jane's Navy International*, August 22, 2013.

48. "Thailand, China to Jointly Develop Multiple Rocket Launchers," *The Economic Times*, April 28, 2012.

49. "China Offers Thailand Collaboration on Missiles, Armoured Vehicles," *Jane's Defense Weekly*, November 3, 2013.

50. As in the case of general trade, arms sales and military-industrial cooperation can also create new tensions, such as those between China and Russia over the former's questionable adherence to the terms of agreements. But the impact will be generally positive.

CHAPTER 5

CAPACITY FOR INNOVATION: TECHNOLOGICAL DRIVERS OF CHINA'S FUTURE MILITARY MODERNIZATION

Richard A. Bitzinger
Michael Raska

DEFINING CAPACITY FOR INNOVATION

Innovation is generally seen as critical, if not central, to military modernization. Throughout history, process of innovation—that is, the process of turning ideas and invention into more effective products or services (in this case, the creation of more effective militaries)—was at the heart of gaining military superiority over a rival (or rivals). This includes the introduction of new ways of fighting (i.e., the phalanx, used to great effectiveness by the Greek city-states in antiquity), of organization (i.e., the *lévee en masse* of the French Revolution), or of technology (i.e., the so-called "gunpowder revolution" of the 16th century, or aviation and mechanization in the 20th century). Accordingly, while the literature on military innovation has portrayed innovation through multiple facets, it has been conceptualized primarily in the context of major military change in relation to existing ways of war.[1] Stephen Rosen, for example, conceptualized military innovation in the context of major "change that forces one of the primary combat arms of a service to change its concepts of operation and its relation to other combat arms, and to abandon or downgrade traditional missions."[2] Rosen differentiated between major military innovations (MMIs) and technological innovations, with MMIs further subdivided into peacetime and wartime processes. Theo Farrell and Terry Terriff also distinguished major military change or "change in the [organizational] goals, actual strategies, and/or structure of a military organization," and minor change or "changes in operational means and methods (technologies and tactics) that have no implications for organizational strategy or structure."[3] More recently, Michael Horowitz equated major military innovations as "major changes in the conduct of warfare, relevant to leading military organizations, designed to increase the efficiency with which capabilities are converted to power."[4] Dima Adamsky, too, focused on disruptive military innovation through the lens of military-technical revolutions (MTRs) or revolutions in military affairs (RMAs), when "new organizational structures together with novel force deployment methods, usually but not always driven by new technologies, change the conduct of warfare."[5]

Inherent in the above definitions is the emphasis on the theory, process, and debate of radical/disruptive change, a large-scale RMA-oriented innovation defined by the synergy of technological change, military systems development, operational innovation, and organizational innovation.[6] However, in a historical perspective, most military changes concomitant with select military innovations have arguably followed a distinctly less than revolutionary or transformational path, consisting of incremental, often near-continuous, improvements in existing capabilities.[7] In other words, while major, large-scale, and simultaneous military innovation in military technologies, organizations, and doctrines have been a rare phenomenon, military organizations have progressed through a sustained spectrum of military innovation ranging from a small-scale to large-scale innovation that have shaped the conduct of warfare.[8]

Military innovation can therefore take multiple facets and rarely proceeds in a synchronized rate, path, or pattern. Given the prevailing external and internal variables — enablers and constraints that shape the capacity of states to integrate, adapt, and utilize military innovation under local circumstances, military innovation is not sequential nor does it follow a particular model. Generally, however, we can distinguish between two types of innovation: (1) **disruptive** and (2) **sustaining**. According to Peter Dombrowski, Eugene Gholz, and Andrew Ross:

> Sustaining innovations are defined by improvements in product quality measured by familiar standards: they offer new, better ways to do what customer organization have been doing using previous generations of technology.[9]

On the other hand, disruptive innovations "establish a trajectory of rapid performance improvements that . . . overtakes the quality of the old market-leading product even when measured by traditional performance standards."[10] In other words, disruptive innovation changes nearly everything about doing business — in this case, the business of war. At the same time, however, disruptive **military innovation must be always viewed in a relative context** — through the lens of the **competitive dimension** reflected in the efforts to develop effective counterinnovation strategies and measures. In such view, military innovation is always contextual, relative, and limited in duration.

Accordingly, a capacity for military innovation can be conceptualized as an input, process, and outcome.[11] Input factors include "**hard innovation capa-**

bilities" — input and infrastructure factors intended to advance technological and product development such as research and development (R&D) facilities, manufacturing capabilities, access to foreign technologies and markets; and "**soft innovation capabilities**" — process-related innovation activities, including political, institutional, relational, social and ideational factors that shape innovation.[12] These are embedded in **defense management processes** in the planning, organizing, and controlling armed forces and their supporting systems to achieve national security objectives; in the development of advanced, reliable, cost-effective **defense industrial base** capable of producing innovative defense technologies, products, and services; and ultimately, **combat proficiency and capabilities** to engage in a range of military operations, and the potential to integrate and exploit innovative concepts, organizational structures, and technologies in combat. A capacity for innovation can be then viewed in the context of **strategic, organizational and operational adaptability** – not only in detecting new sources of military innovation, but more importantly, changing military posture quickly and easily over time in response to shifts in geostrategic environment, military technology, the realities of cost, performance, and organizational behavior and national priorities.[13]

CHINA'S SEARCH FOR INNOVATION: HISTORICAL PATH DEPENDENCE

Although military innovation/modernization is typically a "holistic" event, incorporating technological change with changes in organization, doctrine, and tactics, technology is still generally the starting-point for innovation, and therefore it will be central to this chapter. The People's Republic of China has, going back to its founding, strived to become self-reliant in the development and manufacture of arms.[14] The current phrase to express this desire for autarky in defense production and acquisition is, according to Tai Ming Cheung, 自主创新, or "innovation with Chinese characteristics."[15] Bates Gill and Taeho Kim argue that China's desire to wean itself off foreign dependencies for armaments actually goes back more than 150 years, when the country was too weak militarily to fend off the encroaching Western powers.[16] For most of its history, however, the results of these endeavors have been decidedly mixed. Even with sizable economic inputs, access to foreign technologies, and considerable political will, China, up until the late-1990s, experienced only limited success when it came to the local design, development, and manufacture of advanced conventional weapons. Most systems were at least a generation or two behind comparable military equipment being produced at the time in the West or in the Soviet Union, and problems with quality and reliability abounded. In addition, overcapacity, redundancy, inefficient production, and, above all, a weak defense R&D base all conspired to impede the development of an advanced indigenous arms production capability. Overall, these circumstances left China in the unenviable position of pursuing great power status with a decidedly "Third World" arms industry.

To be sure, the Chinese have long been aware of the deficiencies in their defense technology and industrial base, and they have undertaken several rounds of reforms since the late-1980s in order to improve and modernize their military innovation and R&D processes. Most of these efforts fell well short of their intentions, however, because they failed to tackle the basic if endemic problems facing the defense industry: lack of competition, lack of accountability, excess capacity, lack of capital, lack of human skills, and a "statist" corporate culture. These prior failures make the post-1997 reform efforts even more significant, because they, more than earlier attempts, have tried to attack the very nature of Chinese arms development, production, and acquisition. This will enable these efforts to, first, inject rational, requirements-based planning into the arms procurement process, and, second, to spur the defense state-owned enterprises to act more like true industrial enterprises. These efforts therefore will: (1) be more responsive to their customer base (i.e., the People's Liberation Army [PLA]), and (2) reform, modernize, and "marketize" their business operations.

These goals in particular are central to the PLA's new requirements—as laid out in China's 2004 defense white paper—for fighting limited local wars under conditions of informatization.[17] This, in turn, is linked to a "generation leap" industrial strategy when it comes to armaments development and production—that is, skipping or shortening the stages of R&D and of generations of weapons systems. This process, according to You Ji, entails a "double construction" approach of mechanization and "informatization" in order to concurrently upgrade and digitize the PLA.[18] This "two-track" approach calls for both the near-term "upgrading of existing equipment combined with the selective introduction of new generations of conventional weapons"—a so-called "modernization-plus" approach—together with a longer-term "transformation" of the PLA along the lines of the information technologies-led revolution in military affairs (RMA).[19] Cheung argues that this plan was formalized in both the 2006-20 Medium- and Long-Term Defense Science and Technology Development Plan and the 11th Five-Year Defense Plan, both of which emphasized acceleration of PLA modernization and a new defense R&D drive.[20] Part of this two-track approach also depends on China's "latecomer advantage" of being able to more quickly exploit technological trails blazed by others, as well as avoiding their mistakes and blind alleys.[21]

One of the most important developments of late was the demotion of old Commission of Science, Technology, and Industry for National Defense (COSTIND) to an ancillary role in coordinating defense R&D, and, at the same time, creation of a new PLA-run General Armaments Department (GAD), which was intended to act as the primary purchasing agent for the PLA, overseeing defense acquisition and new weapons programs. As a 2005 RAND report put it, the GAD is part of a process "to create a system that will unify, standardize, and legalize the [Chinese] weapons procurement process."[22] As such, the GAD is supposed to ensure that local arms producers meet PLA requirements when it comes to capabilities, quality, costs, and program milestones. The GAD was given the authority to implement a "robust" regulatory, standards, and evaluation regime that would enforce quality control and performance, and incentivize competition and innovation.[23] More importantly, the establishment of the GAD exemplified a major change in how the Chinese approached defense innovation. According to Cheung, since the mid-1980s, the Chinese military research, development, and acquisition (RDA) system has gradually transitioned from a "technology-push" model (i.e., weapons programs driven mainly by what the defense industries can deliver) to a "demand-pull" type—that is, driven by PLA requirements, and "ensuring that military end-user needs are being served."[24] This process was only fully implemented with the creation of the GAD, which gave the PLA leading authority over defense innovation and R&D. In particular, the GAD had the ability to concentrate R&D funding on "select high-priority projects," with the intended effect of injecting a modicum of competition among R&D institutes when it came to winning R&D work.[25] Concurrently, COSTIND's role in overseeing the defense industrial base was substantially reduced, basically to "the making and administration of government policies toward the defense industry."[26] Oversight and administration of the defense industry enterprises was placed under a new organization, the State-owned Assets Supervision and Administration Commission (SASAC), which reports directly to the State Commission (the PRC's chief administrative authority). This diminished status was followed by COSTIND's eventual demotion in 2008 from a ministerial level entity to a bureau within the Ministry of Industry and Information Technology (MIIT), subsequently renamed the State Administration of Defense Science, Technology, and Industry (SASTIND).[27]

Additionally, China in the late-1990s began to seriously pursue the idea of leveraging advanced technologies and manufacturing processes found in the commercial sector in order to benefit defense R&D and production. According to many analysts, such civil-military integration (CMI) is a central feature of defense industry reform.[28] CMI is viewed as a fast (or at least faster) and ready means to shortcut the R&D process when it comes to advanced weapons systems; to cherry-pick civilian manufacturing practices in high-tech sectors (e.g., computer-aided design and manufacturing [CAD/CAM], program management tools, etc.); exploit dual-use technologies (e.g., space systems for surveillance, communication, and navigation) to support the military; and, in particular, to take advantage of the latent capabilities found in commercially based information technologies (IT) in order to harness the IT-based RMA. Such civil technologies could be both domestically developed or obtained from foreign sources via joint ventures, technology transfer, or even espionage.[29]

This new strategy is embodied in the principle of "locating military potential in civilian capabilities" ("寓军于民"), enunciated at the 16th Party Congress in 2003.[30] Subsequently, this strategy has been made a priority in the last several Five-Year Defense Plans, as well as the 2006-20 Medium- and Long-Term Defense Science and Technology Development Plan. These plans all emphasize the importance of the transfer of commercial technologies to military use, and they call upon the Chinese arms industry to not only develop dual-use technologies, but to also actively promote joint civil-military technology cooperation. Consequently, the spin-on of advanced commercial technologies both to the Chinese military-industrial complex and in support of the overall modernization of the PLA has been made explicit policy.[31]

The key areas of China's new focus on dual-use technology development and subsequent spin-on include microelectronics, space systems, new materials (such as composites and alloys), propulsion, missiles, computer-aided manufacturing, and particularly information technologies. Over the past decade, Beijing has worked hard both to encourage further domestic development and growth in these sectors **and** to expand linkages and collaboration between China's military-industrial complex and civilian high-technology sectors. Factories were also encouraged to invest in new manufacturing technologies, such as CAD, computer numerically controlled (CNC) multi-axis machine tools, computer integrated manufacturing systems (CIMS), and modular construction in shipbuilding, as well as to embrace Western management techniques. In 2002, for example, the Chinese government created a new industry enterprise group, the China Electronics Technology Group Corporation, to promote national technological and industrial developments in the area of defense-related electronics. Defense enterprises have formed partnerships with Chinese universities and civilian research institutes to establish technology incubators and undertake cooperative R&D on dual-use technologies. Additionally, foreign high-tech firms wishing to invest in China have been pressured to set up joint R&D centers and to transfer more technology to China.

"INDIGENOUS INNOVATION" STRATEGY

Over the past decade, China's military modernization has gradually progressed with the advances in China's civilian science and technology base, which in turn has been increasingly linked to global commercial markets and scientific networks. Technology transfers, foreign R&D investment, and training of Chinese scientists and engineers at research institutes and corporations overseas are part of China's "**indigenous innovation**" drive to (1) identify, (2) digest, (3) absorb, and (4) reinvent select technological capabilities, both in civil and military domains.[32] In order to advance indigenous defense science and technology (S&T), China has embarked on an aggressive campaign to acquire and exploit foreign technologies. According to William Hannas, James Mulvenon, and Anna Puglisi, this process of foreign technology acquisition is part of an unprecedented and aggressive effort, directed by the central Chinese government—a "deliberate, state-sponsored project to circumvent the costs of research, overcome cultural disadvantages, and 'leapfrog' to the forefront by leveraging the creativity of other nations."[33] China, they assert, is engaged in a multipronged effort to gain foreign advanced technologies through both legal and illegal means. These include exploitation of open sources, technology transfer and joint research, the return of Western-trained Chinese students, and, of course, industrial espionage (both traditional and, increasingly, cyber espionage). Hannas, Mulvenon, and Puglisi document a number of cases whereby Chinese intelligence organizations stole technology and other defense secrets from the West, and these were ostensibly incorporated (or will be incorporated) into Chinese weapons systems.[34]

China's "indigenous innovation" strategy is embedded primarily in the 2006 National Medium to Long-term Plan (MLP) for the Development of Science and Technology (2005-20).[35] The MLP is Beijing's most ambitious S&T plan to date with special long-term total funding estimated at 500 billion yuan (U.S.$75 billion). The plan is as a follow-up to the highly acclaimed National High Technology Program ("863") launched in March 1986—the most important China's civilian-military R&D program next to the "Two Weapons, and One Satellite" S&T development plan of 1956-67.[36] The 863 Program featured a concurrent development of dual-use technologies applicable in both civilian and military domains. The program had initially focused on developing seven strategic priority areas: laser technology, space, biotechnology, information technology, automation and manufacturing technology, energy, and advanced materials. In the mid-1990s, China expanded these areas in size, scope, and importance, shifting its trajectory toward cutting-edge technological products and processes.[37] The 863 Program is ongoing, funding projects such as the Tianhe-1A and Tianhe-2 supercomputers.[38] In the process, China is benchmarking emerging technologies and similar high-tech defense-related programs in the United States, Russia, India, Japan, Israel and other countries.[39]

Central to the MLP are 16 National Megaprojects—vanguard S&T programs—"priorities of priorities"—designed to transform China's S&T capabilities in areas such as electronics, semiconductors, telecommunications, aerospace, manufacturing, pharmaceuticals, clean energy, and oil and gas exploration. The megaprojects include both civilian and military areas, with 13 listed and three "unannounced" areas classified. Indeed, the 16 Megaprojects have been a source of considerable controversy and debates both in China and abroad, given the continuing structural, technological, and manufacturing challenges that inhibit disruptive innovation in Chinese defense S&T system. The debate has also focused on the three classified megaprojects. Recent analysis suggests three prime candidates for the military megaprojects:[40]

Shenguang Laser Project for Inertial Confinement Fusion.

The Shenguang (神光 Divine Light) laser project explores the inertial confinement fusion (ICF) as an alternative approach to attain inertial fusion energy

(IFE) — a controllable, sustained nuclear fusion reaction aided by an array of high-powered lasers. The lasers essentially heat and compress pellet-sized targets typically containing two hydrogen isotopes, deuterium and tritium, sending shock waves into the center and releasing energy that heats the surrounding fuel, which may also undergo fusion. Shenguang aims to achieve such "burn" — fusion ignition and plasma burning — by 2020, while advancing research in solving the complex technological challenges associated with controlling the nuclear reaction.[41]

Shenguang's target physics, theory and experimentation, began as early as 1993. By 2012, China completed the Shenguang 3 (Divine Light 3), a high-powered super laser facility based in the Research Center of Laser Fusion at the China Academy of Engineering Physics — the research and manufacturing center of China's nuclear weapons located in Mianyang. In this context, Shenguang has two strategic implications: it may accelerate China's next-generation thermo-nuclear weapons development, and advance China's directed- energy laser weapons programs.[42]

Second Generation Beidou Satellite Navigation System.

The second prime candidate for China's "unlisted" megaprojects is likely the Beidou-2 Satellite System (BDS), formerly known as the Compass Navigation Satellite System (CNSS). According to *IHS Jane's*, by the end of 2012, China had 16 operational Beidou satellites in orbit — six geostationary satellites, five Medium Earth Orbit spacecraft, and five satellites in Inclined GeoStationary Orbits covering the Asia-Pacific region. By 2020, Beidou 2 envisions a full-scale system of at least five geostationary and 30 non-geostationary satellites providing a global coverage in two modes: free "open" services available to commercial customers with 10-meter location- tracking accuracy, and restricted "authorized" services providing positioning, velocity and timing communications estimated at 10 centimeter accuracy for the Chinese government and military.[43]

Beidou 2 satellites, developed by the China Academy of Space Technology, are also designed with effective protection against electromagnetic interference and attack. Notwithstanding its wide commercial utility, the BDS will enable the PLA to significantly enhance its global navigation, tracking, targeting capabilities, providing guidance for military vehicles, ballistic and cruise missiles, precision-guided munitions, as well as unmanned aerial vehicles. Most importantly, the BDS eliminates China's dependency on the U.S. GPS and Russia's GLONASS satellite navigation systems that could be deactivated in select areas in times of conflict.[44]

Hypersonic Vehicle Technology Project.

While data on China's hypersonic research remains scarce, there are signs that China is developing conceptual and experimental hypersonic flight vehicle technologies such as hypersonic cruise vehicles (HCV) capable of maneuvering at Mach 5 speeds (6,150+ kilometers [km] per hour [/h]), and flying in near-space altitudes. Andrew Erickson and Gabe Collins analyzed China's *Shenlong* (神龙 Divine Dragon) spaceplane project, including its apparent test flight in 2011 and noted subsequent profusion of Chinese research articles on the subject.[45] Similarly, Mark Stokes from

the Project 2049 Institute identified new research institutes focusing exclusively on the design and development of hypersonic test flight vehicles, including the
10th Research Institute (also known as the Near Space
Flight Vehicle Research Institute) under the China
Academy of Launch Technology (CALT)—China's
largest entity involved in the development and manufacturing of space launch vehicles and related ballistic
missile systems. The Qian Xuesen National Engineering Science Experiment Base in Beijing's Huairou dis-
trict is also one of China's key HCV research centers.[46]

Taken together, China's government views "indigenous innovation" strategy as mutually supporting both PLA's military modernization as well as the
country's economic future to achieve a long-term
sustainable growth, efficiency and productivity gains,
while mitigating serious problems including labor
shortages, stretched resource supplies, unequal distribution of income, social tensions, and unprecedented
environmental pollution. In October 2010, the State
Council formerly announced its decision to target
"seven strategic industries" for focused development:
(1) energy saving and environmental protection; (2)
new generation information technology (IT); (3) biotechnology; (4) high-end equipment; (5) new energy;
(6) new materials; and, (7) new energy cars.[47] These
focus areas are perceived as the forefront of a new
round of information revolution, bringing new and
significant growth opportunities for China's economy. From 2010-15, China reportedly planned to invest
$1.5 trillion to boost the development of seven strate-
gic emerging industries.[48] Inherently, these have the
potential to propel the next wave of China's military
innovation. Technological breakthroughs in alternative energy sources, nano-materials and new compos-

ites, propulsion technologies, bio-medicine can fulfil multiple purposes and have applications in diverse military domains for the PLA.

ASSESSING CHINA'S CAPACITY FOR INNOVATION

Today, China's defense industrial base is certainly much more capable than it was in the late-1990s. The weapons systems coming out of its factories and ship-yards are vastly superior to what was being produced less than 15 years ago. Progress in innovation at the level of defense R&D is undeniable; at the same time, production facilities are humming, and the defense industry is turning unprecedented profits. What then are the keys to China's recent successes as a developer and manufacturer of advanced armaments, therefore? Notwithstanding the range of factors shaping com-prehensive innovation capabilities, two factors have been perhaps the most critical in the developments of China's defense, science, technology and innova-tion (DSTI) system: money and technology. In the first case, China's dramatic and continuing expansion in defense spending has meant more money for innova-tion, more money for R&D, more money to increase procurement (and therefore production runs), and more money to upgrade the defense industrial base with new tools, new computers, and new technical skills. China has experienced double-digit real (i.e., af-ter inflation) growth in defense spending nearly every year since the late-1990s. Even according to its own official national statistics, which most expert observ-ers believe substantially understate spending levels, China's defense budget from 1999 to 2008 expanded at a rate of 16.2 percent per annum.[49] Most recently, in March 2013, Beijing announced that it would allocate 740.6 billion yuan, or U.S.$119 billion for defense, an increase of 10.7 percent over 2012. Overall, since 1997, Chinese military expenditures have increased at least 600 percent in real terms. As a result, since the late-1990s, China has moved up to become the second-largest defense spender in the world, outstripping Japan, France, Russia, and the United Kingdom (UK); only the United States currently spends more on defense.

The impact on defense R&D and procurement has been equally astounding. In real terms, PLA annual spending on equipment procurement has increased from around U.S.$3.1 billion in 1997 to an estimated U.S.$40 billion in 2013. Of this, perhaps U.S.$5 billion to U.S.$7 billion is dedicated to defense R&D. This likely makes China the second highest spender in the world in terms to procurement and perhaps the second or third highest when it comes to defense R&D spending.[50] This upward trend is likely to continue for some time. In May 2006, for example, Beijing approved a 15-year national development plan for defense science and technology, with the goal of "transforming the PLA into a modernized, mechanized, IT-based force" by 2020.[51] This program is intended to boost military R&D spending, focusing on high-technology weapons systems (and specifically on "IT solutions"), supporting advanced manufacturing technologies, and cultivating collaborative international defense R&D efforts.[52] Arguably, if anything has had a positive impact on the defense industry, it is this explosion in defense spending—by increasing procurement and therefore production; by expanding R&D spending; and by subsidizing the upgrading and modernization of arms manufacturing facilities. Consequently, China's defense industrial base is better suited than ever to absorb and leverage advanced, militarily relevant technologies and therefore provide the PLA with the advanced military systems it requires.

In addition to greater resources being made available to underwrite armaments production, the acquisition of new technologies — and especially foreign technologies — has had a significant effect on the growth and modernization of the Chinese military-industrial complex. China has undertaken several initiatives in recent decades to advance its military S&T base. These include the 863 Program (launched in 1986 to promote research into such areas as information technologies, spaceflight, lasers, new materials, biotechnology, and automation), the Torch Program (intended to commercialize new and advanced technologies, as well as establish technology incubators and science parks), and, most recently, the 2006-20 Medium- and Long-Term Defense Science and Technology Development Plan. Concurrently, it has greatly expanded its S&T education program, training a new generation of defense scientists, engineers, and technicians.[53]

Money and technology, of course, go hand-in-hand. Ian Anthony once stated that arms production is a "capital- and technology-intensive industry,"[54] and capital is a critical enabler of technology acquisition. Consequently, more than any structural, organizational, or cultural reform initiatives — or even greater efforts at civil-military integration — China's success as an emerging producer of advanced conventional weaponry is due mostly to a rather traditional, even prosaic strategy: throwing more money and technology at the problem of military modernization. It may be less glamorous than radical reform, but then again, one cannot argue with this approach's accomplishments. At the same time, however, critical weaknesses remain. The Chinese arms industry still appears to possess only limited indigenous capabilities for cutting-edge defense R&D, and Western armaments producers continue to outpace China when it comes to most military technologies, particularly in areas such as propulsion (aircraft/missile engines), navigation systems and defense electronics, and high-end composites.

Indeed, the high entry and technological barriers coupled with technical challenges in acquiring extensive knowledge and experience, as well the limited number of cutting-edge technological enterprises preclude Chinese defense manufacturers to make significant strides toward disruptive/revolutionary innovation. These barriers can be seen in the R&D and production of select advanced materials and composites, including high-end aluminum alloy products, aramid fiber, carbon fiber, high performance steel, nitrocell, titanium alloy, and tungsten alloys. Only a few Chinese companies are qualified suppliers of technologies required for the production of high-performance materials that are essential for the next generation of engines, target detection systems, navigation systems, and many other subsystems used in diverse weapon platforms. For example, high-end aluminum alloy products require a large hydraulic press which is both cost-intensive and difficult to manufacture. Currently, China only has five domestic companies capable to make such press machine.[55] Similarly, in the production of aramid fiber used in armor plates in tanks or engine cases on aircraft, China still relies on imports for roughly 70 percent of its consumption (including 30 percent for defense). Currently, China has only two domestic makers of aramid fiber (Suzhou Zhaoda and

Tayho), which commenced production in 2010 and 2011, respectively. China's most domestic makers of carbon fiber are also new, without the necessary long-term experience to stabilize product quality.[56]

Overall, China is still more of a "fast follower," always playing technology "catch-up," or else be niche innovator when it comes to military R&D. Again, this is not necessarily a bad strategy to pursue. As Hannas, Mulvenon, and Puglisi put it:

> China's genius, as it were, is in putting together a system that capitalizes on its practical skill at adapting ideas to national projects, while compensating for its inability to create those ideas by importing them quickly at little or no cost.[57]

Additionally, it may be acceptable to be niche innovator if one's military is only looking to gain asymmetric niche advantages, such as the PLA using an antiship ballistic missile (ASBM) to attack aircraft carriers.

Consequently, China's capacities to innovate, and those drivers and enablers of innovation, may not have to differ much from each other, depending on the three potential military futures for the PLA, i.e., a PLA focused on regional issues, a globally expeditionary PLA, or a weakened PLA. To take the last scenario first, a weakened PLA would most likely continue to muddle through with its present—and perhaps even diluted—process of modest, incremental modernization, with a focus perhaps more on innovating mainly for the sake of a defensive defense posture; such a future would likely witness **reduced** commitments and efforts, both technological and funding-wise, than have been taking place within the Chinese military-technological industrial base over the past 15 years or so. Instead, given China's current (ambitious) trajectories when it comes to military R&D and technology, it is more likely that present innovation capabilities and activities would more closely match a PLA focused on a regionalized military capacity. Many of the innovations and military systems coming out of Chinese armaments enterprises more fit a PLA that is striving to be an assertive force in and around its near-abroad, both offensively and defensively (the latter epitomized by its growing anti-access/area denial [A2/AD] capabilities). In this regard, therefore, the limitations to China's military-industrial complex, when it comes to innovation, do not present nearly as great a challenge. It is only in the case of the PLA attempting to become a truly globalized and expeditionary that the Chinese innovation system still lets down the military. The PLA still lacks many of the basic building blocks of a truly global force (sustained and sizable power-projection capabilities, long-range strike, global reconnaissance capacities, etc.). To be sure, some of these requirements are driving innovation in the Chinese military (e.g., hypersonics, satellite navigation, stealth, etc.), but it will be decades before the Chinese could obtain such a global operational capacity — and it may be that China does not even desire such a capacity, in which case the military innovation system will not be driven to deliver one.

STRATEGIC AND OPERATIONAL IMPLICATIONS

The Chinese defense, science, technology, innovation, and industrial base has made undeniable advancements over the past decade and a half in terms of developing, manufacturing new, relatively modern military systems. As long as the defense budget continues to grow and the Chinese continue to be able to acquire and exploit foreign technologies, this pace of defense development and production will likely quicken in the decades ahead. U.S. Under Secretary of Defense for Acquisition, Technology, and Logistics Frank Kendall recently alluded to China's growing technological prowess when he testified before Congress that the U.S. military is "being challenged in ways that I have not seen for decades," adding that "technological superiority is not assured and we cannot be complacent about our posture."[58]

At the same time, however, it would be premature to argue that China will catch up to the defense-technological state-of-the-art any time soon. To employ Tai Ming Cheung's analytical framework, while the Chinese defense S&T base is perhaps proficient at the lower tiers of innovation — i.e., duplicative imitation, creative imitation, creative adaptation, and incremental adaptation — the higher levels of innovation — architectural innovation, modular innovation, and radical innovation — still eludes it for the most part. To reiterate, China is still more of a "fast follower," or, at best, a niche innovator when it comes to military R&D. In a sense, therefore, China's defense innovation system remains stuck in a version of the "pockets of excellence" conundrum that it suffered through in the 1980s and 1990s. This time around, however, these pockets of excellence are not necessarily sectoral (such as shipbuilding and missiles), but rather promising breakthroughs in certain technological niches: ASBMs, stealth aircraft, hypersonics, etc.; even then, most of these innovations remain at the prototype stage, and there are no guarantees that they will ever be operationally deployed. Even if some or many of these prototypes are turned into working weapons systems, it could still be some time before they deployed in sufficient quantities so as to be military "game-changers."

Again, however, being a "creative adaptor" or a niche innovator is not necessarily a bad strategy to pursue. If China is mostly keen, at this juncture, in achieving an A2/AD,[59] then a vigorous and directed process of **sustaining innovation**—what Peter Dombrowski has termed a "modernization-plus" approach—could be sufficient for the PLA to achieve its operational objectives. Moreover, China's defense innovation process has always been less about finesse than it has been about brute force, i.e., throwing a lot of resources—especially money and manpower—at a limited number of programs. This is as true today as it was in the 1950s and 1960s, when China pursued its "two bombs and one satellite" project. The primary difference today is that China possesses the resources to pursue a broader range of weapons programs. Still, most of these projects are about catching up or finding asymmetrical A2/AD counters, rather than engaging in radical, transformative innovation.

Consequently, it may not take that much innovation for the PLA to pose challenges to the Asia-Pacific security structure, or the to regional balance of power. The PLA's current operational guideline is to fight "Limited Local Wars Under Conditions of 'Informatization,'" entailing short-duration, high-intensity conflicts characterized by mobility, speed, and long-range attack; employing joint operations fought simultaneously throughout the entire air, land, sea, space, and electromagnetic battlespace; and relying heavily upon extremely lethal high-technology weapons. PLA operational doctrine also increasingly emphasizes preemption, surprise, and shock value, given that the earliest stages of conflict may be crucial to the out-come of a war. In this context, China's long-term DSTI programs reflect not only Beijing's scientific aspira-tions, but also changing strategic priorities and PLA's long-term operational requirements embedded in the concept of "diversified missions" (The Diversified Employment of China's Armed Forces) that are vital to China's "core interests." Ever since the late-1990s, the PLA has been selectively upgrading its existing weapons systems and platforms, while experiment-ing with the next generation of design concepts. These can be seen in the gradual modernization of China's nuclear and conventional ballistic missiles, integrated air, missile, and early warning defense systems, elec-tronic and cyber warfare capabilities, submarines, sur-face combat vessels and the introduction of fourth/ fifth generation of multirole combat aircraft.[60] With the qualitative shifts in "hardware," the PLA has been also revamping its "software" — military doctrine, or-ganizational force structure, and operational concepts that are now focused on "local, limited wars under informatization."[61]

In particular, the prevailing emphasis in Chinese strategic thought is on "integrated networked attack and defense" air, sea, land, cyber and space operations that would amplify PLA capabilities in terms of early warning, intelligence, and information superiority, firepower, mobility, and operational reach. By 2030, for example, Chinese air power doctrine envisions conducting independent air campaigns within 3,000-km radius of China's periphery — shifting its primary missions from traditional land-based air defense, in-terdiction, and close air support operations, toward deterrence and strategic strike at sea. In this context, PLAAF's concept of "integrated attack and defense" — joint counterair strike campaigns in conjunction with the Second Artillery's ASBM capabilities are seen as vital in defending China's territorial and sovereignty claims, as well as in limiting potential adversaries (U.S.) strike, access options, and maneuver capabilities. Consequently, in potential future conflict flashpoints such as the Taiwan Strait, Korean Peninsula, East and South China Seas, selected PLA units may be able to mitigate, at least to a limited extent the traditional operational advantages and unrivaled freedom of action of U.S. forces in East Asia.

As such, the PLA has acquired or is in the process of acquiring a number of new high-tech weapons systems, including 4th generation fighter aircraft, large surface combatants, new nuclear and diesel-electric attack submarines, precision-guided munitions (including land-attack cruise missiles and supersonic antiship missiles), airborne early warning aircraft, air-to-air refueling aircraft, improved air defenses, and the like. Moreover, in accordance with the principles of "informatization," the Chinese military has put considerable emphasis on upgrading its command, control, communications, computers, and intelligence surveillance and reconnaissance (C4ISR) assets — including launching a constellation of communication, surveillance, and navigation satellites — while also developing its capabilities to wage "integrated network electronic warfare" — an amalgam of electronic warfare (jamming the enemy's communications and intelligence-gathering assets), and offensive information warfare (disrupting the enemy's computer networks), and physical attacks on the enemy's C4SIR network. In addition, similar to the U.S. Army's "Land Warrior" program, the PLA is reportedly experimenting with "digitizing" its ground forces, right down to outfitting the individual soldier with electronic gadgetry in order to provide him with real-time tactical C4ISR.

Ultimately, the PLA hopes to turn itself into a modern, network-enabled fighting force, capable of projecting sustained power far throughout the Asia-Pacific region, and which, in the U.S. Department of Defense's (DoD) words, would "pose credible threats [sic] to modern militaries operating in the region." But is what the PLA doing technically a radical process of transformation? In fact, there is very little evidence that the Chinese military is engaged in a transformation-like overhaul of its organizational or institutional structures. The bulk of the PLA ground forces, for example, remain traditional infantry units. The PLA's highly hierarchical and top-down command structure does not seem to have changed, and even the Pentagon acknowledges the PLA's deficiencies when it comes to things like jointness. It is also worth noting that much of the transformational activities being undertaken by the Chinese military are still very nascent and even experimental, and we possess only a vague idea as to the PLA's paths and progress in many areas of informatization, such as information warfare or digitization, or whether these programs will ever be effectively implemented.

Moreover, recapitalizing the Chinese military with modern equipment—and in particular pursuing improvements in C4ISR—does not, in and of itself, constitute an RMA-like transformation; on the contrary, acquiring these systems makes perfect sense even without worrying about "transforming the force." A military does not need to believe in the RMA in order to appreciate the importance of precision-guided weapons, modern fighter jets and submarines, and better intelligence. On the whole, therefore, the PLA seems to have done a better job adopting the **rhetoric** of transformation while pursuing a "modernization-plus" approach to transforming itself. China's current military buildup is ambitious and far-reaching, but it is still more indicative of a process of **evolutionary**, **steady-state**, and **sustaining** – rather than disruptive or revolutionary – innovation and change. Not that this is necessarily a wrong path for the Chinese military, nor is it one that should not give other nations considerable cause for close attention. Perfection, it is said, is the enemy of good enough, and even absent a full-blown transformation, the PLA is adding considerably to its combat capabilities. For better or for worse, the PLA is emerging as a much more potent military force, and that, in turn, will increasingly complicate regional security dynamics in the Asia-Pacific and even beyond.

ENDNOTES - CHAPTER 5

1. Stephen Peter Rosen, *Winning the Next War: Innovation and Modern Military*, Ithaca, NY: Cornell University Press, 1994.

2. *Ibid.* p. 134.

3. Theo Farrell and Terry Terriff, ed., *The Sources of Military Change: Culture, Politics, Technology*, Boulder, CO: Lynne Reinner Publishers, 2002, p. 5.

4. Michael Horowitz, *The Diffusion of Military Power: Causes and Consequences for International Politics*, Princeton, NJ: Princeton University Press, 2010, p. 22.

5. Dima Adamsky, *The Culture of Military Innovation: The Impact of Cultural Factors on the Revolution in Military Affairs in Russia, the US, and Israel*, Palo Alto, CA: Stanford University Press, 2010, p. 1.

6. Andrew Krepinevich, *The Military-Technical Revolution: A Preliminary Assessment*, Washington, DC: Center for Strategic and Budgetary Assessments, 1992, p. 3.

7. Andrew Ross, "On Military Innovation: Toward an Analytical Framework," *IGCC Policy Brief*, No. 1, 2010, pp. 14-17.

8. Tai Ming Cheung, Thomas Mahnken, Andrew Ross, "Frameworks for Analyzing Chinese Defense and Military Innovation," Policy Brief No. 27, San Diego, CA: University of California, San Diego, September 2011, p. 80.

9. Peter J. Dombrowski, Eugene Gholz, and Andrew L. Ross, "Selling Military Transformation: The Defense Industry and Innovation," *Orbis*, Summer 2002, p. 527. See also Clayton M. Christensen, *The Innovator's Dilemma*, New York: HarperBusiness, 2000.

10. *Ibid.*, p. 527.

11. Tai Ming Cheung, ed., *Forging China's Military Might: A New Framework for Assessing Innovation*, Baltimore, MD: Johns Hopkins University Press, 2014, p. 24.

12. *Ibid.*

13. Paul Davis, "Defense Planning in an Era of Uncertainty: East Asian Issues," Natalie Crawford and Chung-in Moon, eds., *Emerging Threats, Force Structures, and the Role of Air Power in Korea*, Santa Monica, CA: RAND, 2000, pp. 25-47.

14. The Chinese defense industry has been the object of considerable study in recent years. See, for example, Richard A. Bitzinger *et.al.*, "Locating China's Place in the Global Defense Economy," Tai Ming Cheung, ed., *Forging China's Military Might*; Mikhail Barabanov, Vasiliy Kashin, and Konstantin Makienko, *Shooting Star: China's Military Machine in the 21st Century*, Minneapolis, MN: East View Press, 2012; Tai Ming Cheung, "The Chinese Defense Economy's Long March from Imitation to Innovation," *Journal of Strategic Studies*, Vol. 34, No. 3, June 2011; James Mulvenon and Rebecca Samm Tyroler-Cooper, *China's Defense Industry on the Path of Reform*, prepared for the U.S.-China Economic and Security Review Commission, October 2009; Tai Ming Cheung, "Dragon on the Horizon: China's Defense Industrial Renaissance," *Journal of Strategic Studies*, Vol. 32, No. 1, February 2009; Tai Ming Cheung, *Fortifying China: The Struggle to Build a Modern Defense Economy*, Ithaca, NY: Cornell University Press,

2008; Richard A. Bitzinger, "Reforming China's Defense Industry: Progress in Spite of Itself?" *Korean Journal of Defense Analysis*, Fall 2007; Evan S. Medeiros, Roger Cliff, Keith Crane, and James C. Mulvenon, *A New Direction for China's Defense Industry*, Santa Monica, CA: RAND, 2005; Keith Crane, Roger Cliff, Evan S. Medeiros, James C. Mulvenon, and William H. Overholt, *Modernizing China's Military*, Santa Monica, CA: RAND, 2005; Evan S. Medeiros, *Analyzing China's Defense Industries and the Implications for Chinese Military Modernization*, Santa Monica, CA: RAND, February 2004; David Shambaugh, *Modernizing China's Military: Progress, Problems, and Prospects*, Berkeley, CA: University of California Press, 2002, pp. 225-283; John Frankenstein, "China's Defense Industries: A New Course?" James C. Mulvenon and Richard H. Yang, eds., *The People's Liberation Army in the Information Age*, Santa Monica, CA: RAND, 1999; Richard A. Bitzinger, "Going Places or Running in Place? China's Efforts to Leverage Advanced Technologies for Military Use," Susan Puska, ed., *The PLA After Next*, Carlisle, PA: Strategic Studies Institute, U.S. Army War College, 2000; John Frankenstein and Bates Gill, "Current and Future Challenges Facing Chinese Defense Industries," *China Quarterly*, June 1996.

15. Cheung, "The Chinese Defense Economy's Long March," p. 326.

16. Bates Gill and Taeho Kim, *China's Arms Acquisitions from Abroad: A Quest for "Superb and Secret Weapons,"* Stockholm, Sweden: Stockholm International Peace Research Institute, 1995, pp. 2-3, 8-18.

17. See "Chapter 3: Revolution in Military Affairs with Chinese Characteristics," *China's National Defense in 2004*, Beijing, China: State Council Information Office, 2004, available from *www.fas.org/nuke/guide/china/doctrine/natdef2004.html*.

18. You Ji, "China's Emerging National Strategy," *China Brief*, November 24, 2004.

19. Cheung, "Dragon on the Horizon," pp. 30-31.

20. *Ibid.* See also Richard A. Bitzinger, "Modernizing China's Military, 1997-2012," *China Perspectives*, No. 2011/11, November

2011, pp. 7-8; and Richard A. Bitzinger, "China's 'Revolution in Military Affairs': How Fast? How Furious?" *Stockholm Journal of East Asian Studies*, December 2007.

21. Ji, "China's Emerging National Strategy."

22. Keith Crane *et al.*, *Modernizing China's Military*, p. 165.

23. Cheung, "Dragon on the Horizon," pp. 30, 36.

24. Tai Ming Cheung, "Innovation in China's Defense Research, Development, and Acquisition System," Policy Brief No. 20, *Study of Innovation and Technology in China*, September 2011, pp. 35-36.

25. *Ibid.*

26. Cheung, "Dragon on the Horizon," p. 36.

27. *Ibid.*, pp. 36-38; Barabanov , Kashin, and Makienko, *Shooting Star: China's Military Machine in the 21st Century*, pp. 3-4.

28. Eric Hagt, "Emerging Grand Strategy for China's Defense Industry Reform," Roy Kamphausen, David Lai, and Andrew Scobell, eds., *The PLA at Home and Abroad: Assessing the Operational Capabilities of China's Military*, Carlisle, PA: Strategic Studies Institute, U.S. Army War College, July 2010, pp. 481-484; Brian Lafferty, Aaron Shraberg, and Morgan Clemens, "China's Civil-Military Integration," Research Brief 2013-10, *Study of Innovation and Technology in China* (SITC), January 2013, pp. 58; Mulvenon and Tyroler-Cooper, *China's Defense Industry on the Path of Reform*, pp. 57-58.

29. Hagt, "Emerging Grand Strategy for China's Defense Industry Reform," pp. 514-518; Mulvenon and Tyroler-Cooper, *China's Defense Industry on the Path of Reform*, pp. 35-37, 38-43; Cheung, "Dragon on the Horizon," p. 47.

30. Mulvenon and Tyroler-Cooper, *China's Defense Industry on the Path of Reform*, p. 5.

31. Hagt, "Emerging Grand Strategy for China's Defense Industry Reform," pp. 481-484.

32. Cheung, "The Chinese Defense Economy's Long March from Imitation to Innovation," pp. 343-344.

33. William C. Hannas, James Mulvenon, and Anna B. Puglisi, *Chinese Industrial Espionage: Technology Acquisition and Military Modernization*, New York: Routledge, 2013, p. 78.

34. See *Ibid.*, Appendix I, pp. 256-270.

35. "China Issues S&T Development Guidelines," *Xinhua*, February 9, 2006, available from *english.gov.cn/2006-02/09/content_183426.htm*.

36. Ministry of Science and Technology of the PRC, "National High-tech R&D Program, 863 Program," Bejing, China, available from *www.most.gov.cn/eng/programmes1/200610/t20061009_36225.htm*.

37. Tai Ming Cheung, *Fortifying China: The Struggle to Build a Modern Defense Economy*, Ithaca, NY: Cornell University Press, 2008, pp. 193-196.

38. Brian Tsay, "The Tianhe-2 Supercomputer: Less than Meets the Eye?" *SITC Bulletin Analysis*, July 2013, available from *escholarship.org/uc/item/1839q9q8*.

39. DoD Defense Science Board, *Task Force Report: Resilient Military Systems and the Advanced Cyber Threat*, Washington, DC: Office of the Under Secretary of Defense for Acquisition, Technology, and Logistics, 2013.

40. Andrew Erickson and Gabe Collins, "Spaceplane Development Becomes a New Dimension of Emerging U.S.-China Space Competition," *China SignPost*, No. 62, August 16, 2012.

41. Michael Raska, "Scientific Innovation and China's Military Modernization," *The Diplomat*, September 3, 2013.

42. *Ibid.*

43. Jon Grevatt, "China Outlines Satellite Navigation System Plans," *IHS Jane's Defense Industry*, October 20, 2013.

44. Mark Stokes and Dean Cheng, "China's Evolving Space Capabilities: Implications for U.S. Interests," Report Prepared for The U.S.-China Economic and Security Review Commission, April 26, 2012, available from *origin.www.uscc.gov/sites/default/files/Research/USCC_China-Space-Program-Report_April-2012.pdf*.

45. Andrew Erickson and Gabe Collins, "Spaceplane Development Becomes a New Dimension of Emerging U.S.-China Space Competition," *China SignPost*, No. 62, August 16 2012.

46. Mark Stokes and Dean Cheng, "China's Evolving Space Capabilities,"pp. 17-23.

47. "China to Nurture 7 Strategic Industries in 2011-15," *Xinhua*, October 27, 2010.

48. "China Eyes New Strategic Industries to Spur Economy," Reuters, July 23, 2012.

49. "China Plans to Boost 2009 Military Spending by 14.9%," *Bloomberg*, March 4, 2009.

50. In 2009, for example, France spent approximately U.S.$14 billion on procurement and U.S.$5.8 billion on defense R&D; that same year, the UK spent U.S.$10.9 billion and U.S.$4.2 billion, respectively, on procurement and R&D. *Defense Data of EDA* (Economic Development Administration) *Participating Member States in 2009*, Washington, DC: EDA, p. 11. China defense R&D budget is unknown, but based on its overall military spending, it is not unreasonable to assume that the Chinese allocate anywhere between U.S.$5 billion and U.S.$10 billion on military R&D.

51. Ben Vogel, "China Embarks on 15-Year Armed Forces Modernization Program," *Jane's Defense Weekly*, July 1, 2006.

52. *Ibid.; 2011 Report to Congress*, Washington, DC: Office of the Secretary of Defense (OSD), 2011, p. 45.

53. Cheung, "Dragon on the Horizon," pp. 52-54.

54. Ian Anthony, "The 'Third Tier' Countries: Production of Major Weapons," Herbert Wulf, ed., *Arms Industry Limited*, Oxford, UK: Oxford University Press, 1993, p. 365.

55. The five hydraulic press makers include Shanghai Heavy Machinery, China First Heavy Machinery, China Second Heavy Machinery, North Heavy Industrial, and China Heavy Machinery Research Institute.

56. David Cui, Tracy Tian, and Katherine Tai, "China: Defense, Defensive in an Age of Turbulence," *Bank of America Merrill Lynch Equity Strategy Brief*, January 30, 2014.

57. Hannas, Mulvenon, and Puglisi, *Chinese Industrial Espionage*, pp. 241.

58. "China threatens US military superiority: Defense official," *AFP*, January 29, 2014.

59. According to the A2/AD operational concept, a defending force would first attempt to restrict the enemy's ability to enter a war zone ("anti-access"), through such actions as aerial or sea blockades, or blocking landing operations; should anti-access efforts fail or being only partly successful, one would then attempt to disrupt or impede the enemy's ability to operate freely in the war zone ("area-denial").

60. Anthony H. Cordesman, Ashley Hess, Nicholas S. Yarosh, *Chinese Military Modernization and Force Development*, Washington, DC: Center for Strategic and International Studies, 2013.

61. Andrew Erickson and Michael S. Chase, "Informatization and the Chinese People's Liberation Army Navy," Phillip Saunders, Christopher Yung, Michael Swaine, and Andrew Nien-Dzu Yang, *The Chinese Navy: Expanding Capabilities, Evolving Roles*, Washington, DC: Institute for National Strategic Studies, 2011, pp. 247-287.

ALTERNATIVE FUTURES FOR THE PEOPLE'S LIBERATION ARMY

CHAPTER 6

THE PEOPLE'S LIBERATION ARMY IN 2020-30 FOCUSED ON REGIONAL ISSUES

Bernard D. Cole

The views in this paper are the author's alone and do not represent those of the National War College or any other agency of the U.S. Government.

INTRODUCTION

This chapter describes a Chinese military in the decade 2020 to 2030 that is focused on regional issues and prepared for conflict on China's periphery, particularly its maritime frontier. The People's Liberation Army (PLA) budget, organization, doctrines, training and personnel, platforms, and space-based assets will be addressed.[1]

These elements are meaningful indicators of the PLA's focus a decade and more hence; in fact, they reflect China's leaders' view of the utility of the military instrument of statecraft. A regionally focused PLA will require different systems and organization than will a globally focused military; this chapter argues that the former overshadow the latter.

That said, the future PLA will address missions identical in name—deterrence and power projection for instance—but different in requirements and intention. Missions are not the drivers in military developments, as much as are the intended theaters of operations—regional rather than global.

The "region" in this chapter is defined as the waters lying within the first and second island chains.

The first encompasses the Yellow, East China, and South China Seas and is delineated by a line from the Kuriles through Japan, the Ryukyus, Taiwan, the Philippines, and then west through Indonesia. The second adds much of the Philippine Sea to that previously mentioned and is delineated by a line from the Kuriles through Japan, the Bonins, the Marianas, Palau, and then west through Indonesia.

THE PLA BUDGET

The assessment period encompasses the 14th and 15th Five-Year Plans (2021-25 and 2026-30) used by Beijing to evaluate, adjust, and guide its economy. Although China's economy is not without potentially serious problems, continued economic growth is a viable assumption.

Beijing announced the PLA's 2013 budget as 720.2 billion yuan (U.S.$114.3 billion), a 10.7 percent increase from the 2012 budget. Almost all observers think this is a significantly underestimated figure, but Dennis Blasko has offered a reasonable conclusion to the different budget estimates:

> Whatever the true numbers may be, the Chinese military has much more money to spend on fewer troops than it did 15 years ago. At the same time, personnel, equipment, and training costs for a more modern, technologically advanced military are significantly higher than in previous decades . . . the growth of the defense budget in fact appears to be coordinated with the growth of the Chinese economy. . . . If need be, the government could increase spending even faster. . . .[2]

Increasing military budgets are consistent with Beijing's official policy "that defense development should be both subordinated to and in the service of the country's overall economic development, and that the former should be coordinated with the latter." Thus, PLA budget growth has followed China's gross domestic product (GDP) and inflation rate; it has not diverted massive funding away from important civilian projects necessary for maintaining economic development.[3] This paradigm should continue into the next decade and to mid-century, barring an unforeseen, major national security emergency.

Four factors support a continually increasing Chinese defense budget:

1. President Xi Jinping's apparent determination to ensure continued growth and reduce income disparities by maintaining high government spending.[4]

2. China's emergence as the world's second leading economy, increasing global military presence, and determination to act and gain recognition as a global power.[5]

3. Beijing's actions in support of maritime and insular territorial claims demonstrate its determination not to waver on sovereignty issues.[6]

4. The influence of the military commanders, determined to continue modernizing their forces.

A regionally focused PLA will not require Beijing to make the large investments demanded for a global military. It will not change its current modernization process to try to match the United States ship for ship, or missile for missile, but will continue focusing on strategic, essentially defensive capabilities.

A decision to increase, decrease, or maintain the present percentage of the national budget dedicated to the PLA will be driven much more by political than economic concerns. Future military modernization in

China will not be determined by economic resources, but by political decisions.

THE REGION

"East Asia" is a description that rolls off the tongue for an area on which a 2025 PLA would focus, but that is too easy, just as "Indo-Pacific" is too broad. China's current strategic military interests focus on defense of the homeland, to include all 14 of its land borders, as well as the vast maritime expanse to its east, into the Philippine Sea, and to the south, to the Singapore and Malacca Straits.

The most immediate maritime concern is the "three seas," or "near seas," composed of the Yellow, East China, and South China Seas, which cover the water area inside the "first island chain."[7] The island chain construct is credited to Admiral Liu Huaqing, who in the mid-1980s described it as bounding an area over which the PLA Navy (PLAN) should aspire to exert control by 2020. Liu's concept of "control" is not the same as classic Mahanian "command of the sea," but aims for the capability to control specific areas for specific periods of time.

The PLAN did not meet Liu's 2000 date for controlling the area within the first island chain, but was close to that goal in 2014, by virtue of its increasingly sophisticated surveillance capabilities, expanded submarine fleet, and missile arsenal headlined by the near-initial operating capability (IOC) of the DF21 antiship ballistic missile (ASBM).[8] This mix of capabilities, including the PLA Air Force (PLAAF) and Second Artillery, means that the goal of sea control is not a function of just the PLAN, but of the entire PLA.

REGIONAL ISSUES

Taiwan's status was the PLA's most crucial planning contingency in 2014, but is likely to continue subsiding in crisis intensity, as discussed later. The PLA's missions focused on border defense will retain their priority.[9] These are both continental and maritime, extending through the three seas today but out to Liu's "second island chain" by 2030. This line defines an area over which the PLA should aspire to exert control and includes much of the Philippine Sea, in addition to the near seas. It is a vast ocean expanse, extending approximately 1,800 nautical miles (nm) eastward from the Asian mainland, sometimes described as the "middle sea."[10]

It would also establish an extensive defensive security structure by the 100th anniversary of the founding of the People's Republic of China (PRC) in 2049.[11] The 2006 defense white paper included this goal in a list of modernization target dates, as "the strategic goal of building informationized armed forces and being capable of winning informationized wars by the mid-21st century."[12]

Military Forces as an Instrument of Chinese Statecraft.

Beijing has not hesitated to defend national security interests, including its maritime claims. PLAN ships defeated Vietnamese units to consolidate Chinese control of the Paracel (Xisha) Islands in 1974 and several Spratly (Nansha) Islands in 1988. Less dramatic PLA engagements in the South China Sea have included the seizure of Mischief (Meiji) Reef in 1995 and Scarborough Shoals (Huangyuan Dao) in 2012 against Philippine claims.[13]

Chinese government and perhaps commercial ships under government direction have also confronted other nation's vessels, ranging from fishing craft to U.S. survey ships on many occasions. These confrontations have included very aggressive Chinese actions, resulting in the loss of life and significant damage. In one incident between China and South Korea, a South Korean Coast Guard officer was murdered when he boarded a Chinese fishing boat.

Confrontations involving both civilian-manned and PLAN craft have become commonplace in the East China Sea between Japanese and Chinese vessels and aircraft. No loss of life has occurred — although the risk may be increasing with each confrontation. [14]

The past 4 years' events in the East and South China Seas demonstrate Beijing's use of uniformed and civilian services to enforce its maritime and insular territorial claims. That is not unique to China, of course, but Beijing's apparent faith in its ability to control such incidents and prevent unintended escalation are both unrealistic and troubling. [15]

Japan, India, and the United States are viewed as posing threats of various degrees to China's national security. [16] The first is both a historic enemy and as a current contestant to sovereignty and resource issues in the East China Sea; India's nuclear arsenal is threatening to Beijing's ally, Pakistan, as well as to China itself; while the United States is the only nation with the economic, political, and military power to frustrate China's ambitions.

Additionally, Beijing faces an East Asia generally pursuing naval modernization. Japan and South Korea continue to improve their already formidable naval and coast guard capabilities, while Vietnam, Singapore, Malaysia, Indonesia, and Australia are engaging in long-term modernization of their submarine fleets and other naval units. The Indian Navy aspires to a very ambitious modernization program based on a future force of three aircraft carrier battle groups and nuclear powered submarines.[17]

President Xi Jinping's statement that "We are strongly committed to safeguarding the country's sovereignty and security, and defending our territorial integrity" is not just rhetoric, but addresses an obvious and lasting strategic goal.[18]

PLA PERSONNEL

PLA Army.

The army (PLAA) dominates the military in terms of command and numbers. There are indications, however, that this dominance will change by the middle of the next decade. First, China's 2004 defense white paper stated that:

> The PLA will promote coordinated development of firepower, mobility and information capability, enhance the development of its operational strength with priority given to the Navy, Air Force and Second Artillery Force (PLASAF) in order to strengthen the capabilities for winning both command of the sea and command of the air, and conducting strategic counter strikes.[19]

Second, at the Chinese Communist Party's (CCP) Eighteenth Party Congress, in November 2012, President Hu Jintao emphasized that the army would be yielding influence to the other services. Hu asserted:

we must make major progress in modernizing national defense and the armed forces . . ., striving to basically complete military mechanization and make major progress in full military IT [information technology] application by 2020. . . . We should attach great importance to maritime, space and cyberspace security . . . enhance the capability to accomplish a wide range of military tasks, the most important of which is to win local war in an information age.[20]

Third, writing about the Decision of the CPC Central Committee . . . at the 3rd Plenary Session of the 18th CPC [Communist Party of China] Central Committee, General Xu Qiliang reported "it is imperative to . . . lay stress on strengthening the building of the Navy, Air Force, and Second Artillery."[21]

Then, in November 2013, a senior Military Region (MR) commander described a future, more balanced PLA, with the army being deemphasized in favor of the navy and air force.[22] Finally, in January 2014, Chinese military analysts described a "new joint command system" reflecting "naval prioritization."[23]

The PLA of a half-century ago focused on continental threats and missions; logically, the army dominated. China's national security concerns in 2014 are concentrated on the maritime arena, which should empower the PLAN and PLAAF. It also lends weight to the Second Artillery's conventional capabilities. A maritime, eastern orientation will continue with the unresolved status of Taiwan, disputes with Japan, and South China Sea issues.

These indicators mean reduced army personnel numbers, with increased navy, air force, and Second Artillery Force manning. It likely will lead to a lessening of army influence and budget allocation, with concomitant increases in the other services' shares of budget resources and leadership positions. This reorientation, in recognition of 21st century strategic goals, will allow a reorganization of PLA infrastructure, to include simplifying the MR structure.

Changes in PLA organization by 2025-30 should include interservice rotation among many of senior command positions. For instance, an admiral in command of the Guangzhou MR would recognize the PLAN's leading role in confronting South China Sea challenges. Similarly, a PLAAF or Second Artillery general in command of the Nanjing and Jinan MRs would be directly in control of the air- and missile-focused forces responsible for exercising anti-access/area denial (A2/AD) operations within the first island chain—particularly the East China Sea.

PLA MISSIONS IN 2025

Hence, the PLA in the next decade will reflect a more balanced personnel and resource structure among the three primary services, with the navy and air force gaining at the army's expense. The Second Artillery likely will maintain its present position— with personnel and resources sized only to ensure the presence of a viable, effective nuclear and conventional deterrent force.

The most important future PLA development will be continuation of the post-2000 improvements in personnel management. Professional military education (PME) and training for all ranks will continue to increase in flexibility and professionalism—maximizing the accuracy and honesty of training and exercise evaluation and reporting.

Two important challenges confront the PLA. One is the elimination of corrupt accession, assignment, and promotion practices. Second is the PLA's decade-long attempt to develop a professional, career noncommissioned officer (NCO) corps. The extent of this effort's success should be apparent by the mid-2020s.[24]

China's working age population—the prime pool for military entrants—is expected to begin declining as early as 2015, described as "a drastic decline in the young labor force," despite recent decisions relaxing the "one-child policy."[25] However, in view of the burgeoning need to find more and more jobs for the country's increasing work force and continuing conscription means that future manpower resources will not be a limiting factor on future PLA manning.

Homeland Defense.

Homeland Defense obviously will remain the primary mission for all services and branches. However, increased attention to developing jointness and the continued increase in ballistic and cruise missile capability noted earlier may well lead to the establishment of a separate command responsible for that mission. This would be a "supported command," without its own forces but empowered to secure operational forces from the different services to carry out its mission.

The maritime defense mission will remain primarily a PLAN responsibility, but will require greater naval aviation capability and coordination with the PLAAF. The newly organized coast guard forces will gain in coherence and capability over time and their operations will be increasingly influenced by the PLAN. Required defense of China's recently announced air defense identification zone (ADIZ), the acquisition of aircraft carriers and advanced surface combatants, all with flight decks, will shift more of this mission to seaborne aviation assets, both rotary and fixed-wing.

Nuclear Deterrence.

Nuclear deterrence will remain a vital PLA mission, with the Second Artillery in the lead, but with a division of labor with the PLAN, the service responsible for the actual operation and maintenance of ballistic missile submarines, and with the PLAAF, responsible for the actual operation and maintenance of nuclear weapons-capable aircraft. Second Artillery control of nuclear-capable intercontinental missiles will be unchallenged, but as the navy and air force acquire longer range and more sophisticated conventionally armed cruise and regional ballistic missiles, Beijing may decide that these weapons embody too much political impact to be left in the hands of the individual services. Establishing a more centralized, joint command and control authority over long-range missiles would be a logical step.[26]

Power Projection.

Employing military power to enforce sovereignty claims includes power projection, a phrase often used to describe a navy mission. It should more accurately be defined in whole-of-military terms.

PLA power projection capabilities in 2014 take several forms, including amphibious assault by army or marine corps troops transported by navy or commercial vessels' air and missile strikes launched from the sea or from territorial possessions against a foreign force or country, or by the threat of such force being exercised.

These capabilities will increase, as China continues modernizing its military. PLA power projection effectiveness will also improve as a result of "lessons learned" from the more-than-5 years of PLAN deployments to the Gulf of Aden and beyond.[27]

Presence.

Presence, or employing military forces as a diplomatic instrument, is as old as naval history — the Athenians employed their own and allied maritime forces throughout the Peloponnesus on this mission. China has deployed its naval vessels on diplomatic port visits since the mid-1970s, when PLAN ships conducted port calls throughout Southeast Asia. The pace of interregional port calls will continue to increase until, by 2025, PLAN warships and support vessels call routinely in East Asian countries.

PLAN warships joining the large, biannual, multilateral rim of the Pacific (RIMPAC) exercise in Hawaiian waters in the summer of 2014 were a significant Chinese demonstration of both presence and power projection. This major exercise likely signaled a new naval balance in Asian-Pacific waters for both China and the United States.[28]

Maintaining Order at Sea.

This mission has been part of PLAN and coast guard operations since the organizations were founded. The PRC's early years included PLA defensive operations against Nationalist raids; seizing islands held by those forces; fighting piracy and other criminal activities in riverine and littoral waters; and enforcing customs regulations, conducting salvage, navigation, and safety of life operations. These included participation by the People's Armed Police (PAP) and other national agencies, as well as provincial and municipal authorities.

China's military and civilian ability to ensure order at sea has been significantly improved. The 2013 reorganization of coast guard-like services has yet to have a significant impact, but eventually should provide a rational, effective organization for executing these missions. It also represents a trend of civil-military integration that will continue, while the impressive acquisition of ships and aircraft will provide the platforms necessary to ensure maritime order and security.

Significant command and control arrangements were apparently left unresolved by this reorganization. Operational requirements and bureaucratic inertia will continue to drive integration of various "coast guard" organizations into the administrative control of a national ministry, while operational control gravitates to the PLAN.[29]

Nontraditional Missions.

The PLA will increase its participation in "military operations other than war" (MOOTW).[30] These include noncombatant evacuations (NEO), humanitarian assistance and disaster relief (HA/DR), and peacekeeping.

NEO.

The Libyan NEO in 2012, when 48,000 Chinese citizens were evacuated, was just the latest NEO; between 2006 and 2010, 6,000 Chinese citizens were evacuated from Chad, Haiti, Kyrgyzstan, Lebanon, the Solomon Islands, Thailand, Timor-Leste, and Tonga.[31]

NEO operations are difficult to predict; Beijing's willingness to participate in such operations, perhaps in cases where no or very few Chinese citizens are among foreigners threatened in a situation of violent civil unrest or natural disaster, will likely increase.

Humanitarian Assistance and Disaster Relief (HA/DR).

Hospital ships, large amphibious ships, and large transport aircraft increase the PLA's ability to conduct HA/DR missions throughout East Asia and beyond during times of man-made or naturally caused emergencies to relieve human suffering. The PLAN's modern hospital ship, *Peace Ark*, has by 2014 carried out long voyages to the Indian Ocean, the Southwest Pacific, and the Caribbean Sea.[32] The ship also is an ideal platform for Beijing to employ in the event of a domestic catastrophe in one of its coastal or riverine provinces.

The PLAN in 2014 deploys just three large amphibious ships, Yuzhao-class landing platform docks (LPD), named *Kunlunshan*, *Jingganshan*, and *Changbaishan*. At least two or three more of these very capable vessels soon will join the fleet.[33]

Expansion of the HA/DR mission for the air force will be enhanced by acquisition of additional large cargo aircraft capable of long-range flights. These may include additional Il-76 aircraft acquired from Russia, but are more likely to consist of advanced models of the Chinese-manufactured Y-20 aircraft.[34]

China was deficient in HA/DR capability when the December 2004 tsunami struck Southeast and South Asia; capacity had improved significantly when Typhoon Haiyan struck the Philippines in November 2013, but Beijing lacked the political willingness to engage. The two cases are different, but, as of 2014, China has yet to employ the PLA in providing humanitarian relief from a disinterested position.

Extensive PLA participation in HA/DR missions will result from a political decision by Beijing; the military capability is already present. The Chinese government will have to decide that participation in HA/DR operations, especially those not concerned directly with succoring Chinese citizens, is in the national interest.

Counterpiracy.

Piracy and other criminal activity at sea and in coastal areas has historically been a continuing problem in East Asian waters. Much news reporting has resulted from the PLAN's deployments to the Gulf of Aden and beyond since December 2008. This mission has demonstrated China's ability to conduct long-distance military operations over an extended period of time.

Piracy will persist, but is best described in 2014 as "manageable," a description that will remain apt in 2030. Its prevalence, however, may rise or decline in conjunction with rising or falling economic prosperity among professional sea goers, especially in coastal waters. In any case, these missions in littoral waters will decrease for the PLA in the next decade, if the new coast guard units develop administrative coherence and operational capability in nonmilitary law enforcement at sea and on regional rivers.

Counterterrorism.

The PAP and Ministry of Public Security (MPS) civilian police forces have been primarily responsible for domestic incidents Beijing classifies as terrorism, although the PLAA may be called upon in extreme cases.[35] Very few terrorism incidents have occurred at sea; the PLAN would be assigned to resolve such incidents if beyond the capability of the Coast Guard or other maritime security organization, but this will remain a minor mission for the navy.

Maintaining Civil Order.

Societal peace and order is a bottom-line mission for all Chinese security forces, from local police to the PLA. This mission ties directly to countering terrorism. The PLA will retain ultimate responsibility for domestic stability.

Taiwan.

Taiwan probably will not be a primary operational concern for the PLA by the end of the next decade. Resolution of the island's status vis-à-vis the mainland before 2030 is supported by several factors. One is the increasingly intertwined economic and social relationship between the island and the mainland.[36]

Second is the lack of clear sentiment among Taiwan's population in favor of formally declaring independence.[37] This is seen in the Taiwan government failing since at least 2000 to have made dramatic efforts to improve the island's military capabilities.

Third is the lack of international support for a formally independent Taiwan, reflected in the declining number of nations that recognize the Republic of China.[38] Fourth is Taiwan's inability to gain entry into international organizations without the support of the PRC.

Fifth is the de facto decline in U.S. support for an independent Taiwan, which exacerbates the point about Taipei's defense posture referenced previously—relying on Washington to defend the island will not be an effective policy in the long term.

Three Seas.

The PLA's headline-grabbing strategic issues of 2014 are unlikely to have been resolved by the middle of the next decade, including disputed sovereignty claims over land features and ocean areas within the East and South China Seas. Very little prospect exists that China will achieve a settlement with Japan over their conflicting continental shelf claims in the East China Sea, although a *modus vivendi* is possible.

There is even less chance that they will agree on Senkaku/Diaoyu Islands sovereignty, an issue that rests largely on nationalism, although many analysts view these land features as a crucial part of the first island chain, serving in Japanese hands to constrain PLAN operations.[39] In both cases, the lack of material benefit will not prevent a military confrontation between China and Japan occurring during the next decade and a half, but reduces that possibility.[40]

The South China Sea disputes are more substantive, important, and complex than those in the East China Sea. The PLA has long been used by Beijing to enforce territorial claims and expel forces perceived as encroaching on China's sovereignty, including 1974, 1988, 1995, 2005, 2007, 2012, and 2013.

THE PEOPLE'S LIBERATION ARMY

Organization.

PLA reorganization has received attention in the wake of the fall 2013 Third Party Plenum, often featuring a reduction in the number of MRs from seven to perhaps four theaters.[41] The navy, with three fleets, has direct administrative links to just three MRs—Jinan, Nanjing, and Guangzhou. If two or all of these are combined, presumably their assigned fleets might be combined into two—a North Sea Fleet focused on Japan and a South Sea Fleet focused on the South China Sea.

What will the PLA look like in 2025-30 if the services become "more balanced"? A regionally focused PLA will not require an army even as large as the 2014 force, absent unexpected conventional warfare on China's northern or western borders. The 2014 army of mixed divisions and brigades will continue reorganizing into brigades, with increased special forces and aviation units, and reduced headquarters personnel.

A smaller PLAA might well shift at least two more divisions to a primary amphibious role; its mission in the maritime arena outlined earlier and the acquisition of more and larger amphibious warships would enable it to fulfill the adage of "a projectile fired by the navy."[42] There is no evidence that the current marine corps of just 12,000 personnel will be expanded.

PLAAF and Naval Aviation.

A future, regionally focused PLA will deploy enhanced naval and air force capabilities to confront national security concerns about the Diaoyutai, Taiwan, and the South China Sea.

The air force would realign with a new MR structure. Each associated air force will continue to focus on defense of the homeland, using a national ADIZ covering both East and South China Seas. This will likely be a mission of both the PLAAF and Naval Aviation, but with a central controlling organization in each MR, and with cross-MR coordination.

By the middle of the next decade, the PLAAF and Naval Aviation inventory will include low-observable aircraft derived from either the J-20 or J-21. Less certain is whether the J-21 is destined to become Naval Aviation's primary carrier aircraft. The J-15 is currently filling that role but reportedly is so weight-restricted at launching from the ship's ski-jump ramp that its significant redesign or replacement is likely, perhaps by a version of the Russian-designed Su-33.[43]

Homeland defense will focus on the maritime theater, the area delineated by the island chains. These enclose China's littoral waters, in which a doctrine of A2/AD would be exercised, requiring increased numbers of airborne warning and control aircraft (AWACS), aerial refuelers, cruise missile launching aircraft, short-range ballistic missiles, and, especially, anti-submarine warfare (ASW) aircraft.

The PLA also is acquiring increasing numbers of unmanned aerial vehicles (UAVs), which will play increasingly important roles, particularly in surveillance and targeting, and which offer significant advantages when compared to manned aircraft.[44] UAVs offer several advantages in reduced procurement and maintenance costs, personnel manning, and even plausible deniability. They are by themselves, however, suited to regional rather than global employment.[45]

PLAN.

One very significant MR realignment would be combining the Jinan and Nanjing regions, with the PLAN disestablishing the East Sea Fleet, and the North and South Sea Fleets dividing the former fleet's area of responsibility. As far as force structure is concerned, the navy would continue its present, impressive pace of warship construction.

China's ship building programs support the concept of a regionally focused PLAN. The first aircraft carrier, *Liaoning*, provides increased airpower at sea but with a "ski jump" flight deck is limited in its aircraft capability. China's indigenously designed and constructed carriers may have the catapults necessary for greater airpower generation, which would engender significantly higher costs, in terms both of financial and personnel resources.[46] Should China build larger, flat-deck, catapult-equipped carriers, it would indicate a more global than regional intent for its fleet missions. Similarly, the low number of replenishment-at-sea (RAS) ships in the PLAN, currently just six, indicates regional missions, not involving distant deployments on a regular basis.[47]

The 2030 surface fleet will center on three or four aircraft carriers, all indigenously constructed, 18 air defense destroyers with Aegis-like anti-air warfare systems, and 36 frigates and corvettes equipped primarily for ASW, with defense of sea lines of communication their primary mission.[48] This major acquisition program in a regionally focused PLA reflects as much national pride as it does national security requirements.

A force of 50-60 attack submarines will be maintained, not more than ten nuclear powered, but twice that number equipped with air-independent-propulsion (AIP) conventional power plants. The conventionally powered boats will retain as a primary mission enforcing A2/AD within the first island chain, but as more AIP submarines join the fleet, the PLAN will begin extending its operations into the Philippine Sea, moving toward a goal of regularly patrolling out to and beyond the second island chain.

Nuclear attack submarines (SSNs) are more expensive to build and much more expensive to maintain and operate than attack submarines; the basic justification for building the former is to assign them to long-range missions.[49] Hence, a regionally focused PLAN will not require that a significant percentage of its submarine force be nuclear powered.

The PLAN faces several challenges to improve its numerically large submarine force's capability. A particular challenge for China's naval architects is to improve their boat's covertness; the current fleet of nuclear powered submarines is surprisingly noisy, greatly increasing their detectability by opposing forces.[50] Conventionally powered submarines are inherently quieter and more difficult to detect, if their equipment is properly maintained.[51]

By 2025, China should be able finally to deploy nuclear powered ballistic missile submarines (SSBN), a goal unfulfilled in 2014, after 3 decades of effort. At least two or three Jin-class SSBNs are already operating in the South Sea Fleet, but lacking their main battery of JL-2 missiles. Even when successfully tested and loaded onboard, these missiles will be incapable of reaching mainland U.S. targets except from narrow ocean areas.[52]

Construction of the major submarine base at Yalong Bay, near the city of Sanya on Hainan Island, and the existing naval base at Yulin, may indicate that China will opt for a Soviet-style "bastion strategy" for operating its SSBNs, once a longer-range missile becomes operational.[53] Although locating the SSBNs at Hainan may just be due to the South China Sea offering the steep sea floor gradient that allows submarines to submerge into deep, safe waters almost immediately upon leaving the island's southern ports.

Beijing could have these submarines patrol continuously, as did the United States and the Soviet Union during the Cold War, or they might choose to have the boats leave homeport for patrol as a signal, during times of crisis. The maritime element of China's early warning infrastructure — especially a seabed listening and monitoring system — also would play an important role in defending the bastion against intruders.[54]

ASW capability is key PLAN weakness, while the U.S. submarine force is its navy's most lethal element. By 2020, however, the U.S. Navy is predicted to deploy a total of just 39 SSNs.[55]

The Second Artillery.

The current arsenal of approximately 72 intercontinental ballistic missiles (ICBMs) is organized into seven brigades, including one DF-4, three DF-5A, one DF-31, and two DF-31A units. The older missiles will have been mothballed by 2030, and the Second Artillery is likely to deploy only DF-31A or DF-41 brigades.[56] The number of missiles and brigades will remain approximately the same, unless Beijing believes that the U.S. and allied anti-ballistic missile defense structure is significantly improved.

The size of China's ICBM nuclear force will continue to be determined by a policy of "credible minimum deterrence."[57] The 2014 strength of approximately 400 missiles, ranging from the DF-3A to the DF-15, may remain in 2025-30, but will be affected by at least three factors. First is Beijing's confidence in the effectiveness of its missile force; second is its view of the effectiveness of U.S. and other nation's countermeasures. Third is Beijing's evaluation of its security environment; even if regionally focused, the PLA's missile inventory will have to recognize India's potential for employing nuclear weapons.

The short- and medium-range ballistic missiles inventory is more likely to increase, as are the air- and sea-launched cruise missiles in which China "has invested heavily" in a program described by the Pentagon as "the most active in the world."[58]

Systems Improvements.

The PLA is emphasizing cyber operations and space-based systems, which define the 21st century command, control, communications, computers, surveillance, and reconnaissance (C4ISR) environment, as well as anti-satellite (ASAT) weapons. PLAN commander Wu Shengli's insistence in 2008 on access to space-based systems to support the navy's deployments to the Gulf of Aden was followed by his 2009 statement that "the Navy will move faster in researching and building new-generation weapons to boost the ability to fight in regional sea wars under the circumstances of information technology."[59]

Future developments are likely to focus on systems integration to maximize the effectiveness of the complex system of systems that characterize modern warfighting platforms. A recent report emphasized the PLA's continued difficulties in this area; it decried the lack of jointness and even teamwork between units, noting that "without standardization, there is no informatization" and demanding that "each military branch [must] completely remove its 'departmental selfishness' barriers."[60]

PLA writings frequently call for greater jointness in capabilities and doctrine. The need and call for jointness will continue, as the military gains in capability and expanded mission scope.

Strategy.

Beijing has not issued a "national security strategy," "military strategy," or "maritime strategy," as such. In each case, however, documents are available that delineate China's strategic concerns. The regionally focused PLA of the next decade will be primarily occupied with the maritime concerns mentioned previously.

Applicable documents include the 1998 *National Ocean Policy of China* and the series of biennial defense white papers, published from 1998 to 2014. The tenets of maritime strategy discerned in these documents include developing and defending coastal and offshore economic resources, "reinforcing oceanographic technology," and establishing a "comprehensive marine management system." Other points noted are to "harmonize national and international law," integrate China's agencies responsible for maritime security, coordinate traditional and nontraditional maritime security concerns, and deploying a navy of "new types of submarines, frigates, aircraft, and large support vessels."[61]

CONCLUSION

The Dream.

Military modernization has been linked to the PRC's 100th anniversary by all three post-Deng Xiaoping presidents. President Jiang Zemin spoke in the late-1990s of making important progress in military modernization by mid-century, while President Xi Jinping has set 2049 for the fulfillment of the "China dream." The goal is "to recapitalize China's armed forces to achieve mechanization and partial informatization by 2020."[62]

The PLAN and other maritime enforcement agencies should have the capability to confront threats to China's claimed fisheries, sea bed resources, and economic interests connected to sea lines of communication by 2025, a significant achievement. At the end of the next decade, Beijing may believe its naval and coast guard forces strong enough to control East Asian regional sea lanes. This would strengthen Chinese ambitions to turn the "three seas" into a "no-go" zone if it suits.

The congressionally mandated Office of the Secretary of Defense report on the PLA for 2013 sums up current and possible near-term developments in China's military. It states that:

> the PRC continues to pursue a long-term, comprehensive military modernization program designed to improve the capacity of its armed forces to fight and win

short-duration, high-ntensity regional military conflict, . . . Its military modernization has also become
increasingly focused on investments in military capabilities to conduct a wider range of missions beyond
its immediate territorial concerns, including counterpiracy, peacekeeping, humanitarian assistance/disas-
ter relief, and regional military operations. . . . These
missions and capabilities can address international security challenges, [as well as] more narrowly defined
PRC interests and objectives, including advancing territorial claims and building influence abroad.[63]

When—or will—the PLA be able to meet these goals
and control the huge maritime area delineated by the
second island chain?[64]

While it took the PLA approximately 2 decades
(1996-2014) to close in on the 2000 goal attributed to
Liu Huaqing, that process has engendered a momentum enhanced by the continuing growth of China's
economy, development of Chinese defense industries,
and the increasing PLA budget. Hence, the ability to
control—or for the PLA to estimate that it can control—the water area delineated by the second island
chain may be effective by 2030. Again, this does not
mean classic "command of the sea," but the ability
to use a specific area of the sea for a specific period
of time.

A PLA focused on global operations would require weapons systems not necessary for a military
focused on regional issues, especially those inherent
in China's long maritime frontier. First, the regionally
focused navy will continue to build many more conventionally than nuclear powered submarines, given
the respective ranges of each. Second, fewer replenishment ships are also appropriate to a PLAN focused

on regional rather than far-sea operations. Third, a navy built around even three aircraft carriers would be focused on regional issues, since the conventional wisdom that three such ships are required to maintain one in full operational status remains realistic. Another relevant factor is the requirement for two aircraft carriers to operate together to conduct the 24-hour a day flight operations typically required in a far-sea scenario. This implies that a globally oriented PLAN would incorporate at least six carriers.[65] Finally, a significantly increased inventory of heavy-lift aircraft in the PLAAF would indicate Beijing's intentions to operate more consistently at greater distances. None of these "global" systems appear immediately in the offing.

Predicting Chinese military capabilities and intentions for a decade or more hence of course is constrained by fundamental unknowns; even a regionally focused PLA will continue certain out-of-area operations, to include ship visits to Western Hemisphere and European ports. Furthermore, the Indian Ocean presence represented by post-2008 counterpiracy deployments, as well as exercise participation, will continue.

First, corruption and bureaucratic complexity are problems hindering PLA effectiveness. In the words of one observer:

It's not just corruption. More than three decades of peace, a booming economy, and an opaque administrative system have taken their toll as well, not to mention that the PLA is one of the world's largest bureaucracies -- and behaves accordingly.[66]

Second, the PLA's position within China's "national command authority" faces an unknown future. Ellis

191

Joffe once said there was no reason why Chinese military officers could not be both professionally competent and politically reliable. Nonetheless, continuing Mao Zedong's declaration that "Our principle is that the Party commands the gun and the gun must never be allowed to command the Party" remains a concern of China's succeeding leaders. For instance, three of Jiang Zemin's "Five Sentences on Army Building" addressed political reliability of the military.[67]

More recently, President Xi Jinping demanded the army's "absolute loyalty, purity and reliability." The military, he continued "should absolutely follow the command of the CPC Central Committee and the Central Military Commission at any time and under any circumstances, . . ."[68]

The near-complete absence of uniformed personnel in the most senior CCP organs attests to PLA subservience to civilian leadership, with little significant change from the 2006 observation that "senior uniformed military leaders are primarily focused on military issues."[69] The danger of a developing feeling in the PLA that only it understands what is required to protect *la patria* is possible but not on the horizon.

Third and most importantly, future PLA capabilities will be influenced by Beijing views of China's strategic situation. The immediate regional concerns posed by Taiwan, the East China Sea, and the South China Seas greatly outweigh more distant issues, such as counterpiracy, counterterrorism, NEO, or HA/DR. Furthermore, the Asian maritime picture in 2030 will present China with a challenging venue of capable, modernizing navies. Beijing's efforts to build a dominant regional military force are not assured of success. Not only will the Japanese Maritime and Air Self-Defense Forces continue to acquire and deploy state-of-the-art weapons systems and platforms, but even Vietnam, for instance, will have deployed at least six Kilo-class submarines, MiG-29 aircraft, and Russian-designed frigates armed with modern cruise missiles.

China's military modernization over the next decade and a half will be impressive. It should not be constrained by budget or other resource shortages, including personnel availability. However, its political drivers—national security concerns—logically will be more regional than global.

A PLA focused on but not necessarily restricted to an East Asian regional arena will continue modernizing its command and control structure, and will become increasingly aware of international factors. Service rivalries will always be present, but PLA jointness will increase both operationally and in military command positions. As noted previously, MR commanders will quite possibly include navy and air force officers by the end of the next decade.[70]

A regionally focused PLA in 2030 will have developed into a smaller, but more professionally competent military. "How effective will it be in combat" is an impossible question to answer with assurance, but the PLAN's increasing operational experience certainly indicates greater competence, as does the evolving personnel and unit education and training system. The question is not one of PLAN versus the U.S. Navy or the Japan Maritime Self-Defense Force but the degree to which Beijing believes its forces must be engaged—to win decisively or to "teach a lesson"—in a given scenario.

The PLAN and PLAAF will have increased their share of budget and personnel resources; the Coast Guard and other ancillary forces will have developed into coherent, increasingly competent forces. The strategic goal of controlling events within the three seas will be largely achieved and the next goal of controlling events within the second island chain will have made impressive progress.[71] In regional terms, China will have completed the near-unprecedented development into both a continental and maritime military power.

ENDNOTES - CHAPTER 6

1. My chapter is based on personal observation of PLA developments during the past 20 years, extended discussions with PLA officers and analysts, and learning from many China hands. I especially thank Ken Allen, Tom Bickford, Dennis Blasko, John Corbett, Dave Finkelstein, Paul Godwin, Roy Kamphausen, Mike McDevitt, Eric McVadon, Susan Puska, Alan Romberg, Stapleton Roy, Michael Swaine, Scott Tanner, Cynthia Watson, and Larry Wortzel.

2. Zhou Erjie, "China Defense Budget to Grow to 10.7 Pct in 2013: Report," *Xinhua*, March 5, 2013, available from *news.xinhuanet.com/english/china/2013-03/05/c_132207943.htm*, accessed December 5, 2013. Sweden's SIPRI estimates the 2013 military budget at 1.5 times higher than reported by Beijing, or about U.S.$171.5 billion; South Korea's KRISS applies a 1.5 to 2.0 multiple; India's IDSA gives an estimate of U.S.$187 billion; Great Britain's IISS estimated China's 2011 defense budget at U.S.$136.7 billion, although Beijing's figure for that year was U.S.$90.2 billion. Jane's Information Group in 2012 estimated China's defense budget would increase from $119.80 billion to $238.20 billion between 2011 and 2015, a figure larger than the defense budgets of all other major Asian nations combined, but still smaller than the estimated U.S. 2013 defense budget of $525.40 billion. Dennis J. Blasko makes his point in "An Analysis of China's 2011 Defense Budget and Total Military Spending: The Great Unknown," *China Brief*, No. 11, Issue 4, Jamestown Foundation, March 11, 2011, available from *www.jamestown.org/single/?no_cache=1&tx_ttnews%5Btt_news %5D=37631&tx_ttnews%5BbackPid%5D=517#.UqTo_I4aU00*, accessed December 8, 2013.

3. This discussion, including the previous quote, relies on J. Taylor Fravel and Dennis J. Blasko, "Xi Jinping and the PLA," *The Diplomat*, March 19, 2013, available from *thediplomat.com/2013/03/xi-jinping-and-the-pla/*, accessed December 29, 2013.

4. See for instance, Arthur R. Kroeber, "Xi Jinping's Ambitious Agenda for Economic Reform in China," Washington, DC: The Brookings Institution, November 17, 2013, available from *www.brookings.edu/research/opinions/2013/11/17-xi-jinping-economic-agenda-kroeber*, accessed December 8, 2013.

5. Supporting facts include China's prominent role in global economics; major role supporting United Nations peacekeeping operations; prominent roles in or with the Shanghai Cooperative Organization, Association of Southeast Asian Nations, the Arctic Council, and other multilateral organizations; and an apparent determination to accompany its growing stature with the military historically deployed by global powers; more than 5 years' continuous naval deployments to the Gulf of Aden and beyond; and an understandable determination to have the capability to defend the homeland and associated national security interests and areas.

6. See, for instance, "Xi Jinping Vows Peaceful Development While Not Waiving Legitimate Rights," CCTV report, January 30, 2013, available from *english.cntv.cn/program/china24/20130130/102378.shtml*, accessed December 8, 2013. Also see "Xi Jinping Stresses Diplomatic Work With Neighboring States," *The Nation*, November 1, 2013, available from *www.nation.com.pk/international/01-Nov-2013/xi-jinping-stresses-diplomatic-work-with-neighbouring-states*, accessed December 8, 2013.

7. The "near seas" recently were described as "nearly 875,000 square nautical miles" by Jesse Karotkin, "Trends in China's Naval Modernization," Testimony Before the U.S.-China Economic and Security Review Commission, Washington, DC, January 2014, available from *www.uscc.gov/sites/default/files/Karotkin_Testimony1.30.14.pdf*, accessed February 6, 2014.

8. See Andrew S. Erickson, *Chinese Anti-Ship Ballistic Missile, (ASBM), Development: Drivers, Trajectories and Strategic Implications*, Washington, DC: The Jamestown Foundation, 2013.

9. Border disputes with India remain unresolved and statements from Beijing and New Delhi promise no early resolution of the Western Sector sovereignty contest over the Aksai Chin area, particularly since it concerns Jammu and Kashmir, or in the Eastern Sector dispute over Arunachal Pradesh. The PLA in 2014 is also concerned with the North Korean border; a collapse of that state would involve employing China's military to safeguard the nation's border, possibly to secure nuclear weapons, and to prevent South Korean or U.S. military forces from encroaching too far north of the 38th parallel. Another strategic border defense issue concerns the Islamic countries to China's west, including the former Soviet republics of Central Asia—Kazakhstan, Kyrgyzstan, and Tajikistan. First, Russian President Vladimir Putin and possibly his successors may not be reconciled to the loss of these former Soviet states from Moscow's domination; second, an aggressive Russo-Chinese contest for the region's energy reserves may supersede the two nations' 2014 "strategic relationship."

10. One nautical mile (nm) equals 1.15 statute miles. The distance from Hong Kong to Agana is 1821.5-nm. See the maps in Kimberly Hsu and Craig Murray, "China's Expanding Military Operations in Foreign Exclusive Economic Zones," U.S.-China Economic and Security Review Commission Staff Research *Backgrounder*, June 19, 2013, available from *www.uscc.gov/Research/china's-expanding-military-operations-foreign-exclusive-economic-zones*, accessed January 18, 2014.

11. Dennis Blasko note to the author, December 30, 2013, highlighted in PLAN exercise report by Bai Ruixue, "If We Run Swiftly in Small Steps, the Many Small Successes We Have Achieved Will Add Up to a Big One," *Liaowang Dongfang Zhoukan*, No. 42, OSC-CHR2013121032596896, Shanghai, November 7, 2013, p. 36:

> In the days to come, [the PLAN] will certainly become stronger than before, but this process will require the continuous explorations and efforts made by successive generations of our navy's officers and men.

Blasko commented that "the idea that it will take 'successive generations' for the PLAN to finish its 'developmental process' [fits] into the PLA's 'Three Step Development Strategy' that sees modernization concluding in 2049."

12. The 2006 defense white paper is available from *www.fas. org/nuke/guide/china/doctrine/wp2006.html#4*, accessed January 18, 2014, quote is in "Section II. National Defense Policy."

13. The Paracels and Spratlys are called Hoang Sa and Quan dao Truong Sa in Vietnamese; Hanoi and Manila call Mischief Reef Da Vanh Kahn and Panganiban Reef, respectively, while the Scarborough Shoal is called Panatag Shoal by Manila.

14. Choe Sang-Hun, "Chinese Fisherman Kills South Korean Coast Guardsman," *The New York Times*, December 12, 2011, available from *www.nytimes.com/2011/12/13/world/asia/chinese-fisherman-kills-south-korean-coast-guardsman.html?_r=0*, accessed December 14, 2013. A particularly egregious shooting incident occurred in 2005, resulting in the death of five Vietnamese fishermen, reported in Jason Folkmanis, "Vietnam Accuses China of Violating Law After Fishermen Killed," *Bloomberg*, January 23, 2005, available from *www.bloomberg.com/apps/news?pid=newsarchive& sid=aXAIKIyrExFU*. The Chinese press reported this incident as Chinese police killing "Vietnamese robbers," in "Eight Vietnamese Robbers Shot Dead in China Sea," *People's Daily*, January 23, 2005, available from *www.chinadaily.com.cn/english/doc/2005-01/23/ content_411498.htm*, both accessed December 14, 2013.

15. See Bernard D. Cole, *Taiwan's Security: History and Prospects*, London, UK: Routledge, 2006, 21 ff; Peng Guangqiang and Yao Youzhi, *The Science of Military Strategy*, Beijing, China: AMS, 2001), Chap. 8, Parts II-IV.

16. The author's conversations with several PLA officers since 1994 have listed Japan, India, the United States, and occasionally Russia as threatening China's foreign security.

17. Discussed in Bernard D. Cole, *Asian Maritime Strategies: Navigating Troubled Waters*, Annapolis, MD: Naval Institute Press, 2013, "Conclusion," 190 ff.

18. Quoted in Shen Dingli *et al.*, "China's Maritime Disputes," New York: Council on Foreign Relations, 2013, available from *www.cfr.org/asia-and-pacific/china-maritime-disputes/p31345*, accessed December 14, 2013.

19. Dennis Blasko reminded me about this declaration. The 2004 defense white paper may be found *https://www.fas.org/nuke/guide/china/doctrine/natdef2004.html*, accessed December 30, 2013.

20. Hu's address is available from *www.chinadaily.com.cn/china/2013npc/2012-11/18/content_16261308_10.htm*, accessed December 29, 2013.

21. Xu Qiliang, "Firmly Push Forward Reform of National Defense and the Armed Forces," Beijing *Renmin Ribao Online*, OSC-CHL20131121127590483, November 21, 2013, p. 6, available from *https://www.opensource.gov/wiki/display/nmp/Renmin+Ribao+-+China*, accessed December 30, 2013. Xu is a Central Military Commission vice-chairman.

22. The MR commander spoke to a small group at the U.S. National Defense University (NDU).

23. Yang Yi, "New Joint Command System 'On the Way'," *Xinhua*, January 3, 2014, available from *news.xinhuanet.com/english/china/2014-01/03/c_133015371.htm*, accessed January 18, 2014.

24. At an earlier Carlisle conference, a former U.S. defense attaché to China expressed doubt about the PLA developing a U.S.-style NCO corps, based on Chinese cultural factors. Non- and commissioned officer training will be the same for a regionally or globally oriented PLA up to a point, that at which long-range/distant sea logistical and C4ISR requirements must be practiced.

25. See Feng Wang, "China's Population Destiny: The Looming Crisis," Washington, DC: The Brookings Institution, September 2010, available from *www.brookings.edu/research/articles/2010/09/china-population-wang*; "China's Population: The Most Surprising Demographic Crisis," *The Economist*, May 5, 2011, available from *www.economist.com/node/18651512*, both accessed January 31, 2014.

26. Similarly, operational control over China's fleet ballistic missile submarines is to a degree not transparent, with the PLAN and PLASAF both having an interest in that capability.

27. Andrew S. Erickson and Austin M. Strange, "No Substitute for Experience: Chinese Antipiracy Operations in the Gulf

of Aden," *China Maritime Studies* No. 10, Newport, RI: U.S. Naval War College, China Maritime Studies Institute, 2014.

28. "PACOM Supports China Invite to RIMPAC 2014," *Navy Times*, September 19, 2012, available from *www.navytimes.com/article/20120919/NEWS/209190323/PACOM-supports-China-invite-RIMPAC-2014*; "China to Attend RIMPAC 2014," *Xinhua*, June 9, 2013, available from *news.xinhuanet.com/english/china/2013-06/09/c_132443566.htm*, both accessed February 2, 2014.

29. "Transcript of PRC National Defense Ministry's News Conference," PRC Ministry of Defense News Conference, in OSC-CHL2013122847385798, December 26, 2013. Continued expansion of PLAN roles was indicated in a December 26, 2013, Ministry of National Defense news statement that reported military exercises in "counterterrorism and counterpiracy, as well as humanitarian assistance and disaster mitigation." A senior State Oceanographic Administration official told the author in April 2014 that, so far, little had been accomplished by the reorganization.

30. A unique PLAN mission is participating in the multi-national escort of ships carrying Syrian chemical weapons. This and other MOOTW missions are discussed in Koh Swee Lean Collin, "Westward Ho: Expanding Global Role for China's Navy," *RSIS Commentary 005/2014*, January 7, 2014, available from *www.rsis.edu.sg/publications/Perspective/RSIS0052014.pdf*, accessed January 18, 2014.

31. China's contribution to the Libyan NEO is described in Gabe Collins and Andrew S. Erickson, "Implications of China's Military Evacuation of Citizens from Libya, March 11, 2011, available from *www.andrewerickson.com/2011/03/implications-of-china's-military-evacuation-of-citizens-from-libya/*; and "35,860 Chinese Evacuated From Unrest-Torn Libya," *Xinhua*, March 3, 2011, available from *news.xinhuanet.com/english2010/china/2011-03/03/c_13759456.htm*, both accessed December 31, 2013. A more complete accounting is in Mathieu Duchatel and Bates Gill, "Overseas Citizen Protection: A Growing Challenge for China," Stockholm, Sweden: SIPRI, February 2012, available from *www.sipri.org/media/newsletter/essay/february12*, accessed February 12, 2014.

32. See, for instance, Glen Mohammed, "'Peace Ark' Drops Anchor," *Trinidad Express Newspapers*, October 9, 2011, available from *www.trinidadexpress.com/news/_Peace_Ark__drops_anchor-133508968.html*; and "Peace Ark Hospital Ship Returns to China," *China Military Online*, October 15, 2013, available from *english.people.com.cn/90786/8425558.html*, both accessed December 31, 2013. The hospital ship also has a combat mission, receiving wounded suffered during power projection operations ashore or as the result of a sea battle.

33. A senior PLAN officer told the author in February 2011 that China planned to build five of these ships.

34. See Zhang He and Li Wei, "SAF Expert: 20 Outperforms Il-76, *China Military Online*, January 21, 2013, available from *english.peopledaily.com.cn/90786/8099537.html*, accessed December 31, 2013.

35. See, for instance, William Wan, "Chinese Police Say Tiananmen Square Crash was 'Premeditated, Violent, Terrorist Attack'," *The Washington Post*, October 30, 2013, available from *www.washingtonpost.com/world/asia_pacific/chinese-police-say-tiananmen-square-crash-was-premeditated-violent-terrorist-attack/2013/10/30/459e3e7e-4152-11e3-8b74-d89d714ca4dd_story.html*; and "Chinese Police Kill Eight in Xinjiang 'Terrorist Attack'," Reuters, December 31, 2013, available from *www.reuters.com/article/2013/12/30/us-china-xinjiang-idUSBRE9BT02V20131230*, both accessed December 31, 2013.

36. See, for instance, Peggy McInerny, "The China-Taiwan Cross-Strait Relationship: Stable But Fragile," Los Angeles, CA: UCLA, May 7, 2013, available from *www.international.ucla.edu/china/article/131770*, accessed January 21, 2014.

37. Polling data vary. See, for instance, Chris Wang, "Less Support for Independence," *Taipei Times*, February 1, 2013, available from *www.taipeitimes.com/News/taiwan/archives/2013/02/01/2003553953*; and Chris Wang, "Taiwanese Prefer Independence Over Reunification," *Taipei Times*, October 31, 2013, available from *www.taipeitimes.com/News/front/archives/2013/10/31/2003575806*, both accessed January 17, 2014.

38. Twenty-two as of January 2014--Belize, Dominican Republic, Burkina Faso, El Salvador, Guatemala, Haiti, Honduras, Kiribati, Marshall Islands, Nauru, Nicaragua, Palau, Panama, Paraguay, Saint Kitts and Nevis, Saint Lucia, Saint Lucia, Saint Vincent and the Grenadines Solomon Islands, Swaziland, Tuvalu, and the Vatican.

39. See Alan Wachman, *Why Taiwan? Geostrategic Rationales for China's Territorial Integrity*, Palo Alto, CA: Stanford, 2007.

40. Fortunately, hubris and nationalism are the chief attractions to both nations. If, however, very significant seabed energy deposits were discovered in the disputed area of the East China Sea, the economic stakes for China and Japan would be raised, with both countries viewing the use of military force as more justified. The U.S. Department of Energy (DOE) 2014 East China Sea oil estimate was 60 to 100 million barrels (mmbbl) of "proven and probable reserve," noting that more accurate estimates are "difficult to determine." The DOE estimate for natural gas in the East China Sea is even less precise: 1 to 2 trillion cubic feet. Chinese National Overseas Oil Company, CNOOC estimates for the East China Sea are 70-160 mmbbls of oil, both "proven and undiscovered," and 300 billion cubic feet of natural gas. By comparison, China's total proven oil reserves were estimated at 20 billion barrels in 2011. Estimates are at available from *www.eia.gov/countries/ analysisbriefs/east_china_sea/east_china_sea.pdf*, accessed December 30, 2013.

41. MR reduction has long been discussed; most recently, in late-2013 and early-2014. See Yoimuri Shimbun, "Reorganization Plan Under Consideration for PLA," *The Japan News*, January 13, 2014, available from *the-japan-news.com/news/article /0000911699*; and Bai Tiantian and Liu Yang, "No Joint Command," *Global Times*, January 6, 2014, available from UtLD-V44aU00, both accessed on January 13, 2014. A summary of recent reports on PLA reorganization is in "Chinese Armed Forces to Undergo Immense Change," *Detachment Report* ASD14C03051, *U.S. Army Asian Studies*, January 4, 2014, in OSC.

42. Britain's foreign secretary in the years leading to World War I, Edward Grey, is credited with saying that "The British army should be a projectile fired by the British navy" in a quote

considered disparaging to the army. Margaret MacMillan, *The War That Ended the Peace: The Road to 1914*, New York: Random House, 2013, p. 399.

43. *The Military Balance 2013*, p. 254, discusses the two stealth aircraft. J-15 limitations are discussed in Gabe Collins and Andrew Erickson, "China's J-15 No Game Changer," *The Diplomat*, June 23, 2011, available from *thediplomat.com/2011/06/chinas-j-15-no-game-changer/*, accessed January 18, 2014.

44. PLA acquisition/employment of UAVs is discussed in Wendell Minnick, "Report: China's UAVs Could Challenge Western Dominance, *Defense News*, June 25, 2013, available from *www.defensenews.com/article/20130625/DEFREG03/306250021/Report-China-s-UAVs-Could-Challenge-Western-Dominance*; Trefor Moss, "Here Come . . . China's Drones," *The Diplomat*, March 2, 2013, available from *thediplomat.com/2013/03/here-comes-chinas-drones/?allpages=yes*, both accessed January 18, 2014.

45. Obviously, drones may be transported great distances by ships or aircraft before launching.

46. As a comparison, the new Indian ski-jump aircraft carrier, *Vikrant*, is being built at an estimated cost of U.S.$2 billion, not including embarked aircraft, while the next U.S. carrier, *Gerald R. Ford*, is reported to cost at least U.S.$13.5 billion, not including aircraft. *Liaoning* will also suffer air conditioning and engineering plant problems common to Soviet-designed ships, unless China replaced these systems during the 8 years it had the ship in dry dock.

47. Beijing would have to build two to three times this number of RAS ships to support a globally oriented navy.

48. The total number of surface combatants in the PLAN in future years is not as important as their capabilities, but in 2013 alone, China reportedly commissioned 17 new combatants, including two DDGs, three FFGs, nine corvettes, two replenishment-at-sea ships, and one minesweeper. See "Opinion: Intensive Commissioning of PLAN Warships In Line With China's Goal to Safeguard its Maritime Rights and Interests," *China Military Online*, January 9, 2014, available from *eng.chinamil.com.cn/news-chan-*

_nels/china-military-news/2014-01/09/content_5727866.htm_, accessed January 18, 2014.

49. U.S. submariners have for decades strongly and successfully campaigned against building other than nuclear powered submarines, based primarily on the logical argument that U.S. submarines must be capable of global operations. At the time VADM William Owens, himself a submariner, had a study conducted in 1992-93 about the feasibility of and rationale for adding SSs to the U.S fleet. No conclusion was offered.

50. The U.S. Office of Naval Intelligence published a report in 2009 that showed China's newest ballistic missile submarine, the Jin-class, generating a significantly higher level of self-noise, Ns than even a 30-year-old Soviet Delta III-class boat. China's newest SSNs, the Shang-class, were shown to generate a significantly higher level of Ns than any other country's SSN. This table is available _blogs.fas.org/security/2009/11/sub noise_, accessed December 30, 2013.

51. I have not been on board a Chinese submarine, other than an old Whiskey-class boat, but my visits to approximately a dozen surface warships have left me with an impression of only average maintenance practices.

52. Hans M. Kristensen, "China's Noisy Submarines," _FAS Strategic Security Blog_, November 21, 2009, p. 2, available from _blogs. fas.org/security/2009/11/subnoise_, accessed December 30, 2013.

53. The Soviet bastion strategy is explained in Christopher A. Ford and David A. Rosenberg, "The Naval Intelligence Underpinnings of Reagan's Maritime Strategy," _Journal of Strategic Studies_, Vol. 28, No. 2, 2005, pp. 379-409.

54. See Lyle Goldstein and Shannon Knight "Wired for Sound in the 'Near Seas'," _Naval Institute Proceedings_ 140/4/1, 334, April 2014, pp. 56-61, for a convincing argument that China is deploying a sea bed surveillance system, which has the potential significantly to enhance its ASW capability in regional waters.

55. See, however, William Murray, "Underwater TELs and China's Antisubmarine Warfare: Evolving Strength and a Cal-

culated Weakness," *China's Near-Seas Combat Capabilities,* CMSI Study 11, Peter Dutton, Andrew S. Erickson, and Ryan Martinson, eds., Newport, RI: Navy War College, 2014, pp. 17-30.

56. Numbers are from *The Military Balance 2013*, p. 287.

57. Jeffrey Lewis, "Minimum deterrence," *Bulletin of the Atomic Scientists*, Vol. 64, No. 3, 2008, pp. 38-41. Also see Brad Roberts, Robert A. Manning, and Ronald N. Montaperto, "China the Forgotten Nuclear Power," *Foreign Affairs*, Vol. 79, No. 4, July-August 2000, pp. 53-63. In an often misinterpreted statement, a Chinese official told Ambassador Chas W. Freeman in 1995 that China no longer feared U.S. use of nuclear weapons in a Taiwan conflict, because of China's own nuclear arsenal. In Freeman's words:

> I did not consider the Chinese statements either threatening or particularly significant. Nor did I interpret them as a reflecting a Chinese fixation with Taiwan. Rather, I heard them as a straightforward deterrent statement, directed at escalation control in Taiwan contingencies. The actual statement was something like: 'you will not continue to threaten us with nuclear attack because we can now retaliate and, in the end, you care more about Los Angeles than you do about Taipei.' That is not easy listening but it's hardly menacing.

January 22, 2014 exchange between Ambassador Freeman and the author. The publicized but erroneous account is in Joseph Kahn, "Chinese General Threatens Use of A-Bombs if U.S. Intrudes," *The New York Times*, July 15, 2005, available from *www.nytimes.com/2005/07/15/international/asia/15china.html?_r=0*, accessed December 10, 2013. The Chinese defense white papers have typically used words like "small but effective nuclear counterattacking force," 2000, "limited nuclear counterattack ability," 2002, "credible nuclear deterrent force," 2006, and "lean and effective deterrent force," 2008. Additionally, *The Science of Military Strategy*, p. 213, states that "deterrence" includes "a limited but effective nuclear deterrence."

58. *Annual Report to Congress: Military and Security Developments Involving the People's Republic of China 2010*, Washington, DC: DoD, 2010, cited in Andrew Erickson and Gabe Collins, "China's Ballistic Missiles, A Force to Be Reckoned With," *The Wall*

Street Journal Online, August 24, 2012, available from *blogs.wsj.com/chinarealtime/2012/08/24/chinas-ballistic-missiles-a-force-to-be-reckoned-with/*, accessed January 22, 2014.

59. Quoted in "Navy Admiral: China to Develop Sophisticated Marine Weapons systems," *Xinhua*, April 15, 2009, available from *news.xinhuanet.com/english/2009-04/15/content_11191749.htm*, accessed January 21, 2014.

60. The PLA's difficulty in overcoming this problem may be seen in sources dating from Bernard D. Cole, *The Great Wall at Sea*, Annapolis, MD: Naval Institute Press, 2001, pp. 111-112; and Xia Hongping, Wei Bing, and Shi Binxin, "Standardization, an Urgent Issue for 'System of Systems' Operations," *Jiefangjun Bao Online*, Beijing, China, OSC-CHR2013121030965419, December 10, 2013, p. 2.

61. The *National Ocean Policy* is an old but apparently still pertinent document, issued in Beijing in May 1998. Also see "China Issues Plan for Maritime Development," *Xinhua*, April 26, 2012, available from *www.chinadaily.com.cn/bizchina/2012-04/26/content_15152578.htm*; the 2012 *White Paper* may also be found at *news.xinhuanet.com/english/china/2013-04/16/c_132312681.htm*, both accessed January 30, 2014.

62. Blasko "note," n. 5, in the full citation found in n. 2 of in this chapter.

63. "Executive Summary," *Annual Report to Congress*, p. i.

64. Defense Minister Chang Wanquan to U.S. Secretary of Defense Chuck Hegel, April 8, 2014: "We are prepared at any time to cope with all kinds of threats and challenges . . . the Chinese military can assemble as soon summoned, fight immediately upon arrival and win any battle."

65. This model assumes one carrier in overhaul, one in training, and one operational. A four-carrier minimum actually may be more realistic, given the transition times required between the three phases.

66. Nan Li, quoted in John Garnaut, "Xi's War Drums," *Foreign Policy*, April 30, 2013, available from *www.foreignpolicy.com/ articles/2013/04/29/xis_war_drums#sthash.t3tT2ymZ.dpbs*, accessed December 29, 2013. A senior U.S. intelligence official commented to the author 2 years ago that in the PLA "if it is valuable, it is for sale."

67. Quoted in Blasko, *The Chinese Army Today*, London, UK: Routledge, 2011, p. 6.

68. Quoted in "Xi Jinping Calls for Powerful Missile Force," December 12, 2012, available from *news.xinhuanet.com/english/ china/2012-12/05/c_132021964.htm*, accessed December 29, 2013. Japan's National Institute of Defense Studies (NIDS) supported this view in its 2012 conclusion that "It is nearly inconceivable that the PLA, as the 'Party's Army,' should take arbitrary action against, or not in line with the will of the senior leaders of the CPC." See *NIDS Security Report 2012*, Tokyo, Japan: NIDS, 2012, p. 54.

69. Blasko, *The Chinese Army Today*, pp. 8, 181.

70. Recent exercises have also demonstrated improved jointness, with PLAAF generals commanding both ground and air units. See, for instance, "CCTV-7 'Junshi Jishi' Recalls Chinese Military's Progress, Incidents in 2013," January 9, 2014 report on "Maneuver-5" and "Mission Action-2013" exercises, in OSC-CHO2014011404757157; "Special Report on Shenyang Military Region Live-Forces Exercise Joint-2013, Part 2," *Shenyang Qianjin Bao*, reported that "the Army and the Air Force took turns playing the main role and director of the joint operations, and this was the first time the Military Region had done so." See OSC-CHR2013121477178103, October 28, 2013, p. 1, both accessed January 30, 2014.

71. This ambition reflects the intensely maritime character of China's defined area of concern, out to the second island chain but again, does not require "command of the sea" in the sense attributed to Alfred Thayer Mahan. Rather, Beijing intends being able to counter military actions it considers threatening to its national security interests.

CHAPTER 7

A GLOBAL EXPEDITIONARY PEOPLE'S LIBERATION ARMY:
2025-30

Oriana Skylar Mastro

Dr. Oriana Skylar Mastro would like to thank Mariangela Taylor, Xingjun Ye, and Elaine Li for their excellent and timely research assistance.

INTRODUCTION

Since the 1980s, the Chinese People's Liberation Army (PLA) has been undergoing a comprehensive reform process to move from a personnel-heavy, low-tech force designed to expel invaders to one that is technology-intensive and focused on operating beyond China's coasts. The PLA is currently focused on traditional warfighting missions, with an emphasis on winning local wars under informationized conditions shaping its military preparedness.[1] While China's ability to project conventional military power beyond its periphery remains limited[2] as China gains greater influence within the international community, it is becoming increasingly focused on modernizing its military capabilities to include "a wider range of missions beyond its immediate territorial concerns, including counterpiracy, peacekeeping, humanitarian assistance/disaster relief (HADR), and regional military operations."[3]

Since 2004, China has increasingly focused on coping with nontraditional security threats and safeguarding the state's development and overseas interests.[4]

This has inspired the Chinese military to increasingly conduct missions beyond its immediate territory, in particular to handle threats to Chinese citizens and economic interests abroad.[5] Chinese armed forces are already emphasizing how they would be employed during peacetime for military operations other than war (MOOTW) to:

> strengthen overseas operational capabilities such as emergency response and rescue, merchant vessel protection at sea and evacuation of Chinese nationals, and provide reliable security support for China's interests overseas.[6]

The PLA's experience to date with such expeditionary operations is limited, but expanding rapidly. Since 2002, the PLA has undertaken 36 urgent international humanitarian aid missions.[7] Chinese naval vessels have engaged in expeditionary goodwill tours such as the 2012 voyage of the PLAN ship *Zheng He* and the 2010-13 "Harmonious Missions" of a hospital ship to provide medical aid in Asia, Africa, and Latin America.[8] To date, China's participation in the anti-piracy operations in the Gulf of Aden is the most notable example of the PLA conducting expeditionary operations. As one Chinese Rear Admiral notes, the main point of the operation was not to combat pirates, as the Chinese navy's main mission was not to attack or detain them, but to protect Chinese overseas economic interests.[9] The mission began in January 2009 when a Chinese naval flotilla consisting of a replenishment ship and two destroyers arrived in the Gulf of Aden off Somalia to protect merchant ships from pirates.[10] Over the course of 500 operations, this force has protected more than 5,000 commercial vessels.[11] The humanitarian aspect of the operation allowed the

PLA to operate outside China and gain valuable deployment experience, without being seen as a threat.[12]

The amount of resources China dedicates to its global missions will be influenced by a number of variables, including the U.S. response to this evolution, and China's relations with regional states such as Japan, North Korea, Taiwan, Vietnam and the Philippines. But domestic and international imperatives could ensure that China develops power projection capabilities regardless. Furthermore, the Chinese leadership is likely to believe that the capabilities necessary for such expeditionary capabilities could also be employed in regional contingencies, thereby increasing the political support for their development. In this chapter, I will outline what doctrine, force structure, and organization and training would most likely characterize a globally expeditionary PLA. The chapter then addresses the implications of a global expeditionary PLA capable of operating to a limited degree overseas for regional and global security.

FUTURE NATURE AND DIRECTION OF CHINESE MILITARY MODERNIZATION

A range of domestic and international factors — from the need to protect overseas Chinese interests to the status of regional issues — could, by 2025-30, compel the PLA to act increasingly globally. A global expeditionary PLA is not inevitable, but one of three possible scenarios of the PLA's development covered in this volume. In this alternative future, by 2025-30 a global expeditionary PLA could be able to project limited power in a limited area for a short duration anywhere in the world. This global expeditionary capability will allow China to play a role in peacekeeping, HADR, and stability operations regionally and globally. China could also develop capabilities such as expeditionary strike groups and special operations to conduct raids, noncombatant evacuation operations (NEOs), security operations, counterblockades, strikes, and amphibious exercises. If the Party leadership mandates the PLA to modernize and train to operate beyond the first and second island chain, the majority of those efforts would be undertaken by the PLA Navy (PLAN) and PLA Air Force (PLAAF). This section addresses the likely developments in doctrine, force posture, and organization and training of a PLA capable of projecting power globally.

DOCTRINE, STRATEGIC GUIDELINES, AND OPERATIONAL CONCEPTS

Doctrinal changes would likely accompany any changes in the direction and focus of Chinese military evolution to account for the addition of global expeditionary missions. Since 1949, China's doctrine has evolved as the Party leadership's threat perceptions and China's ability to meet them have changed.[13] In this future scenario, the state of the international environment, potential threats to China, the most likely type of war and the best ways to fight that war will shift significantly, calling for an addition to the current formulation of "local war under informationized conditions." In terms of equipment, integration, and training, China plans to have the process of mechanization (the deployment of advanced military platforms) and informatization (bringing them together as a network) completed by 2020. Around this time, in this scenario, President Xi Jinping would announce a corollary to local war, win-win global operations, asserting that China must also develop the skills and platforms necessary to project power globally to be a responsible great power. Within the top echelons of government, there would be more discussion and formalization of the basis for MOOTW and a focus on creating the ability to conduct simultaneous operations in different locations globally, in addition to joint operations.

Additionally, Chinese operational concepts will likely evolve to account for shifting priorities and frequency of certain types of missions. For obvious reasons, the joint island landing campaign is the most prominent operation currently found in publicly available Chinese writings. This campaign objective's would be:

> to break through or circumvent shore defense, establish and build a beachhead, transport personnel and material to designated landing sites in the north or south of Taiwan's western coastline, and launch attacks to seize and occupy key targets and/or the entire island.[14]

Strategic air raids designed to leverage the PLA's asymmetric advantages over potential adversaries to achieve localized air superiority is another type of campaign currently at the top of Beijing's priorities.[15] But as the PLA begins to operate farther from China's shores, ensuring its own ability to conduct operations may take precedence over capabilities designed to degrade an adversary's capability. A reprioritization of campaigns coupled with the addition of new campaigns could shift the focus from defense-oriented campaigns to security operations and strikes. By 2025-30, Chinese strike capability could move beyond the Second Artillery to give equal strategic weight to

strikes conducted by the PLA, PLAN and PLAAF—
a doctrinal change that has institutional and strategic
implications.

Lastly, Chinese leaders would begin to consider
the framework needed to build the type of strategic
partnerships necessary for expeditionary operations.
To date, China has been focused on developing relationships that will help it improve its capabilities and
increase its political power. China has already begun
this process, though to a limited degree. For example,
in February 2014, China signed a security and defense
agreement with Djibouti to promote regional stability in the Gulf of Aden region.[16] China participated in
RIMPAC 2014, the biennial naval exercise hosted by
the United States that involves 23 nations. Within the
framework of the Shanghai Cooperation Organization
(SCO), China and other SCO member states have conducted a total of nine bilateral and multilateral exercises.[17] China has also conducted joint exercises with
Thailand, Singapore, Romania, Indonesia, Pakistan,
Belarus, Venezuela, Colombia, Russia, Australia, New
Zealand and Turkey since 2010. [18]

While Chinese leaders have been adamantly against
formal alliances, given the operational necessity of
this global expeditionary scenario, a debate could en-
sue in China about changing its approach, akin to the
way China changed its approach to peacekeeping operations in the 1990s. Chinese strategists are currently
ideologically averse to overseas bases partly due to the
national narrative that only hegemonic powers seek
such arrangements.[19] Though useful in operations, establishing overseas bases or hubs are in direct conflict
with Chinese foreign policy, defense policy, and military strategy.[20] Mutual defense treaties and permanent
bases are therefore unlikely at this stage, but Beijing's

ideology is elastic, and could be reshaped to fit pragmatic realities if required. China could begin to pursue formal treaties to institutionalize arrangements to use facilities in other countries. To maintain the appearance of consistency, Beijing would retain its rhetoric against alliances and put forth strategic guidance that describes these arrangements as win-win agreements between equal partners seeking to enhance stability and security in the region. According to one Chinese naval officer, if China were to go this route, first experts would have to posit and discuss the idea, then revisions would have to be made to the white paper, supported by diplomatic efforts. But he noted it was unlikely China would station troops overseas or operate from overseas bases, because such a change would require major changes to Chinese defense and grand strategy, in addition to a major diplomatic undertaking.[21] Increased multilateral exercises and operations would likely follow to reassure countries that China will not unilaterally pursue changes in the status quo through the use of force.

FORCE POSTURE

In order to conduct global operations, the PLA would start to develop the ability to force open denied air and sea space far from Chinese territory in order to be able to operate beyond immediate periphery and in hostile environments away from friendly ports.[22] In addition to building the relevant air, naval, and ground forces, the PLA will prioritize the systems and skills necessary for joint operations. For any type of expeditionary operation, conducted in peacetime or in war, China will need to make major advances in information warfare—space, cyber, and electronic warfare.

Chinese writings suggest that the PLA believes these three types of technologies not only enable operations, but should also be treated as separate domains that must be seized and denied to an adversary.[23]

In terms of space assets, China will be able to call upon communication and navigation satellites, and a robust, space-based ocean surveillance system in particular for its operations. The PLA also understands that in order to be effective in modern conflicts and MOOTW, it must have the Command, Control, Communications, Computers, Intelligence, Surveillance and Reconnaissance (C4ISR) capacity to carry out joint operations. By 2025-30, a global expeditionary PLA must have made great strides in C4ISR integration including creating a model system to facilitate interoperability of its information technology systems.[24] Digital C4ISR connectivity will revolutionize the PLA's ability to conduct modern combined arms military operations.[25] The incorporation of improved C4ISR networks into training will ensure that the forces are consistently provided with real-time data transmission within and between units, enabling better command and control during operations.[26]

Cyber and electronic warfare capabilities will also enhance China's ability to conduct global operations, especially in contested environments. Currently, China is more focused on cyber warfare as a means to exfiltrate data from vulnerable networks, to serve as a force multiplier when coupled with kinetic attacks, and to target an adversary's networks to constrain its actions or slow its response time.[27] As the Chinese military begins to operate abroad, cyber warfare will become a critical tool in gathering intelligence on potential areas in which the PLA may be required to operate, known as intelligence preparation of the operational environment (IPOE). The PLA will also work to expand their electronic warfare capabilities, which consist of technologies that weaken and destroy electronic equipment and systems and protect one's own electronic equipment and systems. During air operations, these systems would be employed against communication nodes, radars, command centers, and air-defense weapon control systems in particular. If conducting operations at sea, such as a counter blockade campaign, electronic warfare forces would be used against enemy ships and airborne and sea-based anti-missile systems. [28]

While this section focuses on the assets needed to sustain operations far from China's shores, the PLA will simultaneously continue to improve its warfighting capabilities with a focus on regional contingencies. Current plans suggest that by 2020, China will be able to employ satellites and reconnaissance drones; thousands of surface-to-surface and anti-ship missiles; more than 60 stealthy conventional submarines and at least six nuclear attack submarines; increasingly stealthy surface combatants and stealthy manned and unmanned combat aircraft; and space and cyber warfare capabilities. It is also possible that China will invest in additional aircraft carriers.[29] But even as the PLA prepares to fight local wars under high-tech conditions within the region, it will expand its attention on expeditionary capabilities in the air, on the sea, and on the ground.

Air.

China will invest in large fleets of tankers and long-range large transport aircraft for various missions such as NEOs. China has ordered but not taken delivery of four IL-78/MIDAS tankers, but even these can support at most a squadron of Su-30s in combat operations, so the PLA would look to use a more advanced platform by 2025-30.[30] China will be looking to expand its inventory of large transport airplanes capable of carrying large cargo for long-range flights. This may include more IL-76s from Russia, but more likely the advanced models of the indigenously manufactured Y-20 aircraft. The Y-20 should give China the ability to quickly ship troops, vehicles, and supplies over long distances, though the PLA may need to upgrade the engines at some point for the Y-20 to be able to do so efficiently.[31] The PLAAF will also continue to progress in its Airborne Early Warning (AEW), Electronic Warfare, and command and control systems, including significant unmanned aerial vehicle (UAV) development.[32]

In addition to developing and acquiring systems designed to sustain operations abroad, the PLA will continue to progress in traditional warfighting capabilities. The PLAAF will likely phase out its aging H6 fleet. [33] The new H-6K, which was unveiled in 2013, is likely only a stopgap measure. Though China's intentions are unclear at this point, the PLA will likely have a stealthier platform by 2025-30.[34] The PLAAF's 2025-30 inventory will include a low-observable aircraft a low-observable aircraft derived from either the J-20 or J-31.

UAV development over the next 15 years will be significant; the PLA will likely have several massive fleets of mostly cheap drones operated by the ground forces, the General Staff Department (GSD), PLAN, PLAAF, Second Artillery, and Coast Guard.[35] Each will bolster the operational requirements of the respective service or unit they serve.[36] These assets will probably be truck-launched to keep them operationally flexible and survivable, or some could be based on carriers. While most will be used regionally, larger drones could serve as long-range reconnaissance platforms or focus on decoy, jamming, and swarming tactics for penetrating enemy air defense systems in expeditionary operations. However, China will likely continue to suffer from a lack of bases outside China.

Sea.

China's defense white paper articulates the desire to develop blue water navy capabilities for conducting operations, carrying out international cooperation and countering nontraditional security threats, and enhancing capabilities of strategic deterrence and counterattack.[37] But currently, strategic sealift beyond Taiwan is quite limited. China has never possessed a robust capability to transport and land troops under combat conditions.[38] China has three Yuzhao class landing platform dock (LPD) ships, each capable of transporting one battalion of marines and their vehicles and two large multiproduct replenishment ships that carry fuel, water, ammunition, and other supplies.[39] But to be a global expeditionary PLAN, the service will need to increase the number of LPDs as well as the number of large, multiproduct replenishment ships to support long-range patrols.[40] China would also have to address the limitations of inadequate air defense, lack of experience in formation steaming, and lack of ability and training in cross-beach movement of forces to enhance its amphibious assault capabilities.[41] The Chinese navy may also invest to a greater degree in a marine corps as an offshore expeditionary force given the increased need to prepare for amphibious landings and assaults. China's marines will have to expand from the current two brigades of 6,000 men each, but the ultimate level of forces depends on the type of amphibious operations the PLA stresses in 2025-30 and the forces of surrounding countries.[42] China may also put off such investments given the extraordinarily difficult nature of amphibious operations — at this point, only the United States has a robust capability. Even now, China currently has more marines than naval powers such as Australia, Great Britain, and Japan.

Currently the PLAN possesses approximately 77 principal surface combatants, more than 60 submarines, 55 medium and large amphibious ships and roughly 85 missile-equipped small combatants.[43] The PLAN would develop the capabilities and assets needed to protect the sea lines of communication (SLOCs) and engage in operations far from its shores. To that end, the PLAN has already begun the process of retiring legacy combatants in favor of larger, multi-mission ships, equipped with advanced anti-ship, anti-air, and anti-submarine weapons and sensors.[44] China may also commission more carriers, along with their aircraft and UAVs, with the justification that carriers are useful in maritime security operations and operations other than war. These carriers, plus 18 air defense destroyers with Aegis-like anti-air warfare systems, and 36 frigates and corvettes equipped primarily for anti-submarine warfare (ASW), will be tasked with defending the SLOCs.[45]

China may expand the number of attack submarines (SSNs) for sustained patrols in distant waters or to conduct counterblockade operations, though China will rely heavily on conventionally powered submarines equipped with air-independent-propulsion to patrol out to the first and eventually the second island chains. China's economic growth relies heavily on its access to natural resources, and its petroleum comes primarily from the Middle East, which has to pass through a number of vulnerable chokepoints including the Luzon and Taiwan straits and the Strait of Malacca and Strait of Hormuz. China currently cannot project naval control over these chokepoints, but future capabilities may be developed to address this vulnerability. To date, China has stressed anti-surface warfare over ASW. But China may start to focus on developing counterblockade capabilities to protect vital SLOCs, such as more advanced sonar operations and airborne ASW.

Ground.

As China's focus expands from homeland defense to regional contingencies, to global expeditions, the relative role of the PLA Army (PLAA) with respect to the other services will decrease. By 2025-30, the number of active and reserve soldiers in the PLAA will likely be reduced to fewer than two million, unless there is a conventional flare up with India, Vietnam, Russia, or instability on the border with North Korea. The PLAA, however, will still have critical missions within a global expeditionary PLA. The PLAA is reorienting itself already from theater operations to trans-theater mobility focusing on army aviation troops, light mechanized units and special operations forces (SOF), and enhancing building of digitized units, making its units small, modular, and multi-functional to enhance capabilities for air-ground integrated operations, long-distance maneuvers, rapid assaults, and special operations.

China's reluctance to get involved globally on a large scale may translate to a prioritization of development of China's special operations capabilities. China created its elite special forces and Rapid Reaction Units (RRU) in the 1980s. Today, their training extends into more unconventional warfighting missions such as sabotage, and no-contact long range warfare (indirect attacks against an enemy from beyond the line of sight), with the United States and Japan as potential enemies. According to the *PLA Army Daily:*

> Special forces warfare includes detailed battle theories, such as special forces reconnaissance, attacks and sabotage, and comprehensive battle theories, such as integrated land-sea-air-space-electronic combat, all-dimensional simultaneous attacks, nonlinear combat, no-contact long-range warfare, asymmetrical combat, large-scale night combat and 'surgical' strikes.[46]

According to *On Military Campaigns*, one of several special operations missions include:

> raids to kill or capture enemy command personnel (including military and government leaders), or destroy small units in the enemy's rear area or key command and control, intelligence, or logistics systems.[47]

China's Rapid Reaction Forces (RRF) currently consist of army special forces, army aviation units, the marine corps, and airborne troops. They focus primarily on border defense, internal armed conflict, maintaining public order, and conducting disaster relief missions.[48] While all "rapid reaction," the army special forces and airborne troops would split off and develop the core SOF mission, while the marine corps and army aviation will progress to address more traditional warfighting tasks. Chinese writings suggest a traditional understanding of SOF in that they would be used for special reconnaissance, decapitation, counterterrorism, hostage rescue, and also have a psychological effect that will impose caution by increasing the risk of war.[49] Some specific missions include: "prisoner snatch operations; raids on enemy missile sites, CPs, and communications facilities; harassment and interdiction operations to prevent or delay enemy movements; strategic reconnaissance; anti-terrorist operations."[50] The PLA may heavily rely on types of special operations forces to accomplish their goals overseas partly because of the small footprint, but primarily because training and readiness of regular troops will continue to be a weakness of their military forces.[51]

By 2025-30, joint use of special forces with the PLA's amphibious and airborne forces, expected improvements in sealift and airlift capabilities, coupled with the increasing mechanization of airborne and army and marine amphibious units will increase the reach and effectiveness of these forces. By the end of that decade, PLA forces may be capable of capturing ports and airfields in neighboring states, leading to a victorious campaign on land.[52]

ORGANIZATION, TRAINING, AND LOGISTICS

Reforms beyond hardware in terms of organization, training, and readiness must be undertaken as well for the PLA to expand its operational reach. First, China will need to improve the movement of military units within China. The PLA still conducts long distance maneuver training at speeds measured by how fast the next available cargo train can transport its tanks and guns forward.[53] To improve its air and sealift, China will have to mobilize the civilian sector, especially in the area of aviation. Furthermore, the Chinese Communist Party will have to move to strengthened interior ground, air, and waterway lines of communication. The PLA will also have to consider the logistics needed to deploy globally and sustain operations abroad. A reorganization of the current Military Region (MR) system is a necessary step to improve mobility. Since 2010, the PLA has attempted to improve its trans-MR maneuvers by carrying out a series of campaign level exercises and drills, codenamed Mission Action.[54] China could reduce the number of MRs from seven to perhaps four and implement a joint operational command structure.[55] Given the new importance of the PLAN, PLAAF, and Second Artillery, another major step toward "jointness" would be assigning a navy or air force officer as an MR commander.[56]

The PLA will have to consider how to fit global logistics into this MR system; given its diverse set of tasks and missions, the PLA will need to improve its logistical system so that it is flexible, distributed, and nimble.[57] Analysis of past operations such as the PLAN's deployment to the Gulf of Aden demonstrates that the issue of preparedness during emergency, the problem of preserving consumables over long periods of time, and the lack of nearby Chinese facilities/bases to which it can send vessels for maintenance and repair continue to plague long-distance PLAN operations.[58] Because the PLA's ability to force open denied air and sea space far from Chinese territory will likely still be constrained in 2025-30, it will still be challenging to operate beyond its immediate periphery and in hostile environments away from friendly ports.[59] Bringing along military supply ships with 3 months' worth of fuel, food, fresh water, and spare parts, as China did in the Gulf of Aden, will not be a viable strategy if China is to conduct larger, more prolonged, or contested, operations.[60] Overseas bases may be the only way for China to be able to deploy and fight on the high seas; the lack of such resources is one of the major differences between major and minor naval powers.[61] China may need them as forward operating bases and logistics platforms, as well as to conduct amphibious assaults.[62]

Some believe that China wants to build a series of bases in the Indian Ocean to support naval operations along the routes linking China to Persian Gulf oil sources. There, Beijing can pursue access in countries such as Oman, Pakistan, and Burma that are politically insulated from Indian and U.S. pressure. Others believe that the PLAN only wants to have places in the Indian Ocean where it can restock and refuel, rather than its own bases.[63] The latter is probably the more likely scenario, especially given the lessons learned from the Soviet Union's overextension, and the priority of concerns closer to home.[64] Leaving aside China's ideological aversion to overseas bases, it is also important to keep in mind that in these areas, facilities are difficult to defend and host nations may not be sufficiently stable to support operations.[65] Given these obstacles, for China to start prepositioning supplies overseas or establishing institutional arrangements to allow operations from other countries, the driver would have to be more than just the need to operate escort vessels like in a Gulf of Aden type of operation.[66]

The PLA will need to improve training to enhance the ability to conduct multiple joint operations simultaneously. China currently conducts exercises frequently; for example, during the month of January 2014, a three-ship flotilla from the Nanhai Fleet began combat exercises in the West Pacific Ocean and East Indian Ocean.[67] Additionally, nearly 100,000 Chinese soldiers and thousands of vehicles from the 16th and 39th Army Groups of the Shenyang MR mobilized for a winter exercise to prepare for a potential crisis over the Korean peninsula.[68]

However, despite the scale and frequency of these exercises, PLA individual and unit training standards remain low, and are improving only gradually. Currently, PLAAF pilots typically get less than 10 hours of flight time a month and only last year began to submit their own flight plans.[69] China's naval infantry and other amphibious warfare units train by landing on big sandy beaches, an unrealistic environment to train for conflict over disputed islands.[70] Moreover, in recent exercises, PLA troops have lacked the emotional fortitude to succeed in high-pressure situations, possibly one of the reasons for President Xi Jinping's focus on enhancing combat readiness among the PLA.[71] Therefore, Chinese exercises will need to become larger and more complicated coupled with training that is more frequent, intense and realistic for the PLA to become a global expeditionary force by 2025-30.

CONCLUSIONS AND IMPLICATIONS

This chapter presents how the PLA may evolve with respect to doctrine, force structure, organization, and training if it were to transition to a force capable of conducting global expeditionary operations. However, such new and expansive PLA capabilities will have significant implications for China's willingness to use force as well as regional stability.

Propensity to Use Force.

The breadth of capabilities the PLA would acquire to conduct global expeditionary operations could also augment Beijing's options in resolving both global and regional disputes. Augmented sea and airlift, advanced SOF capabilities, a greater number of surface vessels and aircraft, and most significant, operational experience for its forces, could encourage China to expand the scope of its interests and willingness to use force to protect those interests. China could become more forceful, confident in its ability to achieve its objectives by support alone with the backing of its people.

While China may currently have no intention of becoming a global hegemon, the introduction of new capabilities in turn could drive changes in Chinese grand strategy away from limited regional aims. Chinese strategists and netizens have already launched a debate about whether China should aspire to become a global military power. Currently, those debates are couched in discussions about how China should approach its territorial disputes, especially in the East and South China Seas.[72] But influential thinkers such as Colonel Liu Mingfu, a former professor at the PLA National Defense University, writes in his book *China Dream* that China should aim to surpass the United States as the world's top military power.[73] In a March 2010 newspaper poll, 80 percent of respondents responded positively to the question, "Do you think China should strive to be the world's strongest country militarily?" However, less than half of respondents approved of a policy to publicly announce such an objective.[74]

Stability and Balance of Power.

Even if this future scenario spurs a growth in traditional power projection capabilities or increased use of force abroad, the implications for the United States and its regional allies and partners are uncertain. This could create balancing backlash in Asia and instability as incentives for preventive war increase with the rapid shifts in the regional balance of power. However, this future scenario could also create a more assertive China that is positioned to provide public goods to the international community and region, further enmeshing Beijing into the current world order, and reducing the incentives to use force to resolve disputes.

Globally, increased expeditionary capabilities could increase the potential for Chinese interference in issues in which the United States may prefer China's traditional hands-off approach. Chinese interests in the Middle East, Africa, and South America, as well as Beijing's preference for stability over other factors such as human rights, may clash with those of the United States. With increased capabilities, China may take actions in countries around the world that have negative second order effects for U.S. national interests. Furthermore, because Chinese actions are not transparent, Washington has limited sense about what exactly China is doing. This makes it difficult for the United States to adjust its policies accordingly to minimize any potential damage to U.S. interests and maximize its ability to achieve its foreign policy goals.[75]

A number of factors could divert the PLA from developing a global expeditionary force. For example, if China were to engage in a war, even a limited one, retrenchment and rebuilding may follow, delaying the unfolding of this scenario. Furthermore, flare-ups closer to home or the emergence of significant threats to its near-seas interests may make it difficult for Beijing to sustain far seas operations.[76] But as long as China continues to spend a double-digit percentage of GDP on defense spending, and GDP growth continues, even on a more conservative level, China should be able to simultaneously develop traditional warfighting capabilities to address regional challenges and global expeditionary capabilities to confront threats farther from home. In this way, flare-ups or resolutions of persistent regional issues may delay or accelerate this future scenario, but not necessarily prevent it.

ENDNOTES - CHAPTER 7

1. For more on this, see Information Office of the State Council of the People's Republic of China, "The Diversified Employment of China's Armed Forces: V. Safeguarding World Peace and Regional Stability," Beijing, China, 2013, available from *www.china.org.cn/government/whitepaper/2013-04/16/content_28556977.htm*, accessed on May 12, 2014.

2. Office of the Secretary of Defense, *Annual Report to Congress: The Military Power of the People's Republic of China 2005*, Washington, DC: DoD, Executive Summary, available from *www.defense.gov/news/jul2005/d20050719china.pdf*.

3. Office of the Secretary of Defense, *Annual Report to Congress: Military and Security Developments Involving the People's Republic of China 2013*, Washington, DC: DoD, Executive Summary, available from *www.defense.gov/pubs/2013_china_report_final.pdf*. Hereafter cited as DoD China Report 2013.

4. Chen Zhou, *An Analysis of Defensive National Defense Policy of China for Safeguarding Peace and Development*, China Military Science, Beijing, China: Academy of Military Sciences, 2007.

5. *DoD China Report 2013*.

6. "Diversified Employment."

7. *Ibid.*

8. It visited five countries in Asia and Africa and four in Latin America and completed 193 days of voyage, covering 42,000 nautical miles, providing nearly 50,000 people with medical supplies. See Lieutenant Commander Jeff W. Benson, "China: Birth of a Global Force?" *USNI News,* January 7, 2013, available from *news.usni.org/2013/01/07/china-birth-global-force*, accessed on March 25, 2015.

9. Zhang Zhaozhong (张召忠) "中国在海外建军事基地的可能性不大" ("It Is Unlikely for China to Establish Military Bases Abroad"), *Tengxun Xinwen*, January 19, 2010, available from *news.qq.com/a/20100119/002913.htm*, accessed on March 25, 2015.

10. "Chinese Naval Fleet Carries Out First Escort Mission Off Somalia," *People's Daily*, January 6, 2009, available from *english.peopledaily.com.cn/90001/90776/90883/6568232.html*, accessed on May 30, 2014.

11. Andrew S. Erickson and Austin M. Strange, "No Substitute for Experience Chinese Antipiracy Operations in the Gulf of Aden," *U.S. Naval War College China Maritime Studies*, Vol. 10, 2013, p. 1.

12. Richard Weitz, "Operation Somalia: China's First Expeditionary Force?" *China Security*, Vol. 5, No. 1, 2009, p. 31.

13. While Chinese strategists would not term this doctrine, but use terms like military thought, national military strategy, and strategic guidelines, these concepts can be understood as the codification of what military institutions hold as fundamental principles for guiding their actions in pursuit of national objectives.

14. *DoD China Report 2013*, p. 57.

15. For more on the strategic air raid campaign, see Peng Guangqian and Yao Youzhi (eds.), *The Science of Military Strategy* Beijing, China: Military Science Publishing House, 2005, p. 21.

16. Clint Richards, "Could China and Japan Work Together in East Africa?" *The Diplomat,* March 20, 2014, available from *thediplomat.com/2014/03/could-china-and-japan-work-together-in-east-africa*, accessed on May 30, 2014.

17. "Diversified Employment."

18. *Ibid.*

19. Huang Yingxu, (黄迎旭),"未来中国需要什么样的军事力量？"("What Kind of Military Power Does China Need in the Future?"),学习时报 (*Xuexi Shiba,* [*The Study Times*]), available from *www.people.com.cn*, accessed on May 12, 2014.

20. Zhang 2010.

21. *Ibid.*

22. Abraham M. Denmark, "PLA Logistics 2004-11: Lessons Learned in the Field," Roy Kamphausen, David Lai, and Travis Tanner, eds., *Learning by Doing The PLA Trains at Home and Abroad,* Carlisle, PA: Strategic Studies Institute, U.S. Army War College, 2012, p. 317.

23. Peng Guangqian and Yao Youzhi, 战略学, *The Science of Strategy,* Beijing, China: Military Science Press, 2001, p. 358. For more on Chinese recent advancements in information warfare, see Kevin Pollpeter, "Controlling the Information Domain: Space, Cyber, and Electronic Warfare," Ashley Tellis and Travis Tanner, eds, *Strategic Asia 2012-2013: China's Military Challenge,* Washington, DC: National Bureau of Asian Research, 2012.

24. Daniel Alderman, *The PLA at Home and Abroad: Assessing the Operational Capabilities of China's Military,* Carlisle, PA: Strategic Studies Institute, U.S. Army War College, June 2010, pp. 2-4.

25. Richard D. Fisher, *China's Military Modernization Building for Regional and Global Reach,* Stanford, CA: Stanford University Press, 2010, p. 113.

26. China is starting to do this, but given limited realistic training and space systems, the force is fare from informationalized. See *DoD China Report 2013*, p. 58.

27. Pollpeter, p. 172.

28. *Ibid.*, pp. 177-179.

29. "China's Military Rise, The Dragon's New Teeth, A Rare Look Inside the World's Biggest Military Expansion," *The Economist*, August 9, 2013.

30. M. Taylor Fravel, "China's Search for Military Power," *Washington Quarterly*, Vol. 31, No. 3, 2008, p. 135.

31. David Axe, "China's Air Power Future Is Visible in These Two Photos," *Medium*, January 5, 2014, available from *https://medium.com/war-is-boring/645be6841203*, accessed on May 30, 2014.

32. For more on trends in PLAAF modernization, see Lee Fuell, "Testimony before the U.S.-China Economic & Security Review Commissions," Department of the Air Force, January 30, 2014, available from *www.uscc.gov/sites/default/files/Lee%20Fuell_Testimony1.30.14.pdf*, accessed on May 30, 2014.

33. Fravel, p. 139.

34. Wendell Minnick, "China's Future Bomber Requirements Murky," *Defense News*, January 31, 2013, available from *www.defensenews.com/article/20130131/DEFREG03/301310016/China-8217-s-Future-Bomber-Requirements-Murky*, accessed on May 30, 2014.

35. The following discussion on UAVs in based on author's correspondence with Ian Easton, a Research Fellow at the Project 2049 Institute and author with L.C. Russell Hsiao of "The Chinese People's Liberation Army Unmanned Aerial Vehicle Project: Organizational Capacities and Operational Capabilities," Arlington, VA: Project 2049 Institute, March 11, 2013, available from *project2049.net/documents/uav_easton_hsiao.pdf*.

36. For example, Second Artillery would invest in strategic strike UAVs, GSD in national intelligence collecting UAVs, PLAAF in air defense and land attack UAVs, PLAN for anti-ship UAVs, etc.

37. "Diversified Employment."

38. Bernard D. Cole, *The Great Wall at Sea*, 2nd Ed., Annapolis, MD: Naval Institute Press, 2010, p. 152.

39. Fravel, p. 135.

40. Sources suggest that the PLAN currently plans on building a total of five. This would allow Beijing to assign one or more to each of its three fleets—North Sea, East Sea, and South Sea. See *Ibid*.

41. Cole, p. 135.

42. Christopher P. Isajiw, "China's PLA Marines an Emerging Force," *The Diplomat*, October 17, 2013, available from *www.thediplomat.com/2013/10/chinas-pla-marines-an-emerging-force/*, accessed on May 1, 2014.

43. Jesse L. Karotkin, "Trends in China's Naval Modernization: U.S. China Economic and Security Review Commission Testimony," January 30, 2014, available from *www.uscc.gov/sites/default/files/Karotkin_Testimony1.30.14.pdf*, accessed May 30, 2014.

44. *Ibid*.

45. For more on the future modernization of the PLAN, see *Ibid*.

46. Scott J. Henderson, "In the Shadow: Chinese Special Forces Build a 21st-Century Fighting Force," *Foreign Military Studies Office*, July-August 2006, p. 30.

47. Dennis J. Blasko, *The Chinese Army Today: Tradition and Transformation for the 21st Century*, 2nd Ed., New York: Routledge, 2012, p. 132.

48. Andrew N. D. Yang and Colonel Milton Wen-Chung Liao, "PLA Rapid Reaction Forces: Concept, Training, and Preliminary Assessment," James C. Mulvenon and Richard H. Yang, eds., *The People's Liberation Army in the Information Age*, Santa Monica, CA: RAND Corporation, 1999, p. 49.

49. Yuan Lin and Li Chengfeng, "中国特种部队素描" ("A sketch of Chinese Special Forces")，*Conmilit*, Vol. 2, 1998, p. 23; Luo Maofu, Wang Shupeng and Jiang Linfang, "浅谈特种部队战士财务保障" ("Tentatively on Wartime Financial Support for Task Forces"), *Military Economic Research*, Vol. 3, 1996; Zhang Mihua, Zhang Quanli and Ma Chuangang，"提升特种部队完成多样化军事任务能力的几点思考" ("The Instructions of Enhancing the Special Force's Capability to Accomplish Diverse Military Tasks"), *National Defense Science & Technology*, Vol. 5, 2009.

50. Blasko, p. 192.

51. One article articulates the dangerous belief that Special Forces alone can accomplish the critical wartime tasks. Luo Wang and Jiang.

52. Stephen J. Blank, "China's Military Power: Shadow Over Central Asia," *Lexington Institute*, August 2006, p. 8.

53. Ian Easton, "China's Deceptively Weak (and Dangerous) Military," *The Diplomat*, January 31, 2014, available from *thediplomat.com/2014/01/chinas-deceptively-weak-and-dangerous-military/*, accessed May 30, 2014.

54. "Diversified Employment."

55. MR reduction was most recently discussed in the wake of the third plenum. A Japanese news source claims China will reduce the number of MRs to five to enhance its ability to respond swiftly in a crisis. See "China considers revamping military regions: report," *The Japan Times*, January 1, 2014, available from *www.japantimes.co.jp/news/2014/01/01/asia-pacific/china-considers-revamping-military-regions-report/#.UvAX_Xkywgg*, accessed May 30, 2014. Chinese sources deny any planned change. See Bai Tiantian and Liu Yang, "No Joint Command," *Global Times*, January 6, 2014, available from *www.globaltimes.cn/content/835937.shtml#.UtLDV44aUl00*, accessed May 30, 2014.

56. Blasko, pp. 38-39.

57. Denmark, p. 327.

58. *Ibid.*, p. 310.

59. *Ibid.*, p. 317.

60. According to one Chinese RADM, food and water supply were not a problem, the biggest issue was repair and maintenance of the ships (维修设施). Zhang.

61. Wei Tian (卫天), "突破远洋的束缚：中国远洋补给能力及未来发展" ("The PLA-Navy's Deep-Sea Replenishment Capability and its Future"), 舰载武器 (*Shipborne Weapons*), Vol. 10, 2010, pp. 20-35.

62. Chen Chuanming (传明),"中国海军的未来海上基地战略" ("Strategy for China's Future Sea Base"), 现代舰船 (*Modern Ships*), Vol. 10, 2011, pp. 20-23.

63. Ronald O'Rourke, *China Naval Modernization: Implications for U.S. Navy Capabilities—Background and Issues for Congress*, RL-33153, Washington, DC: Congressional Research Service, April 10, 2014, p. 35.

64. Andrew Erickson, *China's Modernization of Its Naval and Air Power Capabilities*, Seattle, WA, and Washington, DC: The National Bureau of Asian Research, 2012, p. 96.

65. *Ibid.*, p. 87. The ideological constraints also permeate strategic thinking; Chinese publications on sustaining naval operations abroad in general put forth more arguments against rather than for overseas basing.

66. Zhang.

67. "Chinese Navy Starts Open Sea Drill," *Sina English*, January 20, 2014, available from *english.sina.com/china/2014/0120/664926.html*, accessed May 30, 2014.

68. "PLA's New Tank Deployed in N Korea Border Exercise," *WantChinaTimes*, January 21, 2014, available from *www.wantchinatimes.com/news-subclass-cnt.aspx?cid=1101&MainCatID=11&id=20140121000012*, accessed May 30, 2014. For more on current annual exercises, see *DoD China Report 2013*, p. 11.

69. Previously, staff officers assigned pilots their flight plans and would not even allow them to taxi and takeoff on the runways by themselves. See Easton, "China's Deceptively Weak."

70. "Chinese troops conduct Normandy style amphibious landing exercise for future military conflicts over islands," *LiveLeak*, September 20, 2013, available from *www.liveleak.com/view?i=ad1_1379695188*, accessed May 30, 2014.

71. Easton, "China's Deceptively Weak."

72. For example, one TV show discusses whether the aircraft carrier would be useful in dealing with the Japanese in the island dispute: available from *v.ifeng.com/mil/mainland/201210/fdf13f3a-8f39-4168-bdbc-2ef0067db861.shtml*, accessed May 30, 2014.

73. For an interview with Col Liu on the topic, see Cheng Gang, "解放军大校主张中国世界第一军事强国" ("PLA Senior Colonel Suggests China to be World's Top Military Power"), *Global Times*, March 2, 2010.

74. *Ibid.*

75. For more on the evolution and drivers of China's noninterference principle, see Oriana Skylar Mastro, "Noninterference in Contemporary Chinese Foreign Policy: Fact or Fiction?" Donovan Chau and Thomas Kane eds., *China and International Security: History, Strategy, and 21st Century Policy*, Vol. 2, Santa Barbara, CA: ABC-CLIO, 2014, pp. 95-114.

76. Erickson, *China's Modernization*, p. 96.

CHAPTER 8

CHINA'S MILITARY FORCE POSTURE UNDER CONDITIONS OF A WEAKENED PEOPLE'S LIBERATION ARMY: ALTERNATIVE MILITARY FUTURES, 2020-30

Daniel Gearin
Erin Richter

The views expressed in this chapter are the authors' alone, and do not necessarily reflect the views of the Department of Defense or any other element of the U.S. Government.

This chapter examines an alternative future in which the People's Liberation Army (PLA) is weakened. We first describe what a weakened PLA might look like; then consider circumstances under which the PLA might become weaker, of which economic factors are treated as the most critical; examine the missions of the PLA; and study the force postures of the PLA Army (PLAA), PLA Navy (PLAN), PLA Air Force (PLAAF), and Second Artillery Force (SAF). The chapter concludes with a discussion of implications of a weakened PLA.

WHAT IS A WEAK PLA?

The PLA described here is one that either struggles with or is incapable of fulfilling its military missions due to a necessary shift in national economic and security priorities from their current trajectory. One or a combination of drivers force Beijing to make tradeoffs in budgeting and force employment to better address more pressing concerns which may include domestic stability and economic development needed to maintain party control. While China will be able to field the majority of equipment and execute force restructuring planned through 2020, new priorities may require the PLA to slow development and production of new combat systems, refocus training, extend maintenance cycles, and make unplanned force reductions. Over time these factors will leave the PLA with a reformed organizational structure and more modern order of battle, but with declining troop proficiency and combat readiness. The PLA will remain capable of prosecuting limited military operations to defend China's sovereignty and territorial claims, but unable to effectively respond to military contingencies outside of China's immediate periphery.

PATHS TO A WEAKENED PLA

There are many potential factors that could lead to a future where China's military is left weakened. We chose to focus on economic and domestic factors as the primary drivers, as we view them to be the most plausible, but provide brief consideration to a few others. A military conflict, which involved significant losses for the PLA or caused Beijing to radically change its perceptions of the international security environment, could result in a weakened PLA. Although the recent tensions among China and its maritime neighbors certainly increase the possibility of accident, inadvertent escalation and the use of force, neither China nor the other maritime claimants appear likely to purposefully initiate a military conflict in the near term.[1] Thus we assume that any military conflict between now and the early-2020s would likely be limited in scope and unlikely to significantly alter the trajectory of the PLA.

A resolution to one or all of the various territorial disputes would also likely alter Beijing's security calculus and impact force allocation decisions. However, recent trends suggest that tensions surrounding these disputes are exacerbating rather than trending toward resolution. Furthermore, successful resolution on a bilateral basis (China's apparent preferred method) would unlikely change Beijing's perception that the United States intends to contain China's rise, and China would continue to field a military capable of projecting power around its periphery.

Alternatively, a more prosperous and confident China could lead Beijing to shed the deep-seated sense of historical victimization and national grievance. Such a change in leadership perception could lead to a more relaxed and nuanced approach to foreign relations, thus no longer requiring as much military might. However, rhetoric of the current administration (which will be in power into the 2020s) inextricably links the vitality of the country with the vitality of the military, suggesting that as the country continues to grow, so too will the military along with it.[2]

Primary Driver.

The most compelling causes for concern for the future of China's military are domestic ones, particularly an economic downturn and the social instability that would like result. While the PLA will have achieved substantial progress in the realm of military modernization into the beginning of the 21st century, we argue that long delayed and much required economic reforms initiated in the mid-2010s will bring about an economic slowdown, inhibiting additional increases in defense expenditures and exacerbating internal stability problems. In the following decade, Beijing would likely begin a series of structural adjustments to realign elements of the Chinese armed forces to better address their most pressing concerns, emphasizing border defense, police, civil engineering, and emergency response missions.[3]

Under these conditions, it is likely that faced with declining military budgets, the production of new combat systems will be slowed or halted, maintenance cycles extended, and maintenance intensive legacy weapons systems purged. The numbers of live training exercises will be reduced and PLA units will increasingly rely on virtual training systems to maintain operational proficiency. The PLA will remain capable of prosecuting limited military operations to defend China's sovereignty and territorial claims, but overall combat readiness will decline. Operational planning will emphasize domestic stability, border defense, and anti-access operations and increasingly rely on its "assassin's mace" systems to ensure territorial sovereignty. These changes will impact the various missions assigned to China's military.

China's Military Missions.

China's official defense white papers state that China's military is tasked with safeguarding national sovereignty, maintaining social stability, accelerating the modernization of the armed forces, and maintaining world peace and stability. Safeguarding national sovereignty is in many ways the most challenging requirement for China's military due to the large number of unresolved sovereignty issues ranging from

Taiwan, various maritime claims, and the border with India. China's various territorial claims span a geographically enormous and diverse area, requiring the Chinese military to be able to move troops across great distances and operate in a wide range of conditions.

If the perception of a PLA with declining combat capability takes hold, regional claimants may attempt to take advantage of the situation by altering the status quo and bolstering their territorial claims. Conversely, if Beijing perceives that its military capability to enforce a territorial claim is in decline, China may attempt a military resolution to a dispute before their chances of success further deteriorate.

Maintaining social stability includes a variety of tasks such as ensuring continued support for the ruling government, preventing widespread domestic unrest,[4] counterterrorism, and disaster relief. While many of these tasks are also managed by paramilitary and civilian organizations (People's Armed Police [PAP], Ministry of Civil Affairs, etc.) they remain major missions for the PLA. If, due to economic and social pressure, widespread domestic unrest threatens perceptions of regime survival, social stability missions will take priority over all other requirements and the military will be expected to play a larger role than it might otherwise have been expected to.

China's goal of accelerating the modernization of the armed forces is in part driven by the desire to have a military commensurate with its overall status in the world. Faced with the choice between the preceding priorities and continued military modernization, China is likely to shift resources away from military modernization in order to address more urgent needs. The relegation of national defense to the "fourth modernization" in 1978 provides precedent for such a decision.

Lastly, the goal of "maintaining world peace and stability" can be viewed as China's desire for its military to engage with and influence the rest of the world. Although the PLA remains a largely regional military, over the years it has increased its visibility on the global stage through counter piracy missions, support to United Nations (UN) peacekeeping operations, navy hospital ship deployments, and various other activities.[5] These activities remain largely symbolic, and China currently has no significant global military capability. A PLA faced with declining resource and expanding domestic requirements would be unlikely to expand upon these current efforts and may even curb such activity if it were viewed as too costly.

These four broad categories cover a large number of various goals and expected tasks for China's military. They also demonstrate the relative importance of each category. National sovereignty and social stability are inherently linked to the survival of the regime. As a result, the military will be unable to shed these requirements, regardless of its actual capability to fulfill them. Conversely, military modernization and engagement with the wider world are natural choices for a country seeking to become a global power, but luxuries when faced with political defeat.

The PLA Army.

The PLA Army (PLAA) is tasked to safeguard national sovereignty, security, and territorial integrity by executing mobile operations and multi-dimensional offense and defense.[6] Core missions include executing offensive and defensive operations and support to military operations other than war (MOOTW).[7] Recognizing the diverse and complex security situations the People's Republic of China (PRC) is likely to face at home and abroad in the coming decades, the PLAA has focused on restructuring and equipping its ground forces to provide flexible military responses to accomplish a wide variety of military tasks.

By 2020, the PLAA will be completing a transition to an army with advanced weapons systems and a modular organizational structure capable of task-organizing units to execute mobile warfare, special operations, and amphibious and airmobile operations.[8] Increased production of attack and transport helicopters,[9] new armored and motorized weapons systems,[10] and a decade of training emphasizing combat readiness, strategic maneuver, and civil-military integration will increase the speed with which the PLA can mobilize and deploy ground units for contingencies.[11] Coupled with improved artillery, air defense, and electronic warfare capabilities supported by a command and control system which enables a common operating picture and real-time data transmissions between units, the ability of PLA ground forces to execute rapid precision-strike operations will be greatly enhanced.[12]

In spite of advanced systems, the PLAA will continue to face major challenges in the human domain of warfare. At this time, with its continued reliance on conscripts and a developmental noncommissioned officer (NCO) corps, the PLA will probably continue to struggle with attracting sufficient numbers of enlisted personnel capable of operating the numerous high tech systems the PLA's "new type combat forces" rely on.[13] Force restructuring in the latter half of the 2010s will likely require several years of training by commanders and staffs before these modular forces can be employed effectively in large joint force operations due to the diverse missions and tasks to which they may be assigned.[14] In addition, corruption and nepotism will continue to hinder the professionalization of the PLA since the majority of PLA officers will continue to serve in one unit for the majority of their career.[15] Promotions will likely continue to be heavily determined by relationships, and officers will have little opportunity for career broadening, likely reducing the flexibility of PLA force employment.

The conditions under which the PLA becomes weak may not have a significant impact on PLA ground force organization and capabilities in the near term, but long-term changes in mission priorities and requirements could dramatically alter the shape of the force by 2030. Even after significant personnel reductions likely to take place in the late-2010s, the ground forces will continue to represent approximately 70 percent of total PLA strength. In addition to its role in offensive military operations, the PLA principally shoulders the task of deterring foreign aggression, ensuring internal stability, and supporting humanitarian assistance and disaster response operations. In most scenarios, leadership concerns about public opinion, nationalism, and domestic satisfaction mean that the PLA will not be able to cut ground force personnel drastically in order to shore up funding shortfalls or focus all available funds on a warfighting mission, should one arise.[16]

Major changes in the international security environment could relieve the PLA of some missions and thereby cost savings. For example, in the event of a rapprochement with Taiwan, the PLA would be relieved of the requirement to execute large scale amphibious landing operations, though maintaining a small number of amphibious capable forces on the eastern seaboard might remain a priority if Japanese relations sour further or Beijing perceives an increasing threat of war on the Korean Peninsula.[17] In the unlikely event of a reunification on the Korean peninsula with a friendly government in Seoul, Beijing may be comfortable with moderate ground force reductions in northern China, particularly of armored units.

More likely is that the deterioration of the domestic security environment will compel Beijing to reapportion forces to better respond to internal security and natural disaster contingencies. The trifecta of a lasting economic, environmental, and health crisis compounded by systemic corruption and persecution of ethnic minorities have the potential to push China's population into widespread unrest. In China's growing urban centers, these effects would be particularly pronounced and threatening to party elites. Under such conditions, the PLA could become decisively engaged in supporting PAP riot control, conducting counterterrorism, and providing humanitarian assistance. Furthermore, it is likely that a portion of PLA ground force units would be transferred to the PAP to enhance security in eastern China.

Increased threats to China's border security such as an influx of North Korean refugees or successful infiltration of foreign-trained Uyghur terrorists could draw operational forces away from training for offensive missions in order to reinforce border defense forces. Major domestic security concerns could also prevent the PLA reorganization from seven MRs to three or four joint theaters.[18] While an outwardly focused PLA would benefit from the consolidation of military capabilities under a joint command headquarters to execute regional operations, an inwardly focused PLA would require more responsive localized military and internal security responses for which the seven MR system was essentially designed.

If the PLA's main operational forces are committed to internal contingencies, it is possible that PLA leaders will be less likely to execute large scale military operations which require significant commitment on the part of ground forces, like compelling Taiwan reunification through invasion. In such cases, the PLA would likely rely on precision strike assets and naval platforms to coerce its adversaries. Under these circumstances, it is possible that PLA ground force will deemphasize training for many offensive tasks and that readiness of armor, artillery, electronic warfare, and point air defense systems will deteriorate as maintenance cycles are extended to preserve operating budgets.

The PLA Navy.

The PLAN is tasked with safeguarding China's maritime security and maintaining the sovereignty of its territorial seas along with its maritime rights and interests.[19] The PLAN has focused on extending its area of operation over the previous decades, moving from a primarily "brown-water navy" to an increasingly "blue-water navy." Owing in part to China's expansive maritime claims, the PLAN greatly expanded its presence within the "first-island chain" during the 21st century, and began participating in a growing number of global deployments under the auspices of counterpiracy, UN peacekeeping, and good will visits. As the service with the most interaction with foreign militaries, the PLAN also serves as the "face of China's military."

By 2020, the PLAN will have a largely modern force more numerous than at any time since the early-to-mid-1990s with significantly enhanced weapons systems.[20] The PLAN will field next generation surface combatants, submarines, and naval aircraft with long-range anti-ship cruise missiles (ASCMs) and sensors to enable the PLAN to achieve sea dominance across the "first island chain." A small number of amphibious ships, one to two aircraft carriers, and carrier-based fighter aircraft will enhance PLAN capabilities to assert and defend China's territorial claims, and combined with a modest replenishment capability, to conduct a greater diversity of out-of-area missions. The PLAN will also achieve a near continuous at-sea nuclear deterrent capability through the deployment of five JIN Ballistic Missile Submarines (SSBNs) armed with JL-2 nuclear capable intercontinental-range submarine-launched ballistic missile (SLBM).[21] Future modernization programs will continue to focus on weapons systems and C4ISR to enhance the PLAN's capabilities to safeguard China's maritime security and conduct international cooperation farther afield.

Considering China's role as both a continental and maritime power and its heavy dependence on the sea to fuel economic growth and domestic consumption, there are few conditions under which the Beijing would consciously choose to sequester PLAN equipment development and operational modernization. Major changes in the regional security environment resulting in significantly closer ties with China's maritime neighbors, while highly unlikely, could lead to reductions in the PLAN's budget and reduce the priority of future weapons development programs. It is also possible that political infighting, a major naval defeat by a regional neighbor, or PRC leadership perceptions of overly aggressive and uncontrolled PLAN operations could result in a decision to curtail PLAN future capabilities, particularly the continued development of aircraft carriers and SSBNs. However, the most likely circumstances under which the PLAN would become significantly weaker are major domestic instability requiring a dramatic shift in military resources or a financial crisis which necessitates significant and long-term military budget reductions.

Under conditions of severe domestic upheaval, PLAN operations are likely to be curtailed for the duration, though it is likely that PLAN vessels will continue to be deployed to defend against intervention or opportunistic behavior by regional actors. Barring a major political shift upon the conclusion of the crisis, PLAN regional operations would likely continue though future naval modernization could be curtailed depending on the long-term economic effects of such a crisis. Long-term disruptions to PLAN budgets could severely hinder programs to develop capabilities to equal or defeat other regional naval actors.

Considering the high cost associated with a number of platforms of limited value for the PLAN's traditional security missions of near-seas defense, the PLAN may slow or delay the construction of new high-end platforms for blue water power projection, most notably the construction of additional aircraft carriers and associated air wings and future variants of ballistic and attack submarines and destroyers. Additional cost savings may be achieved through reductions in operating expenditures and cuts to maintenance and fleet modernization programs.

Under these conditions, outdated platforms could be cut from the force to reduce costs including outdated frigates, patrol craft, and submarines. The PLAN's overall operational tempo could decrease with less out-of-area naval operations and large scale exercises. Maintenance cycles will likely be extended and system upgrades delayed. If operating or maintenance costs are severely cut, the PLAN may have to reduce the number and frequency of patrols to its more distant territorial claims like the Spratly Islands which will likely be routine by 2020.

Long-term reductions in training may have a detrimental effect on the proficiency of PLAN officers and crews as the training and evaluation cycle it depends on to modernize and refine operational capabilities will slow. This is likely to frustrate PLAN goals of improving the integration of naval air, surface, and subsurface capabilities through combined operations and the fusion of information systems as well as overall PLA efforts to fully integrate these systems in support of joint operations. It is possible; however, that funding for improved maritime surveillance and targeting systems and the production of more precise long range precision strike weapons may be sheltered from budget cuts in order to maintain credible regional deterrence in light of a weakened fleet.[22]

With a weaker navy, Beijing may become less confident in its ability to forcefully coerce its maritime neighbors into recognizing the primacy of its territorial claims in the East China Sea and South China Sea. It is possible in such a case that Beijing would alter its approach toward regional claimants to appear more conciliatory, cooperative, or legalistic. At the same time, Chinese reaction to security threats to overseas interests will be to employ a combination of diplomacy and economic coercion rather than to commit military forces. In addition, China's leadership may be unwilling to provide significant support to international humanitarian assistance and disaster relief missions that further strain military budgets and domestic perceptions of military priorities.

The PLA Air Force.

The PLAAF is China's mainstay for air operations, responsible for territorial security and maintaining a stable air defense posture nationwide. In line with strategic requirements for conducting offensive and defensive operations, PLAAF modernization has focused on strengthening the development of the combat force structure that focuses on reconnaissance and early warning, air and missile defense, and strategic projection.[23] In addition, the PLAAF has prioritized development of weapons and information systems to effectively conduct long range precision strike operations.[24] Basic PLAAF wartime missions are to destroy enemy air and air defense forces; weaken enemy ground forces; strike key communication, transportation, political, military, and economic targets; defend against enemy air raids; and to safeguard important targets.[25]

By the early-2020s, the PLAAF will likely have fielded 4th generation,[26] multirole fighters and fighter-bombers, and barring a major disruption in China's military aircraft production industry, will be in the late stages of operationalizing 5th generation fighters.[27] They will have achieved nascent but credible strategic force projection capabilities in the forms of Y-20 large transport aircraft,[28] aerial refuelers[29] and refuelable combat aircraft, and an upgraded bomber fleet capable of carrying new longer range missiles.[30] China's integrated air defense systems will remain formidable and will likely be fortified through the acquisition of the Russian S-400 surface to air missiles[31] and improvements to reconnaissance, data relay, navigation, and communication systems, both air and spaced based. Improvements in electronic warfare, low observable materials, and unmanned aerial vehicle (UAV) technologies will further enhance both PLAAF offensive and defensive capabilities.[32]

In order to streamline air operations from training to mission execution, by 2020 the PLAAF will complete its force realignment to modular brigade and base structures enabling greater integration of air force capabilities and interoperability in joint formations.[33] As the PLAAF transitions to more capable aircraft, this brigade structure will likely allow a PLAAF-wide reduction in the total number of flying squadrons and a more optimal balance of support personnel to aircraft. Reforms to the PLAAFs training, education, and NCO programs will have achieved some success in improving the quality of pilots and technical personnel, though there will continue to be a high ratio of officers to NCOs in technical specialties as the recruitment and development of NCOs will remain a work in progress.[34]

If the PLA experiences major budget reductions PLAAF leaders may need to make hard decisions of how to best balance military capabilities and equipment development. If the cuts occur after 2020, it is possible that PLAAF restructuring programs already carried out could enable moderate savings in operating and training costs and significant personnel savings without major disruption to core warfighting capabilities. Under such conditions, the PLAAF may choose to accelerate the retirement of older aircraft and equipment to include its J-7 and J-8 fighters, cutting the number of aircraft in the PLAAF by nearly half with corresponding cuts to associated personnel and infrastructure.[35] Reductions to air defense and surface-to-air missile units are less likely as they will be required to extend coverage to compensate for the loss of combat aircraft. The PLA could also choose to decrease pay and benefits for its officers and NCOs, however, this would likely exacerbate the problems it is already having in recruiting and retaining high quality technical personnel and risks deteriorating operational readiness over the long term.

A sudden reduction in the number of older aircraft maintained by the force may allow the PLAAF to preserve modernization programs and continue personnel training and retention initiatives, however, it would likely require significant adjustments to PLA planning for major contingencies. It is likely that as the PLA increases the precision of its weapons systems, any military operation against Taiwan will require less combat aircraft for air interdiction and strike missions. Such a dramatic reduction in force will limit PLAAF capabilities to support multiple air campaigns which may be required in high-end contingencies.[36] The PLAAF's ability to support counterintervention, anti-air raid, and border-defense operations effectively could be seriously degraded.[37]

Factional disputes, political infighting, or corruption could also disrupt PLAAF modernization, particularly under conditions of retrenchment. Those acquisition programs championed by the best connected and therefore best resourced officials may receive preference over others regardless of their strategic value. Competition between PLAAF and PLAN officials over missions and budget allocations could also affect production and fielding priorities, particularly for surface strike systems. If PLAAF acquisition and development slow significantly, the cost per platform would likely increase, negating the value of these measures while degrading air capabilities over the long term in relation to regional competitors. These variables could be mitigated through foreign sales, however, if the economic issues disrupting PLA modernization are related to a global or regional economic crisis, this may not be an option.

It is possible that under these conditions, the PLAAF may argue for more aggressive policies toward regional competitors in order to showcase newly developed offensive air capabilities and attract patronage of PRC political elites. This could increase the risk of conflict within the region as PLAAF commanders may request and authorize less restrictive rules of engagement as they become anxious to demonstrate the value of their service to China's overall national defense. Such activities could include more aggressive ISR collection and air intercepts, harassment, and active jamming.

Another possible future, particularly under fiscal constraints, is to shift equipment development programs toward more efficient systems with greater average value. The PLAAF may increase the development of unmanned aerial systems and deemphasize platforms which require trained pilots and flight crews. Without the limitations of human pilots, the PLAAF would be able to develop a wider variety of high altitude, long duration, and hypersonic systems which could provide strategic strike capabilities, potentially at a reduced overall cost.[38] In addition, significant saving could be achieved in personnel costs, since such platforms would likely require less manpower for operations and maintenance.

The long-term transition of the PLAAF toward predominantly unmanned offensive strike platforms would necessitate additional structural and personnel reforms as the training and management requirements differ from the current force. Such a force would also demand major enhancements to PLA C4ISR and data fusion systems as well as signals encryption in order to control multiple platforms effectively in combat with confidence, manage airspace in both peacetime training and during wartime operations, and integrate joint fires at the campaign and strategic levels.

Major changes in international security environments could also greatly impact PLAAF modernization priorities and related resources. One unlikely scenario would be a relatively benign security environment in which the air force concentrates on air defense and ISR missions to maintain security along China's periphery and reduces overall investments in precision strike to a minimum credible deterrence capability.[39] Another scenario is that the Taiwan issue becomes resolved, which would allow the PLAAF to cut the number of fighters in its inventory, particularly dedicated to short range air-to-air missions. While an uncertain regional security environment would still require significant air force capability, contingency planning and platform development could concentrate more on counterintervention capabilities.

Another scenario would involve a major deterioration in China's relationship with Russia before China's defense industries are able to complete transition to domestic production of critical airframes, engines, and components. This scenario would be characterized by a major disruption in trade between the two countries rather than heightened military tensions. Loss of Russian support for the maintenance of air and air defense systems and Russian manufactured engines could degrade PLAAF readiness, particularly if it occurs in the near term or China fails its long-term efforts to develop jet engines independently for military applications.[40]

The Second Artillery Force.

The SAF is responsible for deterring other countries from using nuclear weapons against China, carrying out nuclear counterattack if deterrence fails, and has the mission to conduct precision strikes with conventional missiles.[41] The SAF is the primary operator of China's nuclear arsenal, with the PLAN having a relatively smaller, but growing role in nuclear deterrence. The SAF's primary conventional mission likely involves gaining air and information superiority over Taiwan, either as a coercive tool to deter Taiwan independence or as part of a larger military operation against the island. The SAF also serves as the key operator of asymmetric conventional systems meant to deter the United States from intervening in any conflict involving the PLA.

Under conditions of PLA retrenchment, the SAF is the least likely to be affected by force reductions as the utility of the missile force will experience a relative increase due to the deterioration of the wider military. By 2020, the mission and doctrine of the SAF nuclear force will largely resemble what it is today, absent significant changes in the global nuclear force posture. The SAF nuclear force will remain small in number relative to the United States and Russia, however, the gap will have narrowed with the fielding of additional systems, while the United States and Russia attempt further reductions. It is unlikely China would revise its "No First Use" (NFU) policy in these circumstances, as NFU is politically advantageous, and China's nuclear force posture makes the feasibility of a disarming first strike difficult to impossible. Significant advancements in U.S. ballistic missile defense systems, or precision long range conventional strike systems are possible factors that would alter the SAF nuclear force posture. Either scenario would likely lead to increases of the SAF nuclear force numbers and survivability, as well as domestic BMD and new conventional missile technologies.

The SAF conventional force will remain the primary coercive tool to deter Taiwan independence and third party intervention into a conflict with Taiwan. With the deteriorating ability of the PLAA to conduct a large scale amphibious invasion, the SAF importance in contingency plans against Taiwan will increase and the likelihood of employing the conventional force in demonstrative launches similar to those seen in the mid-1990s will increase. Lastly, declining budgets will mean that the SAF is unable to field conventional systems capable of striking out to the second island chain and a full suite of anti-satellite weapons (ASATs).

Expected modernizations to the nuclear force will be delayed in recognition of the high cost of these systems and the unlikelihood of a nuclear conflict. China will likely complete enhancements to its silo-based intercontinental ballistic missile (ICBM) force, as these systems offer the best rapid response times for China's nuclear force. The SAF will likely deploy additional road-mobile CSS-10 Mod 2 nuclear ICBMs, the most modern road-mobile and survivable nuclear ICBM. But the expected follow-on road-mobile ICBM system, capable of carrying multiple independently targetable re-entry vehicles, will likely be postponed in recognition of the cost and difficulty of continued research and development of this system. Absent significant changes in the nuclear forces of the rest of the world, combined with the continued low probability of a nuclear conflict, Beijing will likely delay additional investments into their global nuclear strike capability.[42] For the regional nuclear force, the SAF will likely opt to retain legacy CSS-5 Mod 2 nuclear MRBMs as their primary regional deterrent and slow the operational testing and deployment of more accurate and survivable follow-on system.

In 2020, the SAF conventional short range ballistic missiles will be more accurate, survivable, and multirole than the earlier generation systems, providing China with the capability to cripple key targets across the strait in the early stages of a conflict. The medium range conventional land-attack and anti-ship ballistic missile systems, the CSS-5 Mod 4 and CSS-5 Mod 5, respectively, will remain China's primary systems for targeting regional military targets and carrier battle groups. Under conditions of PLA-wide retrenchment, the SAF will likely retain a larger inventory of missiles in order to mitigate the loss of regional strike capabilities cause by PLAAF downsizing. This will likely require a significant reduction in the number of live fire training exercises in order to avoid added production costs.[43]

Longer range conventional systems with the capability to strike as far as the second island chain will be fielded in limited numbers, but the prospects for a large ramp-up in the number of these systems is less likely given the associated costs. Thus, the SAF will have a limited capability to strike U.S. military bases as far as Guam, but will lack the ability to sustain strikes for a prolonged period of time.[44]

The SAF's experience with road-mobile missiles and strategic systems make it the most likely operator of China's road-mobile ASAT systems. However, like the longer range conventional systems, the ASAT will only be fielded in limited numbers due to cost considerations. The system will serve as a conventional deterrent, providing the threat of escalating a conventional conflict to the space realm and deterring destruction of China's growing satellite constellation.

IMPLICATIONS

In this scenario, while China will be able to field the majority of equipment and execute force restructuring planned through 2020, new priorities may require the PLA to slow the development and production of new combat systems, refocus training, extend maintenance cycles, and make unplanned force reductions. Over time, these factors will leave the PLA with a reformed organizational structure and more modern order of battle, but with declining troop proficiency and combat readiness. The PLA will remain capable of prosecuting limited military operations to defend China's sovereignty and territorial claims, but unable to effectively respond to military contingencies outside of China's immediate periphery.

Barring reunification, Taiwan will remain the primary strategic direction for Beijing.[45] Concerned that the readiness and proficiency of China's military has declined to a state where it would be incapable of conducting a large scale military campaign that spans the strait, Beijing will rely on coercive plans of action which seek to deter Taiwan from declaring independence. Although Beijing recognizes that its military capability to compel the reunification of Taiwan will be in decline, the risks associated with a large scale conflict, with the possibility of third party intervention, outweigh the calculation that China should utilize their military might before it faces further deterioration.

The perceived significance of sovereignty disputes in the maritime realm will not change in the eyes of Beijing, but their ability to enforce their claims will diminish. The PLAN patrols will be sporadic and more reactive in nature.[46] With the declining ability of the PLA to patrol these areas routinely, the various maritime claimants in the region will be left emboldened and encouraged to take advantage of the situation, making the prospects for conflict more likely.

The weaknesses of the PLA will be most apparent in areas beyond China's periphery, and particularly beyond the second island chain. Despite having air and naval systems that are capable of conducting military operations far from shore, the PLA will remain chained to China's periphery for the host of reasons described above. The United States will remain the preeminent military power in Asia, but China will retain a substantial ability to challenge the United States militarily if a conflict were to break out. Furthermore, China will grow increasingly sensitive to U.S. presence within the second island chain in light of its declining military prestige and the belief that Washington is encouraging various countries in the region provoke Beijing over maritime claims.

Faced with a future in which they will be unable to achieve the strategic goals of "being capable of winning informationized wars by the mid-21st century," Beijing will likely conclude that the "strategic period of opportunity" has closed.[47] How China will respond to this perception is unclear, however, if past is precedent, Beijing's self-perception as a victim of the machinations of Western powers will prevail. Having failed to close the gap with the United States, Beijing will continue to press Washington to accommodate its rise and put the impetus for stable relations on the United States. Beijing's suspicions of U.S. intentions to "contain" China would likely persist, with accusations that Washington was responsible for and benefitted from the end of the "period of opportunity."

Such a situation bodes ill for any effort to "manage" China's rise and encourages it to become a more responsible stakeholder in the region. With its ambitions slighted and position vis-à-vis the United States in a worse state than Beijing had desired, China would be less likely to take on greater responsibility in the region arguing that its domestic problems take precedent. While this is not an argument that a stronger China would result in a more responsible stakeholder and positive influence in the region, it does suggest that a China in decline would be no more willing to accommodate on the issues that are currently of greatest sensitivity (maritime claims, Taiwan arms sales, sensitive reconnaissance operations, etc.).

With respect to Chinese military aggression in general, under conditions of a weakened PLA two possibilities exist. China may accept the new status quo in the short term in order to maintain or regain party control and domestic stability and will have no appetite for external conflict. Under such conditions, Beijing would likely respond to security threats to overseas interests by employing a combination of diplomacy and economic coercion rather than to commit military forces. Direct threats to China's sovereignty and territorial claims, however, may draw more aggressive demonstrations of controlled military deterrence and counterintervention up to and including offensive cyber and counterspace operations.

Alternatively, a strong sense of grievance and offended nationalism may drive China to become more hostile toward the outside world. Perceiving threats on all fronts and blaming foreign powers for its internal chaos, Beijing may be more willing to respond to perceived threats with military force in an effort to shore up its perception as a global power at home and abroad. Under such circumstances, Beijing may further expand territorial claims and execute limited offensive operations against regional actors with a limited ability to contain escalation.

ENDNOTES - CHAPTER 8

1. Jane Perlez, "Philippines and China Ease Tensions in Rift at Sea," *The New York Times*, June 18, 2012.

2. Edward Wong, "China's Communist Party Chief Acts to Bolster Military," *The New York Times*, December 14, 2012.

3. Zhu Ningzhu, "Xi Leads China's Military Reform, Stressing Building of Strong Army," *Xinhua*, March 15, 2014.

4. Although China's defense white papers often include domestic separatist activity (Tibet, Xinjiang) in the national sovereignty section, the likely military responses are similar to what would be required for maintaining social stability, in the views of the authors.

5. Liu Xiaopeng (刘晓朋), "中国海军和平方舟医院船到达菲律宾灾区" ("China's Navy's Peace Ark Arrives at the Philippines Disaster Area"), 新华网 (*Xinhua*), November 24, 2013.

6. "Full Text: the Diversified Employment of China's Armed Forces," *Xinhua*, April 16, 2013.

7. Cui Yafeng (崔亚峰) ed; 陆军作战学 (*Science of Army Operations*), 解放军出版社 (PLA Press), June 2009, p. 152.

8. Jiang Daohong (姜道洪), "瞄准 '五化'：迈开陆军建设转型步伐" ("Aim at the 'Five Goals' of Ground Force Building"), 解放军报 (*PLA Daily*), July 14, 2011, p. 10.

9. Hu Wei and Qiu Boxing, "It Is Heartening To See Our Land-Force Aviation Forces Realize Transformation and Are Ready To Fly—Our Land-Force Aviation Forces, Which Are Referred to as 'Light Cavalry in the Air,' Are Quickening Their Pace in Pushing Forward Their Transformation Into Tactical-Type, Combined Offensive-Transportation, and Main-Battle Assault Forces," 解放军报 (*PLA Daily*), June 15, 2012, p. 1; "Z10 Armed Helicopter in Jingdezhen," *Kanwa Asian Defense Review*, No. 87, January 1, 2012, p. 21.

10. Andrei Pinkov Bangkok, "More Details of T96A MBT Revealed," *Kanwa Asian Defense Review*, No. 92, June 1, 2012, p. 12; Wang Xueping, "The 'King of Land Warfare' Calls For Ability to Strike in the Air," *PLA Daily*, January 19, 2012, p. 10.

11. Hu Haijun, Yang Zurong, "PLA Makes a New Leap Forward in Using Civilian Vessels to Enhance Strategic Projection Capacity; 36,000-ton Roll-On/Roll-Off Ferry 'Bohai Cuizhu' Started Its Maiden Voyage From Yantai," *PLA Daily*, August 9, 2012, p. 3; Wei Jiawei, Liu Zhongshu, and Zhao Weijiang, "Research on Organizing and Commanding Cross-Region Mobile Transportation," *Auto Applications*, June 2011, p. 14; Li Xinyang and Wu Yuanqin, "On the Construction of Resources for Integrated Civil-Military Material Procurement Support, Military Economic Research," Vol. 9, 2011, p. 31; Luo Weiran, Huang Tengfei, and Zhou Dongrui, "An Armored Regiment of the Chengdu Military Region Seeks the Truth and Is Pragmatic in Sorting Through and Correcting New Equipment Training Concepts—'Replacing a Shotgun With a Cannon: Certain 'Sayings' Lack Thought," *PLA Daily*, December 19, 2013, p. 7; Che Yin, You Chengfeng, "Group Army's Weaponry Combat Readiness Rate Hits 96 Percent," *PLA Daily*, February 19, 2013.

12. Ni Eryan, "PLA Quietly Advances Reforms in Organizations and Structures," December 31, 2011, available from Hong Kong Wen Wei Po Online, accessed March 3, 2014.

13. Chen Silin, "Current Difficulty in Recruiting Military Personnel' and 'Difficulty in Recruiting High-Caliber Military Personnel': Main Causes and Countermeasures," *National Defense (Guofang) Magazine*, August 2011, pp. 60-65; Zhang Yuhai, "The Thorough Implementation of the Objective of Building a Strong Army Requires the Constant Improvement of the Quality of Non-Commissioned Officer Selection Work—Military Region Headquarters Department Military Affairs Department Chief Zhang Yuhai Answers Questions on This Winter's Non-Commissioned Officer Selection," *Zhanyou Bao,* November 9, 2014, p. 1; "Conscientiously Building Non-Commissioned Officer Ranks and Using Them Well" *PLA Daily*, November 1, 2012, p. 1; Zhang Liang, Wei Guo, and Liang Shenhu, "Why Is the New Transceiver Not Functioning?—One Experience by a Jinan Military Region Division in Improving the Informatized Attainments of the Officers and Men," *PLA Daily*, September 9, 2013.

14. "PLA Daily on Lanzhou MR Brigade's Enhancement of 'System of Systems' Capabilities," *PLA Daily*, June 16, 2013, p. 1; Ge Chong, "International Peacekeeping Heads to the Open Ocean—Possessing Attack and Defense To Protect Sovereignty; The People's Liberation Army Increases Combat Power—Rebirth Should be a Challenge," October 26, 2013, available on Hong Kong Wen Wei Po Online, accessed April 4, 2014.

15. Dennis J. Blasko, *The Chinese Army Today*, Routledge Press, 2012, p. 64; Mu Muying (穆木英), "解放軍臃散疲堕現狀惡化" ("PLA's Swollen, Dispersed, Exhausted, Degenerated Status Worsens"), 爭鳴 (*Cheng Ming*), December 1, 2013, pp. 11-12.

16. Cortez A. Cooper III, "'Preserving the State: Modernizing and Task-Organizing a 'Hybrid' PLA Ground Force," Roy Kamphausen and Andrew Scobell, eds., *Right-Sizing the People's Liberation Army: Exploring the Contours of China's Military*, September 2007, pp. 250-251.

17. *Ibid.*, p. 270.

18. "中国軍　有事即応型に" ("Chinese Armed Forces Will Change to Be Able to Rapidly Respond to Emergencies"), 読売新聞 (*Yomiuri Shimbun*), January 1, 2014, p. 1.

19. "Full Text: the Diversified Employment of China's Armed Forces."

20. Andrew S. Erickson, "Rising Tide, Dispersing Waves: Opportunities and Challenges for Chinese Seapower Development," *Journal of Strategic Studies*, May 28, 2014, p. 8.

21. *Ibid*, pp. 5-14; Ronald O'Rourke, "China Naval Modernization: Implications for U.S. Naval Capabilities — Background and Issues for Congress," *Congressional Research Service*, June 5, 2014.

22. Ronald O'Rourke, "China Naval Modernization: Implications for U.S. Naval Capabilities — Background and Issues for Congress," Washington, DC: Congressional Research Service, September 30, 2013.

23. "Full Text: the Diversified Employment of China's Armed Forces."

24. Wang Faan, 中国和平发展中的强军战略 (*China's Strategy for Invigorating the Armed Forces amid Peaceful Development*), Bejing, China: Military Science Press, June 1, 2011, pp. 44-113.

25. "Science of Campaigns," *The Diplomat*, 2006, pp. 557-559.

26. Chinese Terminology Differs; What Westerners Call 4th Generation Fighters, The Chinese Call 3d Generation, and So Forth. For the purposes of this chapter, western terminology will be applied.

27. "AMR Air Force Directory 2014," *Asian Military Review*, February 1, 2014, pp. 25-48; OSD, "Annual Report to Congress: Military and Security Developments Involving the People's Republic of China 2013," Washington, DC: DoD, 2013.

28. Huanqiu Wang, "First Anniversary of Y-20 Maiden Flight Reveals More Secret Photos," January 27, 2014, available from *www.huanqiu.com*, accessed February 15, 2014; "Top Five Pieces of News on Chinese Military Aviation in 2013," *PLA Daily*, January 8, 2014.

29. Huanqiu Wang, " Summary: Photos Allegedly Show 1st PLA Il-78 Midair Refueling Aircraft," March 27, 2014, available from *www.huanqiu.com*, accessed January 9, 2014.

30. Wang Wenbin and Zhang Li, "The Warplanes of an Aviation Regiment of the Air Force Stage Assaults on Targets Thousands of Miles Away in a Day of Heavy Rains" *PLA Daily*, April 9, 2014, p. 4; "Long-range Stealth Bomber Under Development," January 9, 2014, available from *www.wantchinatimes.com*, accessed January 9, 2014.

31. "China May Become First Importer of Russian S-400 Missile Systems," *Interfax*, February 20, 2013; "Annual Report to Congress: Military and Security Developments Involving the People's Republic of China 2013."

32. Nanfang Dushi Bao, "Summary: PLA's Second Model Stealth Fighter Reportedly Conducts Another Test Flight," *Nanfang Daily*, July 19, 2013, available from *www.nanfangdaily.com. cn*, accessed March 14, 2014; Minnie Chan: "China Unveils New Fifth-Generation Stealth Fighter," October 31, 2012, available from *www.scmp.com*, accessed January 11, 2014; Ren Yong, Fu Shengjie, and Liu Zhe, "Impact Produced by New Technology Development on the Form of Air-Force-Mounted Combat Operations," *PLA Daily,* January 28, 2010., p. 4; "Annual Report to Congress: Military and Security Developments Involving the People's Republic of China 2013."

33. Kenneth W. Allen, "The Organizational Structure of the PLAAF," Richard P. Hallion, Roger Cliff, and Phillip C. Saunders eds., *The Chinese Air Force Evolving Concepts, Roles, and Capabilities*, National Defense University, 2012, p. 104.

34. Ken Allen, "PLA Air Force Aviation Cadet Recruitment, Education, and Training," *China Brief*, Vol. 12, Issue 5, March 2, 2012; "Names of Two Pilots Killed in Su-27 Fighter Crash Released, Speculation on Causes of Crash," 解放军报 (*PLA Daily*), April 3, 2013; Ge Chong: "International Peacekeeping Heads to the Open Ocean — Possessing Attack and Defense To Protect Sovereignty," *Xinhua*, April 2, 2013; "The People's Liberation Army Increases Combat Power — Rebirth Should be a Challenge," October 26, 2013, available from Hong Kong Wen Wei Po Online, accessed February 2, 2014.

35. "The Military Balance, 2014," London, UK: International Institute for Strategic Studies, 2014.

36. David Shlapak, "Equipping the PLAAF: The Long March to Modernity," Richard P. Hallion, Roger Cliff, and Phillip C. Saunders, eds., *The Chinese Air Force Evolving Concepts, Roles, and Capabilities*, Washington, DC: National Defense University, 2012; "Annual Report to Congress: Military and Security Developments Involving the People's Republic of China 2013."

37. Science of Campaigns, pp. 557-559.

38. Ian M. Easton and L. C. Russell Hsiao, "The Chinese People's Liberation Army's Unmanned Aerial Vehicle Project: Organizational Capacities and Operational Capabilities," Arlington, VA: Project 2049 Institute, March 11, 2013, p. 14; "China's Lijian Stealth Drone Set for Maiden Flight: Report," *Want China Times*, May 24, 2013.

39. Phillip C. Saunders and Erik Quam, "Future Force Structure of the Chinese Air Force," Roy Kamphausen and Andrew Scobell, eds., *Right-Sizing the People's Liberation Army*, pp. 381.

40. *Ibid*, pp. 408-410.

41. "Full Text: the Diversified Employment of China's Armed Forces."

42. "Military and Security Developments Involving the People's Republic of China 2013, Annual Report to Congress," Washington, DC: Office of the Secretary of Defense, 2013, pp. 5, 30-31.

43. *Ibid*, pp. 38, 42.

44. *Ibid*.

45. "主要战略方向与其他战略方向的辩证关系" ("The Dialectical Relationship between the Primary Strategic Direction and Other Strategic Directions"), April 4, 2006, available from *www. chinamil.com.cn*, accessed March 3, 2014.

46. Zhu Hu and Yang Yang, "Destroyer Detachment Party Committee Leads Naval Troops to Work Hard at Modernization," *PLA Daily*, July 28, 1995.

47. Xu Jian, "Rethinking China's Period of Strategic Opportunity," San Francisco, CA: California Institute of Integral Studies, May 28, 2014, available from *www.ciis.org.cn*, accessed June 9, 2014.

IMPLICATIONS FOR THE REGION, WORLD, AND U.S.-CHINA RELATIONS

CHAPTER 9

REGIONAL DYNAMICS IN RESPONSE TO ALTERNATIVE PLA DEVELOPMENT VECTORS

Michael McDevitt

INTRODUCTION – CHINA'S STRATEGIC APPROACH TO ITS NEIGHBORHOOD

In October 2013, a high-level policy symposium was held in Beijing on the topic of China's peripheral region. For the first time, all the political bureau standing committee members attended along with the leadership of China's foreign policy establishment. President Xi Jinping chaired the meeting, and in a speech sketched out a peripheral strategy that combined elements of the past 2 decades approach, focused on economic integration, along with some new ideas. He made the point that the strategic objective remains the same – a stable and peaceful periphery to pursue economic development and his "China Dream." He did make one important caveat directly relevant to the question this chapter is addressing. He said China must also maintain its national sovereignty, security, and economic development interests. In other words, maintaining a stable and peaceful periphery should not come at the expense of China's broader interests.[1]

This suggests that China has concluded that it has no need to compromise on fundamental (core) interests with its neighbors because its comprehensive national power is adequate to maintain "peace and stability" on the periphery, despite the existence of maritime sovereignty disputes. It implies that Beijing can and will exercise a combination of hard and soft power with its neighbors, depending upon what interests are involved. In cases of sovereignty disputes with its neighbors, China will seek peaceful outcomes, but will not compromise on its claims, and, as necessary, be willing to use some aspect of coercion (diplomatic, economic, constabulary, or military) to strengthen its claims while weakening the ability of its neighbors to mount an effective defense.[2]

FRAMING THE ANALYTIC APPROACH

With this appreciation of China's likely approach to its neighborhood as context, when forecasting east and south Asian regional responses in 2025 to different People's Liberation Army (PLA) development objectives, it is important to bound the analyses. This chapter will not address the countries that share a border with China: Russia, Mongolia, the Central Asian states of Kazakhstan, Kyrgyzstan, Tajikistan, or Afghanistan. Nor will it address Bhutan and Nepal. It will not consider China's two closest friendly bordering states, North Korea and Pakistan; although, in the case of North Korea, the behavior of Kim Jong-un in the December 2013-January 2014 time frame implied a less than collegial relationship between Pyongyang and Beijing.[3] It is altogether imaginable that by 2025, the "Young General" may have been consigned to the dustbin of history and a regime more inclined to follow Beijing's advice takes its place; or North and South Korea are engaged in some sort of reunification dialogue.

Of China's remaining bordering neighbors: India, Myanmar, Laos, and Vietnam, this exploration will look more closely at Vietnam and India. While Thailand does not directly border China, it is close enough to the Chinese frontier to be extremely attentive to its relationship with Beijing. All five countries face the difficult strategic reality that because the PLA can either walk or drive to their frontier no matter what vector the PLA takes in the future, these nations face a threat of invasion that cannot be ignored. India and Vietnam have experienced this since 1950. It seems probable that in 2025 Myanmar, Laos, Thailand, and Vietnam will continue to be very careful about taking any action that would so provoke Beijing that China's leaders would feel compelled to "teach them a lesson."

In the case of India, a nuclear weapons state that has been reasonably clear that a portion of its nuclear capabilities target Chinese cities, New Delhi should have less reason to be concerned about a Chinese invasion, and hence less anxiety about PLA developments. In fact, however, the development of a global expeditionary PLA is likely to cause considerable anxiety in New Delhi, a response that will be addressed in more detail.

For China's neighbors fortunate enough to be separated from China by some expanse of ocean, specifically South Korea, Japan, Taiwan, the Philippines, Indonesia, Singapore, Brunei, Malaysia and Australia, the primary threat from the PLA, no matter what form its developmental vector takes, is its naval (including amphibious assault capabilities), air, and conventional missile capabilities. These Chinese capabilities currently far outmatch the defenses of all of the aforementioned states except Japan, and that gap is closing. It goes without saying that China's nuclear weapon capabilities threaten all, and provide China with clear-cut escalation dominance against any nation that does not have a formal alliance with the United States that includes an extended deterrence guarantee, or like India, has its own ability to retaliate in kind.

Finally, when forecasting the responses of China's neighbors to all circa 2025 PLA developmental vectors, some assumptions have to be made about how the ongoing sovereignty disputes between China and its neighbors have played out between today and 2025. If there were violent confrontations between China and one or more of its peripheral states, the neighborhood response to a circa 2025 PLA would almost certainly be very different from a situation where force has not been used. As a working assumption, this chapter posits that the sovereignty and maritime demarcation disputes that have heretofore defied resolution will remain unresolved by 2025. Unresolved does not necessarily mean that today's tensions will persist a decade hence, co-development schemes and a live and let live approach could make these disputes less dangerous. In any event, for the purposes of this chapter, the analysis assumes that none of the tension producing maritime claims will have been settled by the overt use of force, mainly because China is likely to have systematically altered the status quo through nonviolent measures.

THE NEAR NEIGHBORHOOD RESPONSE OF CHINA'S GROWING POWER – NORTHEAST ASIA

South Korea.

In 2025, it seems probable that the Republic of Korea (ROK) military will still be postured against a North Korean invasion, but the ROK navy and air force will also have to consider its powerful neighbors, China and Japan.[4] The U.S.-ROK alliance will remain in place, and operational command transfer will have been put on hold permanently as long as Seoul and Washington judge that the North Korean threat remains credible.[5]

It is beyond the scope of this chapter to speculate about the state of North-South relations, except to note that U.S.-led efforts to halt and then roll back North Korea's nuclear weapons program will not have succeeded by 2025. As a result, the South Korean and, for that matter, Japanese defense budgets, continue to invest heavily in missile defense. South Korea will have joined U.S.-led efforts to integrate U.S.-Japanese-ROK missiles defenses, much to China's displeasure because this missile defense organization could also mitigate the effectiveness of China's nuclear posture against Japan and the United States. But because this is driven by North Korea, Beijing's displeasure has been quietly ignored by Seoul.

In general, Seoul and Beijing have remained on good terms, and the only major security issues South Korea has with China are, first, its continued support of North Korea, which keeps the Kim, or a successor regime, afloat which prevents progress toward reunification.

South Korea does have one other issue with China and that revolves around disputes in the Yellow (West) Sea because the overlapping South Korean and Chinese economic exclusion zones (EEZ) have not been reconciled. Both China and South Korea claim the submerged Iedo/Suyan/Socotra Rock, which is located closer to South Korea in its EEZ, but it is also within China's claimed EEZ. South Korea has raised China's ire by building a maritime research laboratory on the reef.[6] In addition, Chinese fishermen continue to venture into South Korean waters. South Korea continues to ask China to respect the median line between the two countries in the Yellow Sea and restrict fishing to the Chinese side of the median until a permanent settlement of overlapping EEZs can be reached. Throughout the decade low-level skirmishing between South Korean coast guardsman and Chinese fishermen has continued. These differences with China, however, pale in comparison to the historic animosity between Korea and Japan which has grown over the years as South Korea has emerged as a vibrant well-to-do democracy.

Finally, Seoul's ambitions to be perceived as a global player[7] have created the political space for more naval shipbuilding. By 2025, the ROK Navy will be a medium sized highly effective hybrid navy; hybrid in the sense that it combines coast defense missions, especially a renewed focus on shallow water anti-submarine warfare (ASW) against North Korea, with very credible blue-water capabilities such as around 10 AEGIS equipped destroyers and 18 frigates. By 2025, the submarine force will have over 40 years' experience and employ around 18 modern conventionally powered submarines. In private conversations with senior ROK navy officers, they make clear that they see the development of a credible navy as a hedge against Japan.[8]

Whether the poisonous atmosphere between Japan and Korea will persist through the decade leading to 2025 is hard to predict, but South Korea's historic antipathy toward Japan is currently getting worse, not better; while thanks to its growing economy, burgeoning South Korean self-confidence feeds an urge to settle scores.

Finally, the ROK has a powerful incentive to develop blue water naval capabilities regardless of what trajectory the PLA takes. It is very dependent upon international trade, which creates an imperative to protect its sea lanes of communication (SLOCs) with significant naval capabilities. The best example of Seoul's concerns with sea lanes is its active participation in international maritime peacekeeping such as anti-piracy operations in the Gulf of Aden where they are current working with China, Japan and India in organizing convoys through higher threat areas. Like the Chinese, the anti-piracy mission has provided the ROK navy with the first out-of-area mission in its history. The ROK navy has learned how to sustain warships halfway around the world while conducting sustained operations with other major navies.[9]

Japan.

Japan is the country in East Asia most affected by China's military modernization, no matter what vector the PLA takes. Today's PLA is daunting enough for Japan, the PLA Second Artillery Force can reach out and touch Japan with both conventionally armed ballistic missiles, long-range land attack cruise missiles, and of course, with nuclear armed ballistic missiles. China's large submarine fleet poses a really severe threat to Japan's sea lanes. This is not an abstract problem for Tokyo, they lived it during 1944-45.[10] The PLA Air Force (PLAAF) is introducing modern jet aircraft at a rate which that will, on paper, shift the air balance of power to China. Finally, and most strategically important to Japan, is the fact that China area denial and anti-access (what the PLA refers to as counterintervention) capability is becoming more credible by the day; which means that the United States may not be able to fulfill its alliance defense responsibilities because the PLA could keep American reinforcements from arriving from the west coast of the United States in time to be effective.[11]

Clearly, a PLA that in 2025 has continued to improve its regional capabilities means that its "counterintervention" capabilities have been strengthened to the point that Tokyo would have serious doubts regarding the operational credibility of Washington's extended conventional deterrent. From Tokyo's perspective, the ongoing capabilities completion between Washington and Beijing that pits anti-access versus assured access is one that Japan and the United States have to win. For Japan, Washington's ability to solve this problem, with support from Japan because of revised roles and missions, will be an important factor in Japanese calculations regarding building its own second strike nuclear weapons force.

Japan has the third largest economy in the world, so it has the financial resources necessary to afford all the capabilities it needs to be able to defend all of Japan's home islands, including the entire Ryukyu chain. By 2025, Japan will have completed its current shift of strategic focus to the southwest. That will include fielding a regimental sized amphibiously qualified army force specially trained to either defend, or retake any small islands that border the East China Sea. By 2025, the Air Self-Defense Force should have replaced its F-4 Phantom fleet and some of the older F-15s with modern next generation fighters (F-35A and F-15Js) The Japan Air Self-Defense Force will also have to expand its training syllabus, and weapons delivering capabilities in order to support operations by the new Japanese marine force. These plans will continue, no matter what vector the PLA takes. Japan is likely to continue to improve its already world-class ASW capabilities in response to the number of modern submarines the PLA Navy (PLAN) order of battle is likely to have by 2025.[12]

Japan cannot neglect the problems posed by North Korea and, as already mentioned, it will continue to develop its ballistic missile defense capabilities. Having a redundant capability versus North Korean missiles is an important strategic issue for Tokyo. It seems likely that over the next decade, Japan will also develop or buy land attack cruise missiles it can fit on its submarine force. This will provide a limited capability to deal with North Korean missiles before they can be launched.

In short, Japan has strategic issues with the PLA modernization no matter what vector the PLA takes. Clearly, the vector characterized as a "weakened PLA" would probably not be seen by Tokyo as a weakened PLA, rather it would be seen in mere slowing of PLA modernization, which obviously could lessen the urgency to improve the self-defense force. But since a "weakened PLA" is not losing capability, it has just stopped adding it as fast, it seems more likely that Japan will continued to be concerned about living in the shadow of a militarily imposing China.

A Japan-Inspired Multilateral Response?

An expeditionary PLA implies that China would be able to interdict Japan's sea lanes anywhere in the world, not just in the waters around Japan. Tokyo is hedging against an expeditionary PLA by working diligently to improve its military relations with India and Australia. Since all three of these countries would have strategic equities at risk by an expeditionary PLA, it seems plausible that military relations and cooperation between India, Australia, and Japan in 2025 will have developed beyond today's nascent stage. If the PLA continues on the expeditionary vector, some sort of Indo-Pacific multilateral response fostered by Japan and Australia is likely to emerge.[13]

Taiwan.

Currently, Taiwan is in a terrible position when it comes to the military "imbalance" across the Strait. The PRC has the ability to bombard the island with hundreds of missiles, followed by fixed-wing aircraft attacks, and create all sort of mayhem for Taiwan's economy through cyber attacks and expropriation of Taiwanese assets on the mainland. As in the case of Japan, the trajectory of PLA modernization is essentially immaterial to Taipei. The PLA already has what it needs to "punish" Taiwan; and Taipei can do nothing to reverse this situation. Again, as in the case of Japan, the ability of the United States to deal successfully with China's "counterintervention" capabilities has major implications for Taiwan's security. Where Taiwan still has military leverage lies in the fact that so long as the will to resist exists in Taipei, the PLA faces the daunting task of successfully crossing the 100 miles of ocean between the mainland and Taiwan, landing on a defended beachhead, and successfully effecting regime change by invasion.

Taiwan is currently in the midst of a very expensive shift to an all-volunteer force that hopefully will yield a smaller but more effective army that would be able to prevent the PLA from gaining a foothold on the island. An agile army armed with Apache gunships, combined with shore based anti-ship cruise missiles, and fast-attack craft would form a credible anti-invasion capability. Even though the prospect of a Chinese invasion attempt is extremely remote, having this mix of capabilities does introduce an element of deterrence by denial into PLA calculations. Of course, Taiwan totally depends on arms purchases from the United States for those items it cannot produce itself. Over the course of the next decade, both Washington and Taipei will face difficult decisions regarding the modernization of Taiwan's air force. Meanwhile, Taipei is poised to begin the development of its own conventionally powered submarine force. This will be difficult and expensive, but if current plans actually pan out, by 2025, the ROC navy would have a valuable new capability in its anti-invasion arsenal.[14]

THE FAR NEIGHBORHOOD RESPONSE TO CHINA'S GROWING POWER — SOUTHEAST ASIA

PLA modernization over the next decade is likely to provoke the same reactions that have characterized Southeast Asia's response to China's growing power over the past 10 years. They will continue to have a close relationship with America, but they will be careful to try and avoid to be perceived by Beijing as becoming part of an anti-Chinese coalition. The objective is to hedge or balance their relations between Beijing and Washington. China is the largest trading partner of each of its near neighbors, and none of them wants to upset the economic relationship with China. Yet, they look to Washington for moral and security oriented support where they have disagreements with China. In this regard, the reaction of Southeast Asian nations to the disputes in the South China Sea is instructive.[15]

Association of Southeast Asian Nations and Multilateralism.

China's neighbors to the Southeast can be broadly divided into three camps: those on the front lines of the sovereignty issue, especially Vietnam and the Philippines; those with significant interests in the outcome of the territorial disagreement (specifically, Indonesia, Malaysia, Singapore, and Brunei); and those inclined to accommodate China, including Cambodia, Laos, Myanmar, and Thailand. This division was on full display during the November 2012 East Asia Summit, which President Barack Obama attended. The end result of the summit was a split between six countries (the Philippines, Indonesia, Malaysia, Singapore, Vietnam, and Brunei) that favored broader discussion of the SCS, and four (Cambodia, Laos, Myanmar, and Thailand) that did not. Countries without sovereignty disputes with China do not wish to anger China.[16] The result is that it is unlikely that the Association of Southeast Asian Nations (ASEAN) inspired multilateral institutions with a security focus, such as the East Asia Summit (EAS) or the ASEAN Defense Minister Meeting (ADMM+), are likely to be unable to reach a consensus that could be construed as being anti-Chinese. Unless China is particularly maladroit in its regional diplomacy this is likely to be the case in 2025.

Many Southeast Asian countries are counting (hoping) the U.S. rebalance strategy will act as a brake on Chinese assertiveness.[17] As a result, when forecasting 2025, the past is likely to be a prologue. Each ASEAN member will continue to carefully hedge its relationships between Beijing and Washington. Examples of this behavior abound, in April 2012, for instance, U.S. ally Thailand elevated its bilateral relationship with China to "strategic partnership," and in July 2012, it dispatched a senior military delegation to visit China as a minister of defense counterpart. More recently, Thailand opted to include the PLA as a participant in the 2014 Cobra Gold exercise. Vietnam, as a frontline state in the South China Sea (SCS) disputes, has been careful to avoid making its relationship with China any worse, and has seemingly "walled off" its SCS disputes from broader Sino-Vietnam relations. That policy may be revised in the wake of the nasty May 2014 dispute with China over oil exploration in Vietnam's EEZ.

Malaysia and Indonesia have also been careful to balance their engagements with Washington and Beijing. Malaysia held its first bilateral "defense and security consultation" with China in September 2012 and agreed to strengthen military exchanges and cooperation, while, in April 2014, agreed to a "comprehensive partnership" with Washington.[18] Jakarta, for its part, values its "comprehensive partnership" with Washington, but also emphasizes developing good defense relations with China. In August 2012, an agreement was reached with China that permitted Indonesia to produce China's C-705 anti-ship cruise missile under license.[19] Indonesia has also embarked on a gradual military modernization based on co-production understandings so that over time it will create an indigenous defense industrial base.[20] This includes a submarine procurement from South Korea, which would be a very relevant capability if the issue of China's SCS nine-dashed line overlapping with Indonesia's Natuna gas field becomes militarized.[21]

Singapore plays an important role in enabling Washington's rebalance strategy, by agreeing to permit four U.S. Navy warships to be stationed rotationally in Singapore. This gives the United States easy naval access to the SCS, and suggests a more or less permanent U.S. naval presence in the SCS. That said, Singapore is very careful to remain neutral between China and the United States; it rationalizes its 2-decades-old security relationship with the United States as a hedge against Indonesia and Malaysia.[22] At the same time, Singapore is improving its ability to look after its maritime interests. The Republic of Singapore navy is already the best equipped navy in Southeast Asia. It is an example of a how a small navy can transcend its physical limitations and make an important contribution to regional and international security.[23]

The fact that Singapore's modernization is not directly driven by China is an important point. Simply put, Southeast Asia military modernization is not all about China. Regional rivalries are alive and well. Submarine procurement is a good example: Singapore, Malaysia, and Indonesia are embarked on submarine programs that are as much about keeping-up with one another as patrolling their respective EEZs. Nonetheless, submarines like most modern weapons systems are inherently multimission; provided these countries are able to properly maintain them and operate them professionally they also provide an important capability for Malaysia and Indonesia to use in defending SCS claims against Chinese assertiveness. It is worth keeping in mind that by 2025, the SCS, a relatively confined body of water, will be the area where an impressive number of submarines from the littoral states plus China and the United States will operate. Developing some sort of water space management scheme could become a significant ASEAN issue.

The Philippines.

The Philippines is a front-line state in the confrontation with China over SCS sovereignty disputes. Not surprisingly, the government of the Philippines has warmly embraced Washington's rebalance strategy; it has had to. The April 2012 standoff with China over Scarborough Shoal highlighted the fact that it is virtually defenseless at sea or in the air. Because of their security incapacity, the Philippines will hardly notice the difference between a regional PLA, an expeditionary PLA, or a PLA whose modernization momentum has slowed. No matter what the vector the PLA takes, the Philippines will remain woefully overmatched. Moreover, Manila cannot afford a major increase in defense expenditures. As a result, Manila has sought to ensure its security through developing a close security relationship with the United States, and in April 2014, signed an agreement that will allow U.S. military access to five former U.S. bases in the Philippines for the next 10 years.[24] This was the culmination of over 2 years of increased periodic presence of U.S. naval ships, submarines, and aircraft. Particularly important to both parties will be access to the former Cubi Point Naval Air Station in Subic Bay, which will facilitate aerial reconnaissance over the SCS.[25]

However, the U.S.-Philippine security relationship is susceptible to the ebb and flow of Philippine public opinion regarding the "return" of a U.S. military presence versus how assertive Beijing is in its dealings with Manila. Beijing is not happy with Manila's decision to challenge its claims in the SCS at the International Tribunal for the Law of Sea. Whether that unhappiness will persist over next decade, is difficult to predict. It is not difficult to anticipate, however, that as long as

Manila encourages or facilitates an improvement in U.S. military posture along the SCS littoral, that the Sino-Philippine relationship will be difficult.

It is reasonable to expect that, over the next 10 years, the Philippines' maritime and aviation capability will show incremental improvements; but not to the extent that Manila could ensure the security of its maritime claims on its own.

Vietnam.

Vietnam's defense budget has grown by over 80 percent over the first decade of the 21st century. Much of this growth was due to purchases that contribute to its ability to defend its EEZ and disputed claims in the SCS: specifically naval ships and submarines, coastal defense cruise missiles, and surveillance. At the urging of the leadership, the Vietnam People's Army (VPA) has embraced the idea of defense dialogues, strategic partnership agreements, and practical bilateral military cooperation, and has placed a priority on cultivating defense links with neighbors and developing Vietnam's role in multilateral organizations as a critical component of national defense.[26]

Vietnam has not issued a maritime strategy, but Hanoi did publish a defense white paper in 2009, in which the navy's responsibility was described as strictly managing and controlling "the waters and islands in the East Sea under Vietnam's sovereignty" to include maintaining maritime security, sovereignty and sovereign rights, jurisdiction, and national interests at sea.[27]

Vietnam's most newsworthy purchase related to SCS defense has been the six Kilo-class submarines ordered from Russia in 2009, the first of which arrived in

January 2014. Professor Carlyle Thayer, a specialist on the Vietnamese military at Australia's Defense Force Academy, reported in 2009 that Vietnam was seeking a credible deterrent against China, hoping to defend its own claims to the SCS. "It's a very bold step," Thayer was quoted as saying. He continued:

> It has been apparent for some time now that Vietnam's sovereignty is under threat in the South China Sea, and that is something that is painfully felt in Hanoi. Hanoi knows it could never hope to match the Chinese Navy, but it can at least make them think very hard before any attempt to, for example, drive Vietnam off some of their Spratly Islands holdings. Even a few Kilos makes that a very complicated business, indeed, you suddenly have to factor in losing ships.[28]

The May 2014 deployment of a mobile drilling platform by China's National Off-shore Oil Company to an area within Vietnam's EEZ and on its continental shelf has infuriated Hanoi, and is likely to reinforce the need to be able to defend its off-shore resources.[29] Vietnam has not just acquired submarines. It also has ordered four Russian-built Gepard-class corvettes. Vietnam is also producing under license at least 10 550-ton fast-attack craft that are fitted with anti-ship cruise missiles. These will be combined with the so-called Bastion Coastal Defense System, also from Russia, which consists of truck-mounted anti-ship cruise missiles, along with its 20-odd Su-27/30 aircraft that are capable of maritime strike; and four very modern Dutch corvettes of the SIGMA class. Altogether, Vietnam is putting into place a formidable off-shore naval force.[30]

All these off-the-shelf purchases must still be knitted together into an integrated force, with effective surveillance and command and control, but Hanoi's intent is clear. There is little question that Chinese naval capability is the focus of these procurements. Vietnam wants to make certain that it can defend its maritime claims, and that it will avoid a replay of the 1988 South Johnson Reef clash with the PLAN, in which two Vietnamese landing craft were sunk, a third was badly damaged, and more than 70 Vietnamese were killed.

As in the case of Japan, Vietnam is intent on improving its capabilities no matter what vector the PLA takes over the next decade. Vietnam has centuries of experience in dealing with China, including repeated invasions, but dealing with China in the maritime domain is a novel experience for Hanoi. By 2025, most of the ongoing procurements should be in place. This should provide Hanoi with a very reasonable maritime access denial capability. Again, as in the case of other neighbors of China, Vietnam is likely to do what it can to modernize its military no matter what developmental vector the PLA takes. The confrontation that started in May 2014 over drilling for oil in Vietnam's EEZ, and subsequent outburst of public anger at China, has undoubtedly reinforced the need for Vietnam to be able to defend its interests in the South China Sea.

INDIAN OCEAN STATES RESPONSES – AUSTRALIA AND INDIA

Australia.

In 2009 Australia issued a defense white paper that announced plans to add significant capabilities to the Australian Defense Force. It rationalized this across the board modernization plan by offering a somewhat pessimistic picture of Australia's future strategic environment and the potential negative consequences of China's military modernization. It was straightforward:

> China will also be the strongest Asian military power, by a considerable margin. Its military modernisation will be increasingly characterised by the development of power projection capabilities. A major power of China's stature can be expected to develop a globally significant military capability befitting its size. But the pace, scope and structure of China's military modernisation have the potential to give its neighbours cause for concern if not carefully explained, and if China does not reach out to others to build confidence regarding its military plans. . . . If it does not, there is likely to be a question in the minds of regional states about the long-term strategic purpose of its force development plans, particularly as the modernisation appears potentially to be beyond the scope of what would be required for a conflict over Taiwan.[31]

Today, Australia's problem is how to align a very ambitious force structure plans with shrinking, or at least stagnating, defense budgets. The 2013 white paper changed the strategic narrative by sounding more optimistic about China's rise. It did not, however, change the planned force structure. Instead, it deeply cut the defense budget. The reason for this about face, according to a senior analyst at the Australian Strategy Policy Institute is:

> It is not that Australia has suddenly felt more secure. If anything, events in the region have elevated fears that the rise of China will upset the strategic stability upon which Australia's prosperity is built. Nor is there any sense that Australia can relax because the

United States has reasserted its commitment to the Asia-Pacific. Rather the recent retrenchment in Australian defense spending is largely the result of domestic politics. The Australian polity has an acute aversion to deficits and debt.[32]

Upon taking office in October 2013, Prime Minister Tony Abbott vowed to restore defense spending to 2 percent of gross domestic product from its current 1.59 percent over the course of the decade, conditioned by the caveat that the increase would be subject to economic conditions.[33]

Meanwhile, all of Australia's services are pressing on, within budgetary limits, with modernization plans. The Australian army is restructuring the regular army into three multirole combat brigades, one of which is currently designated to be the backbone of a new amphibious capability. The new capability will be centered on two large, Spanish designed 27,000-ton landing helicopter docks, the Canberra class. These two ships are under construction, and will be the largest ships ever in Australia's inventory.

The Royal Australian Air Force (RAAF) also aims to procure a range of highly sophisticated new aircraft. The original plan to acquire 100 F-35A's from the United States will be cut to 72. The former Gillard government also decided to purchase 12 F-18 Growlers, the electronic attack version of the F-18 along with 24 F-18E/F, these are going forward. If these decisions all reach fruition, by 2025 the RAAF would emerge with a second-to-none air combat capability in its immediate neighborhood, and certainly be able to overmatch any PLAN aircraft carrier based expeditionary air power. The RAAF also intends to introduce a new maritime patrol aircraft, the P-8A Poseidon, as well as the new C-27J strategic airlift.

Its submarine force is a key to Australia's strategy for defending its maritime approaches. The current Royal Australian Navy (RAN) Collins class submarines have been an operational disappointment; plagued with reliability problems. There has been considerable debate whether to give up on the Collins class and start a new submarine program, or to make a serious attempt to fix what ails the class and put off starting the new class of 12 submarines to several years in the future. It seems probable that the budgetary situation will dictate that the start of a new submarine program will be delayed. At the same time the RAN also plans to replace its aging ANZAC-class frigates. Moreover, the government has raised the possibility of building a fourth air warfare destroyer as a means to save the domestic shipbuilding industry from losing ship building expertise because of insufficient orders.

Working on assumption that the Abbot government's next Defense Capability Plan will generally sustain Australia's current modernization direction, by 2025, Australia will remain technologically far superior to any Southeast Asian country, and buttressed by its alliance with the United States, will be confident about its security situation vis-à-vis a Chinese expeditionary capability.

India.[34]

India faces a two-front strategic problem with China. It has a disputed frontier that has already been the cause of a ground war and continues to be the trigger for ground and air force posture improvements for India's armed forces. Recent Chinese "provocations" have highlighted the fact that China can mobilize a very large force in Tibet. As a counter, New Delhi decided to establish an 80,000-man mountain strike corps in Panagarah, West Bengal, with supporting air power. The stated objective of this force is to deter a serious PLA incursion.[35] Should deterrence fail, and India and China come to blows on the Northeast frontier, Indian defense officials believe India's geographic location, astride the Indian Ocean sea lanes that China relies upon, is an asymmetric advantage.[36] It provides a way to inflict pain on China that it cannot easily counter. The Indian belief is that its submarine force, land-based air power and surface navy has the ability to create a serious sea lane problem for China.[37]

But Indian strategists worry that this advantage may be short-lived. The main problem is that Indian's sclerotic procurement process will ensure that India will be out-built, and as a result, perhaps as soon as 2025, the PLAN will be able to turn the tables on India. The PLAN will have the capability to interdict the sea lanes which bring oil and other resources from the Persian Gulf and East and West Africa that India needs for its economic development. As the PLAN just demonstrated in late-2013, one of its nuclear attack submarine (SSN) could operate with virtual impunity against India in the Arabian Sea.[38]

The Indian naval view is that, piracy or no piracy in the Gulf of Aden, China is in the Indian Ocean region (IOR) to stay.[39] Piracy provided a chance for China to build its navy and its profile. But, from India's perspective, there is a clear logic governing China's interest in the IOR and, without piracy, the Chinese will find some other reason to justify their presence there.

In short, India is very conscious of the implicit threat posed by across the board Chinese military modernization. They are also very aware of the shortcomings associated with their own procurement processes.[40] Should the PLA embark on the expeditionary vector and begin to operate routinely more substantial forces in the Indian Ocean region, India may be forced to come to terms with its internal defense procurement problems. It will also have to decide how far it wants to move internationally in aligning itself with western democratic sea powers like the United States, Australia, and Japan. Moving further away from its cherished nonaligned (strategic autonomy) heritage would be politically difficult, and is likely to be decided upon only if New Delhi is persuaded its position in the Indian Ocean region is in jeopardy.

What about an Indo-Pacific Multilateral Response to a PLA Expeditionary Capability?

Over the last decade, a number of initiatives have been explored by official government suggestions, as well as research centers in the United States, Japan, Australia, and India suggesting some sort of maritime coalition. For example, the Japanese suggested in 2004 a maritime coalition of democracies in Asia. At the tactical level, this has been manifested by inviting one another to participate in well-established multilateral maritime exercises. The governments in all four countries have taken only hesitant steps in the direction of formalizing such an arrangement because they did not want Beijing to conclude that some sort of an anti-China alliance was forming. However, over the next decade, these nascent steps could become more formal if China pursues an expeditionary emphasis in PLA modernization while continuing its disturbingly assertive approach to dispute settlement with neighbors whose sovereignty claims conflict with China's view of its territory.[41] As its power continues to grow, will China take a similar approach to other neighborhood disputes, ignoring established rules and established dispute mechanisms, while attempting to rewrite or ignore rules that do not favor its interests? The combination of these factors could easily trigger a multilateral hedge against China.

CONCLUDING THOUGHTS

China is not starting with a blank slate when it comes to PLA military capabilities. Beijing already possesses very capable systems that can "reach out and touch" all of its neighbors. This has already triggered reactions by most of its neighbors to improve their security by modernizing their militaries, moving closer to the United States, or both. As a result, a series of security related decisions from regional countries are already in progress that will be relatively unaffected by whatever modernization vector the PLA pursues.

Anxiety regarding China's military modernization is directly related to how China behaves diplomatically, economically, and politically toward its neighbors. Despite the cautions of strategists and military planners to focus on PLA capabilities and not on Beijing's political intentions, which can change in an instant. The reality is that good relations tend to greatly reduce anxiety about military modernization. How China interacts with its neighbors will have major implications on how nervous they become if the PLA proceeds along one of the postulated vectors focused on enhancement.

Obviously, the vector that has the PLA slowing the pace of modernization, if combined with artful Chinese "smile diplomacy," will have the greatest influence on lessening the urgency its neighbors demonstrate in addressing their own modernization programs. But, since many of these programs are well underway today, it seems unlikely that the political establishments in the capitals of China's neighbors would simply halt those plans in the face of a more regionally benign China.

For Japan, South Korea, and the Philippines, the efficacy of their defense treaties with Washington will continue to be questioned in the face of an ever-improving PLA, particularly one that is focused on regional security. South Korea does not share Japan's or the Philippines' sense of insecurity when it comes to China. Many South Korean security analysts think that a united Korea could comfortably co-exist with a powerful Chinese neighbor. The major problem Seoul has with Beijing is China's support for North Korea. EEZ demarcation and fishing disputes are issues that can be managed by both capitals.

Japan, on the other hand, has few choices other than the United States to ensure its security. However, it is important to keep in mind that very bad relations have not been the post-World War II norm for Sino-Japanese relations and by 2025, they could be better. But Japan's growing sense of insecurity in the face of PLA capabilities that has the potential to ruin Japan's economy has finally persuaded Tokyo that China is a long-term threat. If Tokyo's decisionmakers come to believe that the U.S. alliance does not have the capability or political will to underwrite Japan's security, it seems likely it will develop its own nuclear deterrent in the face of a PLA that continues to grow and over-match Japan's conventional forces.

Further afield, an expeditionary PLA will cause Australia and India to look very closely after their own defenses, and spur multilateral approaches as a hedge against Chinese power. In Australia's case, security based on confidence in U.S. alliance rests on a much firmer foundation than the U.S.-Japan alliance because of the realities of geography.[42] Australia is far enough away from the locus of Chinese power to make PLA area denial a not particularly credible threat. India faces the threat from both a regional PLA on its northern frontier as well as an expeditionary PLA in the Indian Ocean. This may convince Indian strategic planners it is surrounded, confronted with a two-front, or if Pakistan is involved, a three-front security challenge.

Finally, I believe that the PLA will continue to improve its regional capabilities as well as improve its expeditionary forces; they are not mutually exclusive and that, at least in the Indo-Pacific region, we will see a PLA well-poised to defend China and its territorial claims; as well as one, that, for the first time since Ming Dynasty's Admiral Zheng He, be able to project power in pursuit of limited aims anywhere along the Indo-Pacific littoral.

ENDNOTES - CHAPTER 9

1. Commentary during RSIS Singapore workshop on "China's Regional Diplomacy," December 9-10, 2013; and Bonnie Glaser, "China's Grand Strategy in Asia, Statement before the U.S.-China Economic and Strategic Review Commission, Washington, DC: Center for Strategic and International Studies (CSIS), available from *csis.org/files/attachments/ts140313_glaser.pdf*.

2. It is important to keep in mind that, barring illness or some massive internal disruption, Xi Jinping is likely to remain China's leader until 2023, which implies great continuity of policies that have his personal imprimatur.

3. Scott Snyder, "China-Korea: Crying Uncle No-More: Stark Choices for Relations," *Comparative Connections: A Tri-annual E-Journal on East Asian Bilateral Relations*, Vol. 15, No. 3, Pacific Forum CSIS, January 2014, available from *csis.org/files/publication/1303qchina_korea.pdf*.

4. For hedging against China, see, for example, Christopher Hughes, "China's Military Modernization: U.S. Allies and partners in Northeast Asia," Ashley Tellis and Travis Tanner, eds., *Strategic Asia 2012-2013, China's Military Challenge*, Seattle, WA: The National Bureau of Asia Research, 2012, pp. 224-227. For hedging against Japan, see "62% of South Koreans View Japan as a Credible Military Threat," *The American Interest*, November 3, 2013, available from *www.the-american-interest.com/blog/2013/11/03/62-of-south-koreans-view-japan-as-credible-military-threat/*.

5. The May 2014 visit by President Obama to South Korea signaled an understanding between the two countries that postponing OPCON transfer until the threat from North Korea abates would be a wise decision. Ellen Kim, "President Obama's Visit to South Korea," *cogitASIA, A blog of the CSIS Asia Program*, April 29, 2014, available from *cogitasia.com/president-obamas-visit-to-south-korea/*.

6. China's East China Sea ADIZ encompassed Ieodo Rock, and, when Seoul asked Beijing to modify the ADIZ boundary, Beijing refused. Seoul responded in kind and expanded its ADIZ to also cover the rock. Lily Kuo, "Will a Tiny Submerged Rock Spark a New Crisis in the East China Sea," *The Atlantic online*, December 9, 2013, *www.theatlantic.com/china/archive/2013/12/will-a-tiny-submerged-rock-spark-a-new-crisis-in-the-east-china-sea/282155/*.

7. Terence Roehrig, "Republic of Korea Navy and China's Rise: Balancing Competing Priorities," Chap. in *CNA Maritime Asia Project Workshop Two: Naval Developments in Asia*, Alexandria, VA: CNA Center for Naval Analyses, 2012.

8. *Ibid.*

9. Michael McDevitt, "The Maritime Relationship," Scott Snyder, ed., *The U.S.-South Korean Alliance: Meeting New Security Challenges*, Boulder, CO: Lynn Rienner Publishers, 2012, pp. 36-39.

10. See for example, Clay Blair, Jr., *Silent Victory: U.S. Subma-rine War Against Japan*, Annapolis, MD: U.S. Naval Institute Press, 2001 Ed.

11. For a short discussion of anti-access area denial, see Michael McDevitt, "The Evolving Maritime Security Environment in East Asia: Implications for the U.S.-Japan Alliance," *PACNET 33*, May 31, 2012, available from *https://csis.org/files/publication/Pac1233.pdf*.

12. Hughes, pp. 203-216.

13. Kei Koga and Yogesh Joshi, "Japan-India Security Cooperation," *The Diplomat*, July 17, 2013, available from *thediplomat.com/2013/07/japan-india-security-cooperation/2/*; and Ministry of Defense of Japan, *Defense White Paper 2013*, Section 2, "Promotion of Defense Cooperation and Exchanges," Tokyo, Japan, available from *www.mod.go.jp/e/publ/w_paper/pdf/2013/38_Part3_Chapter2_Sec2.pdf*.

14. This section is based on Department of Defense, *Annual Report to Congress: Military and Security Developments Involving the People's Republic of China 2013*, Section 5.55-59, Washington, DC, available from *www.defense.gov/pubs/2013_china_report_final.pdf*.

15. There are a number of excellent analyses of Southeast Asia's response to growth of Chinese power and the subsequent U.S. rebalance strategy. The one that I found most helpful and current is Euan Graham, "Southeast Asia in the U.S. Rebalance: Perceptions from a Divided Region," *Contemporary Southeast Asia*, Vol. 35, No. 3, December 2013, pp. 335-332, available from *https://bookshop.iseas.edu.sg/publication/1942*.

16. Natasha Bererton-Fukui, "Sea Tensions Erupt at Asian Summit," *The Wall Street Journal*, November 20, 2012.

17. "The U.S. Rebalance: Potential and Limits in Southeast Asia," *Strategic Comments*, Vol. 18, Comment 49, London, UK, IISS website, *www.iiss.org*, December 2012, available from *www.iiss.org/en/publications/strategic%20comments/sections/2012-bb59/us-rebalance--potential-and-limits-in-southeast-asia-c5a7*.

18. Office of the Press Secretary, "Joint statement by President Obama and Prime Minister Najib of Malaysia," Washington, DC: The White House, April 27, 2014, available from *www.whitehouse. gov/the-press-office/2014/04/27/joint-statement-president-obama-and-prime-minister-najib-malaysia.*

19. "U.S. rebalance," *IISS Strategic Comments.*

20. Richard Bitzinger, "Revisiting Armaments Production in Southeast Asia: New Dreams, Same Challenges," *Contemporary Southeast Asia*, Vol. 35, No. 3, December 2013, p. 384, available from *www.questia.com/library/journal/1G1-354576536/revisiting-armaments-production-in-southeast-asia.*

21. Yoshihiro Makino, "Indonesia buys 3 submarines from South Korea," *Asahi Shimbum*, December 6, 2011, available from *ajw.asahi.com/article/asia/korean_peninsula/AJ201112060032.*

22. As former Singapore Prime Minster Lee Kwan Yew famously put it in his memoirs, "Singapore is a Chinese island in a Malay Sea." See Lee Kwan Yew, *From Third World to First: The Singapore Story 1965-2000*, Singapore: Times Media, 2000, p. 25.

23. Swee Leon Collin Koh, "The Best Little Navy in Southeast Asia: The Case of the Republic of Singapore Navy," Michael Mulqueen, Deborah Sanders, and Ian Speller, eds., *Small Navies: Strategy and Policy for Small Navies in Peace and War*, Farnham, Surrey, UK: Ashgate, 2014, pp. 117-132.

24. Press Briefing by Deputy National Security Advisor for Strategic Communication Ben Rhodes and NSC Senior Director for Asian Affairs Evan Medeiros, Grand Millennium Hotel, Kuala Lumpur, Malaysia, April 27, 2014, available from *www.whitehouse.gov/the-press-office/2014/04/27/press-briefing-deputy-national-security-advisor-strategic-communication.*

25. Simone Orendain, "Philippines Readies for Increased U.S. Presence," December 12, 2012, available from *www.voanews.com/artcilceprintview/1563453.html.*

26. Le Hong Hiep, "Vietnam's Hedging Strategy Against China since Normalization," *Contemporary Southeast Asia*, Vol. 35,

No. 3, December 2013, pp. 353-356, available from *https://bookshop. iseas.edu.sg/publication/1942.*

27. Ministry of Defense, Socialist Republic of Vietnam, "Vietnam National Defense," Hanoi, 2009, available from *admm. org.vn:6789/TempFiles/ba88fe13-f154-48aa-b9b7-27ffaa18b3b4. pdf.* See also Bernard D. Cole, *Asian Maritime Strategies: Navigating Troubled Waters,* Annapolis, MD: Naval Institute Press, 2013, p. 179.

28. Carlyle Thayer, quoted in Greg Torode, "Vietnam Buys Submarines to Counter China," *South China Morning Post,* December 17, 2009, available from *www.viet-studies.info/kinhte/vietnam_ buys_submarines_SCMP.htm.*

29. Carlyle Thayer, "China's Oil Rig Gambit: South China Sea Game Changer?" *The Diplomat,* May 12, 2014, available from *thediplomat.com/2014/05/chinas-oil-rig-gambit-south-china-sea-game-changer/.*

30. Le Hong Hiep, pp. 355-356.

31. *Ibid.,* p. 34.

32. Mark Thompson, "Confusion Down Under: Australia and the U.S. Pivot to Asia," *Asia-Pacific Bulletin,* No. 180, East-West Center, September 18, 2012, available from *www.EastWestCenter. org/APB.*

33. Jason Scott, "Australia Pledges to Lift Defense Spending from 7-Decade Low," *Bloomberg News,* May 13, 2014. available from *www.bloomberg.com/news/2014-05-13/australia-pledges-to-lift-defense-spending-from-7-decade-low.html.*

34. Over the last 5 years, I have directed a bilateral workshop series with India's National Maritime Foundation (an India Navy funded nongovernmental organization) that has focused on Indian Ocean maritime issues and the naval relationship between the United States and India. Many of the insights and analysis found in this section are drawn from the strategic discussions held during these not for attribution events.

35. Ranjit Pandit, "Army Kicks-Off Raising New Mountain Strike Corps against China," *The Times of India*, January 9, 2014 available from *articles.timesofindia.indiatimes.com/2014-01-09/india/46028828_1_new-corps-liberation-army-two-new-infantry-divisions*.

36. An excellent short overview of India's strategic situation, with good maps, is "India as a Great Power: Know Your Own Strength," *The Economist*, March 30, 2013, available from *www.economist.com/news/briefing/21574458-india-poised-become-one-four-largest-military-powers-world-end*.

37. Dr. David Brewster, "Looking Beyond the String of Pearls: The Indian Ocean Is where India Holds a Clear Advantage over China," *India Today*, May 16, 2013, available from *indiatoday.intoday.in/story/indian-ocean-india-china-strategic-rivalry-tensions/1/271324.html*.

38. Sandeep Unnithan, "Hidden Dragon on the High Seas," *India Today*, March 31, 2014, available from *indiatoday.intoday.in/story/china-nuclear-powered-attack-submarine-south-china-sea/1/350573.html*.

39. Staff Report, U.S.-China Economic and Security Review Commission, "China Extends Its Combat Reach into the Indian Ocean," March 14, 2014, available from *origin.www.uscc.gov/sites/default/files/Research/Staff%20Report_China%27s%20Navy%20Extends%20its%20Combat%20Reach%20to%20the%20Indian%20Ocean.pdf*.

40. Debe R. Mohanty, "India's Defense Sector Still Plagued by Corruption," *Strafor*, February 14, 2014, available from *www.stratfor.com/the-hub/indias-defense-sector-still-plagued-corruption*.

41. See for example, Lisa Curtis, Walter Lohman, Rory Medcalf *et al.*," Shared Goals, Converging Interests: A Plan for U.S.-Australian-Indian Cooperation in the Indo-Pacific," *Heritage Foundation*, November 3, 2011, available from *www.heritage.org/research/reports/2011/11/shared-goals-converging-interests-a-plan-for-u-s-australia-india-cooperation-in-the-indo-pacific*; and Ashok Sharma, "The Quadrilateral Initiative: An Evaluation," *South Asia Survey*, Vol. 17, No. 2, September 2010, pp. 237-253.

42. This is not to say there have not been serious debates in Australia over the need to hedge its security by not putting all its eggs in the alliance basket. For the most noted proponent of this point of view, see Hugh White, "Australia's Choice: Will the Land Down Under Pick the United States or China?" *Foreign Affairs*, September 4, 2013, available from *www.foreignaffairs.com/ articles/139902/hugh-white/australias-choice.*

CHAPTER 10

IMPLICATIONS:
CHINA IN THE INTERNATIONAL SYSTEM

Phillip C. Saunders

Views expressed are those of the author and do not necessarily reflect the policies of the National Defense University, the Department of Defense or the U.S. Government. I would like to thank Denise Der and Jessica Drun for research assistance; and Lonnie Henley, Ellen Frost, and Susan Lawrence for helpful comments on the outline and draft.

To analyze China's potential role in the 2025 international system under the three alternative futures considered in this volume, it is first necessary to describe the key elements of the current international system and assumptions about what that system will look like in 2025. China will influence the evolution of the future international system, but Beijing is unlikely to have either the power or the ambition to overturn the current international system and replace it with one that fully matches its interests. China is best understood as a "moderately revisionist" power that will seek reforms that increase its influence within the international system and adjustments of some international rules and norms to better match Chinese preferences.

This chapter begins with a brief description of the current international system to provide a baseline assessment for analysis. The second section describes China's relationship with the current international system and examines Chinese debates about where, whether, and how China should push for change in international rules and norms. The third section considers potential changes in Chinese international behavior under three alternative futures: 1) a People's Liberation Army (PLA) focused on regional issues; 2) a global expeditionary PLA; and 3) a weakened PLA. The conclusion seeks to identify common behavioral elements across the alternative futures and the most important drivers of Chinese behavior toward the international system and regions outside Asia. It also notes the interconnected nature of Chinese bilateral, regional, and global policy and the challenges in assessing any single area in isolation.

THE CURRENT AND FUTURE INTERNATIONAL SYSTEM

Today's International System.

The current international system includes a number of formal governance structures, most of which are parts of the United Nations (UN) system established after World War II. The UN General Assembly and subsidiary UN bodies are important in terms of global political governance, and the UN Security Council is the closest thing to an authoritative global security institution, albeit one where permanent Security Council members have veto power. In economic governance, the International Monetary Fund (IMF) and the World Bank play important roles in maintaining financial stability and fostering economic development, while the World Trade Organization (WTO) defines, and seeks to enforce, global trade rules. Multilateral organizations such as the Group of Seven (G-7), the Group of Twenty (G-20), and the Organization for Economic Cooperation and Development (OECD), although not formally part of the UN system, have become important vehicles for coordinating policy among major global economies. UN institutions are supplemented by international treaties and international law which prescribe rules of conduct in various functional areas and sometimes establish institutions to encourage cooperation and compliance.

In addition to global institutions and treaties, groups of states in different regions have established a variety of regional institutions. Examples include the European Union (EU), the African Union (AU), the Organization of American States, and a range of Asia-Pacific institutions such as the Association of Southeast Asian Nations (ASEAN), Asia-Pacific Economic Cooperation, the Shanghai Cooperation Organization (SCO), and others. Regional institutions vary widely in the extent to which their member states accept formal commitments and rules, with the EU perhaps the strongest example of an institution where member states have given up significant sovereignty to a supranational organization. In most cases, regional organizations have a relatively limited ability to bind their member states.

While most global organizations and many regional ones establish formal rules and norms of behavior, the anarchical nature of the international system can make enforcement problematic, especially when powerful states are involved. Global and regional institutions structure interactions between sovereign states and provide incentives that shape state behavior, but their ability to constrain powerful states is finite. As a result, patterns of international behavior reflect both formal rules and norms and the calculations of individual states about when to adhere to norms and when to violate them.[1] Powerful states like the United

States, Russia, China, and major European countries are often reluctant to accept hard limits on their ability to wield power, preferring looser rules and norms that give them greater ability to use their superior power to shape or dictate outcomes. Powerful states can also often choose which of several overlapping global and regional organizations (or potential new ones) will best serve their interests in particular cases.

One important constraining factor is that powerful states would be much worse off in a world of pure anarchy, where states are so concerned about relative power and security that they are unwilling to engage in much mutually beneficial cooperation (such as trade). Even powerful states are therefore usually careful to preserve existing institutions even if those institutions do not perfectly serve their interests.[2] States are also sometimes willing to accept and adhere to rules that limit their individual power (what John Ikenberry calls "binding") in order to produce cooperative outcomes that advance their broader interests.[3]

The institutions, rules, and norms of today's international system were heavily shaped by the United States, the most powerful country by far after the end of World War II.[4] Since its establishment, the post-World War II international system has been affected by several important developments. One was the post-war economic reconstruction of Japan, Germany, and Western Europe, which strengthened the West in Cold War competition with the Soviet Union. A second was decolonialization in the 1950s and 1960s, which dismantled European colonial empires and greatly increased the number of sovereign states in Asia, Africa, and the Middle East. A third development was the collapse of communism and the break-up of the Soviet Union in 1991, which ended Cold War economic and political divisions and gradually integrated Eastern Europe and former Soviet states into a global economy. A fourth significant development is the EU institutionalization and geographical expansion into an organization that can give European countries a greater collective voice on some issues.

The net result has been a reduction in the U.S. preponderance that existed after World War II, a dramatic improvement in global living standards as countries took advantage of development opportunities in a globalized economy, and a redistribution of global power as rapid and differential growth rates altered the relative power of major states. Germany and Japan were the principal beneficiaries in the 1960s and 1970s, followed by other East Asian countries in the 1980s and China from the 1990s to the present. Major developing countries such as India, Brazil, and Indonesia have become regional powers with aspirations to global power status. It is important to note that the growth of all of today's major powers has required greater integration into the global economy to acquire needed capital, technology, and resources and to take advantage of international markets and the benefits of participation in production networks. Today's major powers can use economic power as leverage to achieve political or security ends, but would make themselves worse off if such efforts destroy or severely damage the foundations of the global economy.

Within the current system, the United States is still the most powerful actor, but has become less willing to bear the burdens and costs associated with global leadership. These costs not only include the U.S. role in maintaining global security, but also U.S. willingness to serve as the "lender of last resort" and to provide market access to keep the global economy functioning.[5] U.S. allies in Europe and Asia helped support the dominant U.S. economic and security role via joint action and participation in institutions such the North Atlantic Treaty Organization (NATO), the OECD, and the G-7. However, the post-Cold War international system also includes powerful countries such as Russia and China that do not share U.S. values or support a permanent U.S. leadership role. Rapid growth in large developing countries such as Brazil and India coupled with Japan's economic stagnation and the impact of the 2008 global financial crisis on the United States and Europe has reduced the relative power of those states supporting U.S. international leadership. The result is a significant reduction in U.S. global authority and ability to dictate outcomes. This reduction is symbolized by the shift from the G-7 to the G-20 as a more inclusive (and hence more legitimate) venue for global economic decisionmaking.[6]

In analyzing the three alternative futures, this chapter draws upon the assumptions about the international system and global technology in 2025 presented in Chapter 2.

CHINA'S CALCULUS OF CHANGE

Over the last 20 years, China has benefitted more than any other country from access to the global economic and governance institutions created and sustained by the United States. These institutions (and a receptive U.S. attitude toward Chinese economic development) have permitted unprecedented rapid growth which has raised living standards, helped sustain the Chinese Communist Party's (CCP) domestic power, and transformed China's position within the regional and global power structure. Although Chinese leaders may have initially hoped to use the international system solely as a means to increase China's national power and automony, China has become increasingly dependent on the functions performed by international institutions in order to sustain economic growth.[7] U.S. policymakers have called upon China to become a stronger supporter of the current international system, most notably in Deputy Secretary of State Robert Zoellick's 2005 call for China to become a "responsible stakeholder" in the international system.[8]

Chinese leaders disclaim any intent to challenge the U.S. leadership role in the international system or any aspirations to replace the United States in that role. Yet, given China's vulnerability to U.S. power, they are reluctant to endorse any steps that will strengthen the foundations of U.S. hegemony or endorse a special leadership role for Washington. Chinese dependence on the United States for critical functions such as protection of China's sea lines of communication constitutes a significant strategic vulnerability. Most Chinese analysts (and policymakers) believe that the United States is committed to maintaining its dominant position and therefore will inevitably seek to constrain China's rise.[9]

Chinese officials and analysts believe that China benefits from a global trend toward multipolarity (defined as power distributed more evenly among the major states and increased willingness of major states to act independently of the United States).[10] Multipolarity gives China more diplomatic freedom to maneuver and makes it less vulnerable to hostile action by the United States, which is still the most powerful actor in the international system and the most able to facilitate or obstruct Chinese goals. Chinese scholars often note that the People's Republic of China (PRC) was not a full participant in the construction of the post-World War II international order and that current international rules are not necessarily optimal for Chinese interests.[11]

Chinese official policy statements seek to reassure the United States that China has neither the capability nor the intent to challenge U.S. dominance. Several studies argue that there is little evidence that China seeks fundamental changes in the current international system, and that the current system serves China's most important interests.[12] Academic studies of Chinese compliance with existing international rules and norms generally find a record of increasing compliance, albeit with exceptions in some areas.[13] Chinese officials and scholars argue that China only seeks reforms in global governance that will make the current system fairer.[14] At the same time, China regularly calls for creation of a more just international economic order (which implies significant changes to current rules and norms and a reduction in U.S. global influence). The People's Bank of China has publicly supported a reduction in the U.S. dollar's role as the global reserve currency, which would weaken the foundations of U.S. financial power.[15]

Chinese scholars and officials have articulated a range of areas where China seeks modifications in international rules and norms. One study identifies three areas where there is widespread Chinese support for change: 1) ensuring that China and other developing countries have more influence in global institutions; 2) increasing the degree to which the United States is constrained by global rules and norms; and 3) reducing the role of U.S. alliances and military deployments that might constrain China.[16] Chinese complaints are usually couched in terms of the need for fairness for developing countries and increased "democracy" in international relations, but the underlying demand is for a Chinese seat at the table and a greater role for Beijing in shaping international rules and norms.

China benefits from its privileged position as a veto-wielding permanent member of the UN Security Council and has resisted efforts to allow countries such as Japan and India similar status. Given Beijing's structural power as a permanent member of the UN Security Council, it is not surprising that China emphasizes the centrality of the UN in global security governance. In practice, China regularly uses its veto power to encourage resolution of conflicts via dialogue, to limit the role of sanctions, and to restrict the ability of the United States and other major powers to use force. Chinese leaders regularly emphasize the importance of respecting national sovereignty and opposing interference in internal affairs and seek to delegitimize military interventions not authorized by the UN.[17] Under the rubric of "respecting choices of development paths," China seeks to reduce the role of democracy as a precondition for participation in global and regional institutions such as the OECD and the International Energy Agency.[18]

China historically has been suspicious of multilateral institutions due to the potential for others to gang up against a weaker China. Chinese leaders have gradually recognized multilateral organizations as important venues for world politics and have learned to effectively synchronize their bilateral and multilateral diplomacy.[19] China generally prefers institutions where it enjoys formal (via veto power) or informal (via consensus decisionmaking) blocking power, which gives Beijing a degree of control over both agenda and outcomes. In regional diplomacy, China appears to have a preference for institutions such as ASEAN+3 where the United States is not represented, and China has greater influence. However, multilateral organizations which exclude the United States are not a viable option for most global issues. China has supported the establishment of some alternative global institutions, such as the BRICS (Brazil, Russia, India, China, and South Africa) group. However, the conflicting interests of the members, and the fact that they all have equally important relationships with the United States, has limited the influence of such alternative institutions.

China and other powers not fully satisfied with the current international system have a range of potential responses. These include:

1. Accept existing rules even if not optimal.
2. Selective noncompliance.
3. Adjust existing rules to better reflect their interests or carve out exemptions.
4. Create alternative institutions with different rules (SCO, BRIC cooperation, regional trade blocs, regional organizations, etc.).
5. Challenge current leader of the international system in order to replace current institutions and rules with new ones.

The first three responses involve working within the current international system, often while seeking to mitigate its negative aspects (via noncompliance or exemptions) or pressing for reforms to disadvantageous rules. The fourth response involves setting up a "parallel universe" of alternative institutions with more favorable rules, norms, and membership. Such parallel institutions would compete with and (if successful) potentially replace existing institutions. Only the fifth option entails a direct and explicit challenge to U.S. leadership of the current international system, a challenge sometimes referred to as a "power transition" and often accompanied by a war between the established hegemon and the rising challenger.[20] Chinese leaders have explicitly disclaimed any intention to challenge U.S. leadership even as China becomes more powerful; such assurances are a critical part of the proposal to build a "new type of major country relationship" between a dominant United States and a rising China.

China has employed the first four responses to different degrees in different issue areas (e.g., global security governance; international trade; international finance; regional security). These four options potentially can be combined or employed to different degrees in different areas. Efforts to change international institutions or rules in one area need not be part of a comprehensive challenge to the dominant power; significant changes are possible without hegemonic war. Some rules have explicit mechanisms that respond to changes in relative power (for example, World Bank and IMF voting shares are a function of the percentage of capital that a country contributes). Others respond to changes in relative power in a de facto manner (for example, increasing Chinese influence within the UN Security Council and General Assembly).

China is not the only country interested in changing international rules. This can either encourage or discourage Chinese attempts at change. If China can build a coalition of powerful, like-minded countries to change international rules, then the costs of pushing for change are shared and therefore reduced.[21] Some argue that the BRICS countries[22] or other groups of developing countries could form such a coalition.[23] On the other hand, change produced through a coalition effort implies goals acceptable to all members; in such circumstances China may not be able to dictate new rules that best match its interests. Moreover, many countries benefit significantly from the current international system and may not support Chinese efforts at reform that might disrupt the functioning of current international institutions.[24]

China is best understood as a "moderately revisionist" power that seeks to reform the international system and adjust international rules and norms to better suit Chinese interests. Chinese support for the current international system is contingent on the costs and benefits of seeking adjustments in global rules and on China's willingness to bear the burdens of a larger leadership role. A stronger China may be inclined to seek more significant revisions of global rules and norms, either on its own or in conjunction with others. However, many Chinese scholars who argue for modest revisions to the current international order cite China's reluctance to take on more international responsibilities, concerns about provoking a confrontation with the United States, and China's lack of sufficient power to remake international rules to better accord with its interests.[25]

Although Chinese leaders will almost certainly continue to try to avoid a direct challenge or a military confrontation with the United States, the more China's relative power approaches U.S. power, the more likely Beijing is to push for adjustments in international rules and norms. Beijing's reluctance to take on what Robert Sutter calls "costs, risks, and commitments" will be a constraint on Chinese ambitions to push

312

for more radical change.[26] Although current Chinese leaders proclaim a willingness to make more global contributions, in practice China has been reluctant to take on binding commitments. Moreover, in times of crisis Chinese leaders often fend off international demands for action by describing their most important responsibility as managing the Chinese economy and the welfare of 1.3 billion Chinese citizens.[27]

Another factor in the Chinese calculus is the degree of confidence Beijing has that China can achieve its national goals within the structure of current international institutions and rules. If China is prospering, more confident and secure Chinese leaders may feel less need to push for changes. On the other hand, a China that is faltering economically and facing internal turmoil will have a greater stake in defending sovereignty and pushing for international rules (on issues such as Internet security and control of information) that enhance the leadership's ability to maintain control.

China's historical experience with imperialism has led it to adopt foreign policy principles that emphasize respect for sovereignty and noninterference in the internal affairs of other countries. Yet, the exigencies of pursuing access to natural resources and protecting concrete Chinese interests overseas have led to deeper Chinese involvement in domestic politics in Burma, South Sudan, and elsewhere.[28] Some Chinese analysts are critical of the ways in which China's policy of noninterference has hindered diplomatic effectiveness in advancing Chinese economic and strategic interests.[29] As Chinese dependence on imports of energy and raw materials increases and the Chinese overseas "footprint" in terms of investments, construction projects, and Chinese nationals working abroad expands, there will be domestic pressure for China to take a more active and assertive international role.[30] China is likely to maintain its formal policy of respect for sovereignty and noninterference, but these policies may be interpreted more loosely if significant Chinese economic and strategic interests are threatened by instability or by political forces hostile to Chinese interests coming to power in important countries.

THREE ALTERNATIVE FUTURES

Alternative Future 1: A PLA Focused on Regional Issues.

> In this future, the PLA's primary mission remains to prepare for conflict on China's periphery, particularly its maritime frontier along the southeast coast and, in particular, to fight a high-intensity war against U.S. military forces intervening on behalf of Taiwan, Japan, Vietnam, or whoever else China is fighting. The Taiwan issue has not been resolved to China's satisfaction, or some other issue has loomed as large as Taiwan was before. The Chinese government has its internal issues well enough in hand to continue prioritizing and funding military modernization. The PLA is not confident that its modernization through 2020 was sufficient to meet the U.S. threat, and out-of-region missions continue to take a back seat as the PLA responds to the previously-unexpected increase in U.S. military capabilities. Regional conflict remains the central focus of PLA military modernization through 2030, and its ability to project power to other regions of the world increases only as an adjunct to developing combat capabilities out to the second island chain.[30a]

This future implies a China that is doing reasonably well economically, that is strategically focused

314

on maritime territorial and political disputes in Asia (including Taiwan's unresolved status), and that has a much more competitive relationship with the United States and with U.S. regional allies. Competition will be most intense within the Asia-Pacific region, which is where China's most important interests are located.[31] Intensified regional competition with Washington will also color China's broader approach to the international system and its ties with other powers outside Asia. A key question for this chapter is the extent to which U.S.-China competition can be contained within Asia, or whether it expands to an intensified zero-sum competition at the global level.[32] Under these circumstances, Beijing is likely to pursue an incremental approach to changes in the international system.

China would likely seek to balance intensified regional competition with Washington with a degree of cooperation outside the region in order to avoid a confrontation with the United States. Beijing would not challenge the U.S. global role directly, but would continue to promote multipolarity, look for strategic partners among other developing countries and major powers, and seek opportunities on the margin to work with others to weaken the U.S. long-term power position (or at least limit U.S. efforts to entrench its dominance). This would include efforts to work with other developing countries to adjust global trade and finance rules in order to better serve the interests of developing countries. China would continue to promote increased use of the RMB as a settlement currency for international trade (thus increasing its international economic influence and reducing the U.S. dollar's global role). Economic tensions between the United States and China and the increasing economic power of major developing countries are likely to make further multilateral trade liberalization difficult at the global level. Trade action may be more intense at the regional level, where China is likely to promote the Regional Comprehensive Economic Partnership (RCEP) as an alternative to the U.S.-backed Trans-Pacific Partnership (TPP). (However, some Chinese economists have warmed to TPP recently, viewing it as akin to WTO entry as a mechanism for forcing China to undertake necessary but politically difficult economic reforms.) China would likely increase its foreign aid, investment, and economic cooperation activities within the Asia-Pacific to increase its regional influence.

China would seek opportunities to demonstrate its contributions to global stability in order to offset the tensions its actions in Asia are producing.[33] This might include a greater willingness to work with Washington on areas of mutual interest, such as nuclear nonproliferation, energy security, sea lane protection, counterpiracy, and other global issues. China's willingness to cooperate with Washington in the UN Security Council would depend on the nature of the issue, with Beijing blocking actions that might adversely affect its important interests, but compromising or acquiescing on other issues where its stakes are lower. China would be reluctant to authorize any U.S. military interventions for fear of setting negative precedents.

Because China would be concerned about limiting the U.S. ability to intervene in its territorial disputes and on sovereignty issues such as Taiwan, Tibet, and Xinjiang, it would continue to emphasize the importance of UN authorization for military interventions and to highlight respect for sovereignty and nonintervention as the dominant norms of international

316

behavior. This would be in greater tension with China's expanding overseas economic footprint in terms of trade, investment, and construction projects. Beijing may become more involved in the domestic politics of resource-rich countries when critical Chinese interests are at stake, but Chinese leaders will try to maintain the fig leaf of noninterference in such cases.

Political instability in individual countries and broader transnational threats such as terrorism and piracy are likely to put Chinese global interests at greater risk than they are today. Despite its focus on the Asia-Pacific and its limited power projection capabilities, China might increase its contributions to UN peacekeeping missions and its cooperation in capacity building efforts with regional organization such as the AU and the SCO. These are measures that might help increase stability in regions outside Asia (thereby protecting Chinese interests), but which would not require large increases in Chinese resource or military commitments.

China would be somewhat deferential to the security interests of major regional powers outside Asia so long as it can maintain the economic access it needs within their regions. (Although other regional powers will likely not have as much influence within their regions as Russia does in Central Asia, the way China has pursued its economic and energy interests in Central Asia, while paying lip service to Russian prerogatives, may be a useful model for Chinese behavior.) China will cooperate with some major regional powers within global institutions to advance common interests of developing countries (sometimes at the expense of the United States and the West) and within regional institutions to maintain stability in key resource-rich countries. China will rely primarily on economic and diplomatic means to pursue its interests outside Asia, but arms sales, security assistance, intelligence relations, and technology transfer are likely to play more prominent roles than in the past. Using these and other tools, China will continue to be willing to cultivate ties with countries that have hostile relations with Washington when this advances concrete Chinese interests. Sino-Indian relations would be something of a wild card in this future, with some possibility of China trying to resolve the border dispute and pursue closer ties so as to keep India out of Washington's orbit.

Alternative Future 2: A Global Expeditionary PLA.

> The PLA's primary focus has shifted to military power projection beyond China's maritime periphery, whether because regional tensions have faded, because the PLA has satisfied Chinese leaders that it has achieved what needs to win regional conflicts, or because unexpected events elsewhere in the world have raised Beijing's sense of urgency about protecting Chinese interests farther afield. The government has internal issues under control and can afford the required new military capabilities. For most of the decade between 2020 and 2030, the PLA focuses on power projection, the details of which we leave to other contributors to explore.[33a]

This future implies a China that is doing well economically and that has resolved tensions with its neighbors, either because it has established clear regional dominance through economic attraction and selective military coercion or because maritime disputes have been resolved peacefully or set aside in favor of economic development. Chinese regional dominance implies a United States with a weakened or dysfunctional regional alliance system and reduced military presence and political influence in Asia. This could produce different U.S. responses, depending on the underlying causes. If this outcome is the result of a lagging U.S. economy and reluctance to sustain U.S. commitments to Asia (e.g., a more isolationist U.S. mood), then U.S. policymakers may encourage greater Chinese contributions to the stability of other regions of the world to make up for reduced U.S. resources and engagement. This implies the potential for greater U.S. cooperation in other regions with a more confident and more capable China. On the other hand, if this outcome is viewed as the product of U.S. policy failure, a rancorous partisan political debate over "who lost Asia" could produce a much more suspicious U.S. attitude toward an expanded and more active Chinese presence in other regions. Significant PLA Navy (PLAN) progress toward blue water navy capabilities—including frequent deployments outside Asia—would also aggravate these concerns. If maritime disputes are resolved peacefully or fade in political importance, then regional developments have no particular implications for U.S. power relative to China. This could be consistent with "peaceful co-existence" between a relatively strong United States and a stable and more confident China.

Chinese leaders enjoying a stable regional security environment, economic growth, and few internal challenges would be relatively confident about the future and have a broader range of choice about their international ambitions. China's success under prevailing international rules and norms might decrease the perceived benefits of pushing for changes in the international system. Even within current rules, China's improved power position will yield greater influence within most international institutions and increased status and prestige at both the regional and global levels. U.S.-China disputes over military activities within China's exclusive economic zone (EEZ) and Chinese efforts to advance maritime territorial claims would not generate the current level of bilateral tensions and strategic suspicions, either because the United States was not conducting such activity or because the two countries had worked out a *modus vivendi*, perhaps based on more parallel and routinized patterns of surveillance.[34]

Much would depend on how Chinese leaders choose to use their increased power to advance (rather than just protect) China's global economic and political interests. China might be willing to take on more international responsibilities (accepting costs, risks, and commitments) and make more contributions to the functioning of the international system. Chinese leaders would expect—and likely receive—a greater voice and more influence in exchange for greater contributions. Alternatively, Beijing might make more active efforts to use its increased power to reshape international rules to better serve its interests, which would produce significant friction with Washington. Even if the gap between U.S. and Chinese power narrows significantly, Chinese leaders are unlikely to seek fundamental changes in the international system both due to the risk of a confrontation with the United States and because a dominant leadership role would require China to assume significant costs and risks both to change the international system and to keep it running.[35] Such a decision would be inconsistent with Chinese practice in avoiding major long-term costs and commitments and Beijing's narrow focus on obtaining concrete benefits for China.

Accordingly, China is likely to seek evolutionary changes in the international system that increase China's influence or advance specific Chinese interests without a direct challenge to Washington. Beijing will promote multipolarity, look for partners among other developing countries and major regional powers to support its desired changes, and decline to shore up U.S. global leadership or support U.S. efforts to improve its long-term power position. China might make more active efforts to defend the rights of foreign countries to choose nondemocratic systems of government and seek to limit political and human rights criteria for international assistance. China would cooperate with other powers to advance common interests of developing countries within global institutions. The net result might be to weaken the economic and political foundations of U.S. leadership, potentially producing a "G-Zero" world without a clear international leader.[36] China will continue to proclaim norms of sovereignty and nonintervention even as its economic interests lead to much deeper involvement in the domestic politics of resource-rich countries in other regions.

A more powerful and confident China might also be less deferential to the political and security interests of major regional powers outside Asia, especially if instability in their regions threatens Chinese investments, citizens, and access to natural resources and markets. The current liberal international order facilitates Chinese access to resources and markets in other regions, but major regional powers such as Russia, India, and Brazil might well seek to limit China's access to regional resources. More likely, a reduction in the willingness of the United States (and limited capacity of great powers and major regional powers) to intervene to resolve civil wars or domestic insurgencies may produce greater instability in countries important to Chinese economic interests.

China will employ a range of instruments to protect its interests outside Asia, including arms sales, deployment of peacekeeping troops, extensive security assistance and military training programs, and intelligence cooperation, especially in politically unstable countries that have critical resources or which host large Chinese investments. In cases of domestic instability, China's initial response will be to work with the host government to improve its capacity to maintain order (and thereby protect Chinese interests). In this alternative future, China's ambassador, defense attaché, and Ministry of State Security station chief may be more important than their U.S. counterparts in most developing countries, and better able to deliver significant resources to help host governments maintain stability. In cases where governments are unable to maintain order, the PLA would help conduct noncombatant evacuation operations to rescue Chinese citizens. If the frequency of such operations increased dramatically, the PLA might become a supporter of greater Chinese political or military involvement to produce stability. The same might be true of counterpiracy or counterterrorism operations. Then-PLA Chief of General Staff Chen Bingde suggested as much in a May 2011 speech, when he cited the strains counterpiracy operations were placing on the PLAN and noted that solving the piracy problem required action on land rather than at sea.[37]

China will become a more important military and diplomatic player in global and regional efforts to respond to regional crises, and may be willing to act outside the UN framework when significant Chinese interests are at stake. (The evolution of the SCO toward norms of "mutual assistance" and periodic multinational counterterrorism exercises might provide a preview of this aspect of China's role.) However, Beijing will still be very selective about when and how it supports outside intervention and which interventions it participates in. In this alternative future, there will be some examples of Chinese-led intervention to restore stability in internal conflicts, usually under a fig leaf of invitation from the UN, a regional organization, or the host government and sometimes as part of an international coalition. However, Chinese political and military leaders perceive U.S. interventions in Afghanistan and Iraq as a significant drain on U.S. wealth and national power, and are therefore likely to be highly selective in where they choose to act and seek to limit the length of any military operations.[38]

Alternative Future 3: A Weakened PLA.

> Chinese leaders are overwhelmed with China's internal problems and the resources available for military modernization have dropped sharply. The PLA has failed to achieve the development it intended, and the decade through 2030 is consumed in a protracted effort to achieve capabilities relative to the United States that it intended to achieve by 2020. Internal missions including disaster relief, internal security, and assistance to civil authorities consume a great deal of the PLA's time. The external situation remains tense, the possibility of conflict has not diminished, and Chinese interests remain threatened in other parts of the world, But the PLA does not have the time or resources to address those challenges as well as it would wish.[38a]

This future implies a China doing poorly economically (and environmentally), with a leadership focused primarily on maintaining domestic control. The ambitious economic reform agenda announced in the November 2012 plenum will have failed to reverse slowing growth. China may become caught in a "middle income trap" where rising costs make labor intensive products less competitive, but where Chinese companies lack the innovation and management skills to produce more advanced products that are competitive in a global marketplace. While a gradual slowdown in growth is the most likely scenario, a major domestic financial crisis could cause a dramatic recession and sudden, widespread economic dislocation, casting doubt on CCP performance in managing the economy. Environmental problems caused by resource intensive growth and poor enforcement of environmental standards will worsen. The Chinese government will have fewer resources available to mitigate the effects of air and water pollution and may be more reluctant to enforce regulations that raise costs and aggravate employment problems by slowing growth. Flagging political support due to faltering performance will make CCP leaders more paranoid about external support for Chinese activists and democracy advocates.

Internal problems will likely heighten concerns about separatism in Tibet and Xinjiang. There may be more incidents of political violence or domestic terrorism directed against local CCP officials and against Ministry of Foreign Affairs officials, Chinese businessmen, and Chinese citizens abroad. The PLA will face increasing demands to help local authorities and the People's Armed Police maintain order and to demonstrate the party's ability to respond to natural disasters and other emergencies. This will absorb an increasing share of flat PLA budgets, and may also interfere with current military modernization efforts by increasing demand for ground troops and derailing attempts to reform the military region system to support advanced joint operations.

In this future, China still has significant tensions with the United States and its regional allies, but Chinese leaders are more focused on defensive goals (such as preventing Taiwan independence and maintaining territorial claims) than on achieving unification or consolidating control over disputed territories. Chinese leaders would be more open to managing maritime territorial disputes through a *modus vivendi* or joint development arrangements, but would also be willing to use demonstrations or limited force to deter challenges or when they feel provoked. China's evident domestic problems, slower growth rate, and more restrained military modernization program would ease regional and global concerns about an aggressive China. They may also ease the over-confidence that has supported more assertive Chinese security and sovereignty policies and fueled nationalist calls for China to punish the United States and other countries for transgressions against Chinese interests.

Within global institutions, China would be prickly and defensive, with narrower goals of fending off external interference (on issues such as human rights, environmental standards, or Internet freedom) that might complicate efforts to maintain control. China would also resist more intrusive economic rules and enforcement of existing rules that might aggravate domestic economic challenges. China would emphasize the importance of sovereignty and noninterference and make common cause with other authoritarian governments and developing countries to protect those interests. Chinese leaders would continue to view the United States as ideologically hostile and rooting for

China to fail, but this suspicion will not greatly limit Beijing's willingness to cooperate on common interests. Chinese leaders might blame "hostile foreign forces" for domestic problems, but they are unlikely to use territorial disputes or external conflicts (e.g., diversionary war) to build internal unity or distract attention from domestic challenges.

China's more constricted global and regional diplomatic agenda would help ease U.S. concerns about China as a rival and open the possibility of broader bilateral cooperation, especially outside Asia. However, China will have fewer concrete things it can deliver, either in economic or military terms. China would be somewhat more deferential to the security interests of the United States and other major regional powers in the hopes of maintaining the economic access it needs and winning assistance in protecting PRC citizens and interests. Beijing would cooperate within global and regional institutions to maintain stability in key resource-rich countries, although it will remain reluctant to authorize military intervention for fear of setting adverse precedents.

China would increase bilateral intelligence and security cooperation with Turkey, Russia, and the Central Asian members of the SCO to help manage separatist threats. Heightened concerns about such threats may increase bilateral tensions with Pakistan if Islamabad is unwilling or unable to crack down on training camps and insurgent activity. Beijing has strong incentives to resolve the border dispute with India in order to gain New Delhi's cooperation in managing the Tibet issue and resisting Islamic separatists.

Slower economic growth would help ease Beijing's current obsession with access to energy and natural resources, as Chinese demand growth slows. China would rely primarily on economic and diplomatic means to pursue its interests outside Asia, but will be more resource constrained than at present. Less expensive security tools such as arms sales, security assistance, intelligence sharing, and technology transfer will play more prominent roles than they do today. Beijing would make efforts to ensure that these activities are coordinated in support of national interests, but low-level economic incentives may produce a return to the days of unauthorized arms sales and proliferation activities. Beijing would be somewhat more sensitive to the concerns of the United States and major regional countries when making foreign policy decisions on issues outside Asia.

CONCLUSION

As a "partial power," China will have significant limitations on its ability to project economic, military, and ideational power outside Asia and to force major changes in international rules and norms on a reluctant United States by 2025, even under the most optimistic assumptions about alternative futures. The ability of the U.S. to maintain its own economic growth, continue technological innovation, support a capable modern military, and continue to play its post-World War II international role will have a major influence on China's international opportunities and constraints. However, a full assessment of the likely role of the United States in 2025 is beyond the scope of this chapter.[39]

Common elements across all three alternative futures include the importance of economic growth in driving the expansion of China's international economic ties (and associated interests), China's desire to avoid a military confrontation with the United States, and the importance of domestic and regional stability in enabling or constraining a more ambitious Chinese international role. The assumption that China will maintain a narrow focus on what is good for China and will lack the ideological appeal needed to build lasting international coalitions will continue to constrain China's ability to build an enduring support bloc across a range of issue areas even if Beijing is more powerful. When the United States seeks to build a coalition for a positive goal, it starts with treaty allies and countries with whom it has cooperated regularly and successfully in the past. There are not many examples of coalitions led by China; the few that exist tend to be coalitions opposing international action (e.g., on human rights or intervention) rather than those catalyzing positive change. Beijing lacks experience in exerting international leadership for positive goals; if Chinese leaders choose to try, they may discover that China is not very good at it.

One major challenge is the interconnected nature of the U.S.-China bilateral relationship, the increasingly competitive U.S.-China relationship in the Asia-Pacific, and China's role as a global power that cooperates with Washington on many issues and simultaneously seeks to weaken U.S. power. Examining any single aspect in isolation is likely to produce a misleading picture, yet the connections between the bilateral, regional, and global levels are not fully understood.[40] Given the impossibility of analyzing all the interactions within the available space, this chapter has focused on the connections judged to be most important in understanding China's relationship with the international system in the three alternative futures. A fuller answer must draw upon the other chapters to draw out the connections between drivers of Chinese policy, future PLA postures, and the implications for future Chinese behavior at the bilateral, regional, and global levels.

ENDNOTES - CHAPTER 10

1. For an overview of international regimes, see Stephen D. Krasner, ed., *International Regimes*, Ithaca, NY: Cornell University Press, 1983.

2. This is the general case considered by Robert Gilpin, *War and Change In World Politics*, New York: Cambridge University Press, 1983.

3. John Ikenberry, *After Victory: Institutions, Strategic Restraint, and the Rebuilding of Order after Major Wars*, Princeton, NJ: Princeton University Press, 2001.

4. John Ikenberry, *Liberal Leviathan: The Origins, Crisis, and Transformation of the American System*, Princeton, NJ: Princeton University Press, 2011.

5. See Charles Kindleberger, *Manias, Panics, and Crashes: A History of Financial Crisis*, New York: Basic Books, 1978.

6. Although the G-20 was a U.S.-Canada initiative, it is widely interpreted in China and elsewhere as a symbol of the increased economic power of major developing countries.

7. See Li Lianqing, *Breaking Through: The Birth of China's Opening-Up Policy*, New York: Oxford University Press, 2009.

8. Deputy Secretary of State Robert B. Zoellick, "Whither China: From Membership to Responsibility?" Remarks to National Committee on U.S.-China Relations, New York City, September 21, 2005.

9. See Kenneth Lieberthal and Wang Jisi, "Addressing U.S.-China Strategic Distrust," John L. Thornton China Center Monograph Series, No. 4, Washington, DC: The Brookings Institution, March 2012; also see Li Xiangyang, "Recognizing the Global Economic Order's Restraint on China's Peaceful Development,"

Contemporary International Relations, May-June 2013, pp. 61-64; and Zhang Ruizhuang, "The Changing World Order and China," *Contemporary International Relations*, May-June 2013, p. 50.

10. This is clearly evident in the way Chinese defense white papers employ positive terms when multipolarity is viewed as increasing and negative terms to describe a slowdown in movement toward a multipolar world. For an illustration applied to the U.S.-Europe transatlantic alliance, see Wang Xiangsui, "Shifts in Global Power Gravity," *Contemporary International Relations*, January-February 2012, pp. 23-34.

11. See Ruan Zongze, "China Should Participate More In Making Int'l Rules," *People's Daily Online*, October 17, 2012, available from *english.people.com.cn/90883/7979484.html*.

12. See Edward S. Steinfeld, *Playing Our Game: Why China's Rise Doesn't Threaten the West*, New York: Oxford University Press, 2010 and Thomas Fingar, "China's Vision of World Order," Ashley J. Tellis and Travis Tanner, eds., *Strategic Asia 2012-13: China's Military Challenge*, Washington, DC: National Bureau of Asian Research, 2012.

13. See Rosemary Foot and Andrew Walter, *China, the United States, and Global Order*, New York: Cambridge University Press, 2008; and Gerald Chan, *China's Compliance in Global Affairs*, Hackensack, NJ: World Scientific, 2009.

14. See the Wang Jisi and Zhang Yunling chapters in Ashley J. Tellis and Sean Mirsky, eds, *The Crux of Asia: China, India, and the Changing Global Order*, Washington, DC: Carnegie Endowment for International Peace, 2013, available from *carnegieendowment. org/files/crux_of_asia.pdf*.

15. "China Reiterates Call for New World Reserve Currency (Update 4)," *Bloomberg News*, June 26, 2009, available from *www. bloomberg.com/apps/news?pid=newsarchive&sid=a5z7pjiZoYpg*.

16. Fingar, pp. 369-371.

17. For a recent illustration of Chinese principles and priorities, see Wang Yi, "China at a New Starting Point," statement at the UN General Assembly, New York, September 27, 2013.

18. *Ibid.*

19. Marc Lanteigne, *China and International Institutions: Alter-nate Paths to Global Power*, New York: Routledge, 2005; and Phillip C. Saunders, *China's Global Activism: Strategy, Drivers, and Tools*, Washington, DC: National Defense University Press, 2006.

20. See Gilpin. For potential applications to the U.S.-China relationship, see Avery Goldstein, *Rising to the Challenge: China's Grand Strategy and International Security*, Stanford, CA; Stanford University Press, 2005; and John Mearsheimer, *The Tragedy of Great Power Politics*, New York: W. W. Norton & Co., 2014, Updated Ed.

21. For an illustration in the economic sphere, see Wang Ying and Li Jiguang, "China and the G20," *Contemporary International Relations*, July-August 2012, pp. 1-14.

22. See Ji Peiding, "BRICS will reshape the International Land-scape," *Foreign Affairs Journal*, No. 107, Spring 2013, pp. 61-70.

23. Although Hong Yousheng and Fang Qing downplay China's potential to lead such a coalition, their favorable com-ments about the potential for developing countries to cooperate in changing international economic rules illustrates this line of argu-ment. See "Shift in the Center of Global Economic Governance," *Contemporary International Relations*, Vol. 22, No. 2, pp. 56-79.

24. Fingar, pp. 342-373.

25. For overviews of Chinese debates, see Fingar; Alison Kaufman, "The 'Century of Humiliation' Then and Now: Chinese perceptions of International Order," *Pacific Focus*, Vol. 25, No. 1, April 2010, pp. 1-33; the contributions in the May-June 2013 issue of *Contemporary International Relations*; and the report from the Na-tional Intelligence Council-CICIR dialogue on global governance.

26. Robert Sutter, *U.S.-China Relations: Perilous Past, Pragmatic Present*, Lanham, MD: Rowman and Littlefield, 2010.

27. This posture characterized China's initial response to the 2008 global financial crisis.

28. See Mathieu Duchatel, Oliver Brauner, and Zhou Hang, "Protecting China's Overseas Interests: The Slow Shift away from Non-interference," *SIPRI Policy Paper* No. 41, Stockholm, Sweden: Stockholm International Peace Research Institute, June 2014.

29. See the analysis and summaries of Chinese writings in "The End of Non-Interference?" *China Analysis*, Asia Centre and European Council on Foreign Relations, 2013.

30. Protecting Chinese national interests overseas is one part of the "New Historic Missions" Hu Jintao gave the PLA in 2004.

30a. This alternate future is from Lonnie D. Henley, "Whither China? Alternative Military Futures, 2020-30," Chapter 2 in this volume, p. 49.

31. For an explication of Chinese interests in Asia and its regional strategy, see Robert Sutter's contribution to this volume; and Phillip C. Saunders, "China's Role in Asia: Attractive or Assertive?" David Shambaugh and Michael Yahuda, eds., *International Relations in Asia*, 2nd Ed., Lanham, MD: Roman and Littlefield, 2014, pp. 147-172.

32. For a sense of what that might look like, see David Frelinger and Jessica Hart, "The U.S.-China Military Balance Seen in a Three-Game Framework," Richard P. Hallion, Roger Cliff, and Phillip C. Saunders, eds., *The Chinese Air Force: Evolving Concepts, Roles, and Capabilities*, Washington, DC: National Defense University, pp. 347-369. For policy advice on ways of managing U.S.-China strategic competition, see Phillip C. Saunders, "Managing Strategic Competition with China," *INSS Strategic Forum* No. 242, July 2009; and Michael D. Swaine, *America's Challenge: Engaging a Rising China in the Twenty-First Century*, Washington, DC: Carnegie Endowment for International Peace, 2011.

33. This echoes contemporary Chinese debates about whether China should significantly expand cooperation with the United States to cement a "New Type of Major Country Relationship" that will limit U.S. efforts to press China within Asia.

33a. This alternate future is from Lonnie D. Henley, "Whither China? Alternative Military Futures, 2020-30," Chapter 2 in this volume, pp. 49-50.

34. See the discussion in Mark E. Redden and Phillip C. Saunders, "Managing Sino-U.S. Air and Naval Interactions: Cold War Lessons and New Avenues of Approach," *China Strategic Perspectives*, No. 5, September 2012.

35. Although the United States derives considerable material and status benefits from being the dominant power, U.S. politicians and policymakers sometimes chafe at the costs of serving as the lender of last resort, the market of last resort, and the global policeman. Such views were one reason for the limited U.S. response to the 1998 Asian financial crisis and complaints about the Obama administration's efforts to stabilize the world economy after the 2008 financial crisis.

36. Ian Bremmer and David Gordon, "G-Zero," *Foreign Policy*, March-April 2011; and Ian Bremmer, *Every Nation for Itself: Winners and Losers in a G-Zero World*, New York: Portfolio, 2012.

37. General Chen Bingde, "Forging a New China-US Military-to-Military Relationship Featuring Mutual Respect, Mutual Benefit, and Cooperation," speech at U.S. National Defense University, May 18, 2011.

38. This might produce some similarities with post-Lebanon U.S. military interventions in the 1980s, which sought limited missions, decisive action, and clear time lines for withdrawal in order to avoid open-ended commitments.

38a. This alternate future is from Lonnie D. Henley, "Whither China? Alternative Military Futures, 2020-30," Chapter 2 in this volume, p. 50.

39. Robert Sutter's writings on China and Asia consistently emphasize the importance of comparing China's strengths and weaknesses against an accurate baseline of U.S. strengths and weaknesses. This advice is even more useful when thinking about China's global and extra-regional influence.

40. One preliminary effort to think about the connections between the three levels is *Maintaining U.S.-China Strategic Stability*, State Department International Security Advisory Board Report, Washington, DC, October 26, 2012.

CHAPTER 11

IMPLICATIONS FOR U.S.-CHINA
STRATEGIC DYNAMICS

Robert Sutter

I would like to thank Lincoln Hines of National Bureau of Asian Research, who provided effective research assistance for this article.

INTRODUCTION

Prediction of future U.S.-Chinese relations over the course of 15 years requires prudence to avoid gross miscalculations. Prudence requires a close look at what can be learned from the development of the relationship up to the present. Careful examination of the recent context of U.S.-Chinese relations highlights factors that determine recent behavior. These determinants have a long history. The likelihood that they will be upset in future years is offset by several realities: the United States and China are very large countries—the largest in the world; their leaders have long-standing priorities; and they exert great and often dominant influence as they interact with lesser powers. The latter countries like Japan, India, Taiwan, and North Korea plausibly could take actions that upset the recent trajectory of U.S.-Chinese relations, but it is more likely that much stronger America and China will shape those lesser powers. Extreme developments such as regime disintegration, international economic collapse or major war also could seriously disrupt U.S.-Chinese relations, but chances seem much more probable that relations will be governed by factors that have shaped them up to now.

FRAGILE BUT ENDURING STRATEGIC EQUILIBRIUM

The end of the Soviet Union and the Cold War destroyed the strategic framework for the Sino-American cooperation initiated by U.S. President Richard Nixon and Chinese Chairman Mao Zedong. Sometimes dramatic crises since that time have seen policymakers, strategists, and scholars in both the United States and China register concern and sometimes alarm over potential conflict. Major turning points included:

- The multiyear virulent popular and elite American opposition to Chinese leaders responsible for the crackdown against demonstrators in Tiananmen Square in 1989.
- The face-off of U.S.-Chinese forces as a result of the Taiwan Straits crisis of 1995-96.
- The crisis in 1999 prompted by the U.S. bombing of the Chinese embassy in Belgrade and resulting mass demonstrations and destruction of U.S. diplomatic properties in China.
- The crash in 2001 of a Chinese fighter jet and a U.S. reconnaissance plane over international waters near China and the resulting crisis over responsibility for the incident and release of the American crew and damaged plane that made an emergency landing in China.
- The explicit and growing U.S.-Chinese competition of influence in Asia featuring U.S. President Barack Obama administration's so-called pivot or rebalancing policy to the Asia Pacific coincident with greater Chinese assertiveness in dealing with differences with the United States and its allies and associates over issues of sovereignty and security along China's rim.[1]

In 2012, growing Chinese-U.S. competition in Asia headed the list of issues that challenged the abilities of Chinese and American leaders to manage their differences, avoid confrontation, and pursue positive engagement. Competition for influence along China's rim and in the broader Asia-Pacific region exacerbated an obvious security dilemma featuring China's rising power and America's reaction, shown notably in the two sides' respective military build-ups.

Hyperbolic attacks on Chinese economic and security policies were features of the Republican presidential primaries. President Obama also resorted to harsh rhetoric, calling China an "adversary." He highlighted his administration's reengagement with countries in the Asia-Pacific region as a means to compete with China in security, economic, and other terms.[2]

China demonstrated state power, short of direct use of military force, in response to perceived challenges by U.S. allies, the Philippines, and Japan, regarding disputed territory in the South China Sea and the East China Sea. Top Chinese leaders criticized American dealing with the disputed claims and also highlighted regional trade arrangements that excluded the United States, seeking to undermine the American-led Trans-Pacific Partnership (TPP) trade pact.[3]

Kenneth Lieberthal and Wang Jisi highlighted pervasive and deeply rooted distrust between the two governments.[4] David Shambaugh concluded that the overall U.S.-China relationship was "more strained, fraught and distrustful." Intergovernmental meetings meant to forge cooperation were becoming more pro-forma and increasingly acrimonious, he said. The two sides wrangle over trade and investment issues, technology espionage and cyber hacking, global governance challenges like climate change an Syria, nuclear challenges like Iran and North Korea, and their security postures and competition for influence in the Asia-Pacific.[5]

Unexpectedly, increased competition and tension in Sino-American relations in 2012 was followed by the California summit in June 2013 and an overall moderation in Sino-American differences. These developments supported conclusions regarding realities seen by a number of American and Chinese experts as defining the current overall strategic equilibrium in the relationship. The experts averred that the equilibrium was characterized by many areas of convergence and divergence amid changing calculations of interests influenced by changing circumstances. Nonetheless, prevailing trends including the constraints on both powers explained below, showed that avoiding serious confrontation and endeavoring to manage differences through a process of constructive engagement remains in the overall interests of both countries.[6] There are three general reasons for this judgment:

1. Both administrations benefit from positive engagement. It supports stability in the Asia-Pacific, a peaceful Korean peninsula, and a peaceful settlement of the Taiwan issue. It fosters global peace and prosperity, advances world environmental conditions, and deals with climate change and nonproliferation of weapons of mass destruction.

2. Both administrations see that ever growing China-U.S. interdependence means that emphasizing the negatives in their relationship will hurt the other side but also will hurt them.

3. Both leaderships are preoccupied with a long list of urgent domestic and foreign priorities; in this situation, one of the last things they would seek is a serious confrontation in relations with one another.

Looking out, few foresee the Obama administration well served, with a more assertive U.S. stance leading to a major confrontation with China. Indeed, the U.S. Government reached out to President Xi Jinping and the new Chinese leadership in holding the California summit and seeking greater engagement through senior level interchange in cabinet-level visits and structured dialogues. Its criticism of Chinese economic practices adverse to American interests remains measured. It has responded firmly when Chinese actions over disputed territory along its maritime rim escalate tensions and endanger stability, underlining America's commitments to regional stability and the status quo. Its posture on the preeminent issue of Taiwan has been supportive of Taiwan President Ma Ying-jeou's reassurance of and greater alignment with China.[7]

Comprehensive treatment requires consideration of possible serious shifts in American policy leading to greater tension in U.S.-Chinese relations. Those possibilities are considered below, but they seem much less likely and important than the more immediate consequences of China's growing assertive role in the Asia-Pacific and what that means for U.S.-Chinese cooperation or conflict. As argued in the next sections, such Chinese assertiveness will remain troublesome but probably will be held in check, allowing pragmatic U.S.-Chinese engagement to endure for the period of this assessment.

CHINA'S TOUGHER STANCE IN THE ASIA-PACIFIC

China's tough stand on maritime territorial disputes evident in the 2012 confrontations with the Philippines in the South China Sea and with Japan in the

East China Sea has endured through China's leadership transition and now marks an important shift in China's foreign policy with serious implications for China's neighbors and concerned powers, including the United States.[8] China's success in advancing its claims against the Philippines and in challenging Japan's control of disputed islands head the list of reasons why the new Chinese policy is likely to continue and perhaps intensify in the future.

Concerned governments recognize that China's "win-win" formula emphasizing cooperation over common ground is premised on the foreign government eschewing actions acutely sensitive to China over Taiwan, Tibet, and Xinjiang, and that the scope of Chinese acute sensitivity had now been broadened to include the maritime disputes along China's rim. They have been required to calibrate more carefully their actions related to disputed maritime territories. Unfortunately, the parameters of China's acute concerns regarding maritime claims remain unclear. Meanwhile, the drivers of China's new toughness on maritime disputes include rising patriotic and nationalist sentiment in Chinese elite and public opinion and the growing capabilities in Chinese military, coast guard, fishery, and oil exploration forces. The latter are sure to grow in the coming years, foreshadowing greater Chinese willingness to use coercion in seeking advances in nearby seas.

For now, a pattern of varied regional acquiescence, protests, and resistance to China's new toughness on maritime claims seems likely. It raises the question about future Chinese assertiveness, challenging neighboring governments with disputes over Chinese claims, and challenging American leadership in promoting stability and opposing unilateral and coercive means to change the regional status quo.

There are forecasts of inevitable conflict between the United States and China as they compete for influence in the Asia-Pacific or of a U.S. retreat in the Asia-Pacific in the face of China's assertiveness.[9] Such forecasts are offset in this writer's opinion by circumstances in China and abroad that will continue to constrain China's leaders. The circumstances are seen to hold back Chinese leaders even if they, like much of Chinese elite and public opinion, personally favor a tough approach in order to secure interests in the Asia-Pacific.

CONSTRAINTS ON CHINESE ASSERTIVENESS

There are three sets of constraints on Chinese tough measures in foreign affairs related to the United States that are strong and are unlikely to diminish in the foreseeable future.

Domestic Preoccupations.[10]

The Chinese leaders want to sustain one-party rule, and to do so, they require continued economic growth which advances the material benefits of Chinese people and assures general public support and legitimacy for the Communist government. Such economic growth and continued one-party rule require stability at home and abroad, especially in nearby Asia where conflict and confrontation would have a serious negative impact on Chinese economic growth. At the same time, the need for vigilance in protecting Chinese security and sovereignty remains among the top leadership concerns as evidenced by the long and costly build-up of military forces to deal with a Taiwan contingency involving the United States and more recent use of various means of state power to advance territorial claims in nearby disputed seas. There is less clarity as to where Chinese international ambitions for regional and global leadership fit in the current priorities of the Beijing leaders, but there is little doubt that the domestic concerns get overall priority.

Domestic concerns preoccupying President Xi Jinping leadership involve:

- weak leadership legitimacy highly depends on how the leaders' performance is seen by popular and elite opinion at any given time;
- pervasive corruption viewed as sapping public support and undermining administrative efficiency;
- income gaps posing challenges to the Communist regime ostensibly dedicated to advancing the disadvantaged;
- social turmoil reportedly involving 100,000-200,000 mass incidents annually that are usually directed at government officials and/or aspects of state policies; managing such incidents and related domestic control measures involve budget outlays greater that China's impressive national defense budget;
- highly resource intensive economy (e.g., China uses four times the amount oil to advance its economic growth to a certain level than does the United States); enormous and rapidly growing environmental damage results;
- need for major reform of an economic model in use in China for over 3 decades that is widely seen to have reached a point of diminishing returns.

The Chinese leadership set forth in November 2013 an ambitious and wide ranging agenda of economic and related domestic reforms. How more than 60 measures set forth for reform will be implemented and how they will be made to interact effectively with one another are widely seen to require strong and sustained efforts of top Chinese leaders, probably for many years.[11] Under these circumstances, those same leaders would seem reluctant to seek confrontation with the United States. Xi's accommodation of President Obama in meeting in California in 2013, and his leadership's continued emphasis on the positive in U.S.-China relations in seeking a new kind of major power relationship underlines this trend. Xi has presided over China's greater assertiveness on maritime territorial issues that involve the United States, but, thus far, the Chinese probes generally have been crafted to avoid direct confrontation with the superpower.

Strong Interdependence.

The second set of limits on Chinese tough measures leading to serious tensions with the United States involves ever growing interdependence in U.S.-Chinese relations. At the start of the 21st century, increasing economic interdependence reinforced each government's tendency to emphasize the positive and pursue constructive relations with one another. A pattern of dualism in U.S.-China relations featured constructive and cooperative engagement on the one hand, and contingency planning or hedging on the other. It reflected a mix of converging and competing interests and prevailing leadership suspicions and cooperation.

Reflecting the dualism, each government used engagement to build positive and cooperative ties while at the same time seeking to use these ties to build interdependencies and webs of relationships that had the effect of constraining the other power from taking actions that oppose its interests. The Council on Foreign Relations was explicit about this approach in a book entitled *Weaving the Net*, arguing for engagement that would over time compel changes in Chinese policies in accord with norms supported by the United States. While the analogy is not precise, the policies of engagement pursued by the United States and China toward one another featured respective "Gulliver strategies" that were designed to tie down aggressive, assertive, or other negative policy tendencies of the other power through webs of interdependence in bilateral and multilateral relationships.[12]

Chinese leaders also are seen as continuing to hedge their bets as they endeavor to persuade the United States and other important world powers of China's avowed determination to pursue the road of peace and development. New Chinese diplomatic and international activism and positivism not only foster a positive and beneficent image for China; they serve an important practical objective of fostering norms and practices in regional and international organizations and circumstances that create a buffer against suspected U.S. efforts to "contain" China and to impede China's rising power. Roughly consistent with the image of the "Gulliver strategy" noted earlier, they foster webs of interdependent relationships that tie down and hamper unilateral or other actions by the U.S. superpower that could intrude on important Chinese interests in Asian and world affairs.[13]

Both sides have become increasingly aware of how their respective interests are tied to the well-being and success of the other, thereby limiting the tendency of the past to apply pressure on one another. In effect, interdependence has worked to constrain both sides against taking forceful action against each other.

China's Insecurity in the Asia-Pacific.

China's insecure position in the Asia-Pacific region poses the third set of constraints on Chinese tough measures against the United States. Nearby Asia is the world area where China has always exerted greatest influence and where China devotes the lion's share of foreign policy attention. It contains security and sovereignty issues (e.g., Taiwan) of top importance. It is the main arena of interaction with the United States. The region's economic importance far surpasses the rest of the world (China is Africa's biggest trader, but it does more trade with South Korea). Stability along the rim of China is essential for China's continued economic growth—the lynchpin of leadership legitimacy and continued Communist rule. Given the previous discussion, without a secure foundation in nearby Asia, China will be inclined to avoid serious confrontation with the United States.[14]

Among Chinese strengths in the Asia-Pacific region are:

- China's position as the leading trading partner with most neighboring countries and the heavy investment many of those countries make in China;
- China's growing web of road, rail, river, electric power, pipeline, and other linkages promoting economic and other interchange with nearby countries.

- China's prominent leadership attention and active diplomacy in interaction with neighboring countries, both bilaterally and multilaterally;
- China's expanding military capabilities.

Nevertheless, these strengths are offset by various weaknesses and limitations. Some Chinese practices alienate near-by governments, which broadly favor key aspects of U.S. regional leadership. Leadership in the region involves often costly and risky efforts to support common goods involving regional security and development. Chinese behavior shows a well-developed tendency under the rubric of the ubiquitous "win-win" formula to avoid risks, costs, or commitments to the common good unless there is adequate benefit for a narrow win-set of tangible Chinese interests.[15] A major reason for China's continued reluctance to undertake costs and commitments for the sake of the common goods of the Asia-Pacific and broader international affairs is the long array of domestic challenges and preoccupations faced by Chinese leaders.

Chinese assertiveness toward several neighbors and the United States have put nearby governments on guard and weakened Chinese regional influence. They have reminded China's neighbors that the 60-year history of the People's Republic of China (PRC) has, much more often than not, featured China acting in disruptive and domineering ways in the region.[16]

China's success in reassuring neighbors and advancing influence in the Asia-Pacific in the post-Cold War period—a period now extending almost 25 years—is mediocre. China faces major impediments, many home grown. China's long-standing practice of building an image of consistent and righteous behavior in foreign affairs blocks realistic policies, especially when dealing with disputes and differences with neighbors and the United States. Most notably, the Chinese government has the exceptional position among major powers as having never acknowledged making a mistake in foreign policy. As a result, when China encounters a dispute with neighbors, the fault never lies with China. If Beijing chooses not to blame the neighbor, its default position is to blame larger forces, usually involving the United States. Adding to this peculiar negative mix, Chinese elites and public opinion remain heavily influenced by prevailing Chinese media and other emphasis on China's historic victimization at the hands of outside powers like the United States, Japan, and others. They are quick to find offense and impervious of the need for change and recognition of fault on their part.[17]

Arguably Asia's richest country and the key ally of the United States, Japan heads the list of China's most important relationships in the Asia-Pacific. The record shows relations seriously worsened to their lowest point amid widespread Chinese violence, extra-legal trade sanctions, and intimidation well beyond accepted international norms over territorial and resources claims in the East China Sea.[18] India's interest in accommodation with China has been offset by border frictions, and competition for influence among the countries surrounding India and in Southeast Asia and Central Asia.[19] Russian and Chinese interest in close alignment has waxed and waned and has appeared to remain secondary to their respective relationships with the West.[20]

Relations with Taiwan changed for the better with the election of a new Taiwan government in 2008 bent on reassuring Beijing. The government was re-elected in 2012, but the political opposition in Taiwan

347

remained sharply critical of recent trends and improved its standing with Taiwan voters.[21]

South Korean opinion of China declined sharply from a high point in 2004, despite close Sino-South Korean economic ties. China's refusal to condemn North Korea's sinking of South Korean warship and North Korea's artillery attack on South Korea in 2010 strongly reinforced anti-China sentiment. Chinese efforts to improve ties with a new South Korean president in 2013 became sidetracked by provocations from North Korea and Chinese advances in disputed territory claimed by South Korea.[22]

South China Sea disputed claims are seriously complicating developing Chinese relations with Southeast Asian countries. China's remarkable military modernization raised suspicions on the part of a number of China's neighbors, including such middle powers as Australia.[23] They endeavored to build their own military power, and work cooperatively with one another and the United States in the face of China's military advances.

Beijing has depended heavily on the direction and support of the Chinese government to advance its influence on the post-Cold War period. Nongovernment channels of communication and influence have been limited on account of China's repeated aggression against neighbors during the Cold War. So-called overseas Chinese communities in southeast Asian countries have represented political forces supportive of their home country's good relations with China, but those same communities have a long and often negative history in southeast Asian countries.[24]

The areas of greatest Chinese strength in Asia—economic relations and diplomacy—also have shown limitations and complications.[25] As half of Chinese trade is conducted by foreign invested enterprises in China, the resulting processing trade sees China often add only a small amount to the product; and the finished product often depends on sales to the United States or the European Union. A Singapore ambassador told Chinese media in August 2013 that 60 percent of the goods that are exported from China and Association of Southeast Asian Nations (ASEAN) are ultimately manufactures that go to the United States, Europe, and Japan. Only 22 percent of these goods stay in the China-ASEAN region.[26] These facts seemed to underscore Chinese interdependence with the United States and allied countries. Meanwhile, the large amount of Asian and international investment that went to China did not go to other Asian countries, hurting their economic development. What is known shows that actual China's aid (as opposed to financing that will be repaid in money or commodities) to Asia is very small, especially in comparison to other donors, with the exception of Chinese aid to North Korea and, at least until recently, Myanmar. The sometimes dizzying array of agreements in the active Chinese diplomacy in Asia did not hide the fact that China remained reluctant to undertake significant costs, risks, or commitments in dealing with difficult regional issues.

North Korea is a special case in Chinese foreign relations. China provides considerable food aid, oil, and other material support. China is North Korea's largest trading partner and foreign investor. China often shields Pyongyang from U.S.-led efforts at the United Nations to sanction or otherwise punish North Korea over its egregious violations of international norms. Nevertheless, North Korea repeatedly rejects Chinese advice and warnings. At bottom, Chinese leaders are loath to cut off their aid or otherwise increase pressure on North Korea for fear of a backlash from the Pyong-yang regime that would undermine Chinese interest in preserving stability on the Korean peninsula.[27]

U.S. Leadership and China's Rise.

Comparing the previously mentioned Chinese strengths and limits with those of the United States listed here underlines how far China has to go despite over 2 decades of efforts to secure its position in Asia. Without a secure periphery and facing formidable American presence and influence, China almost certainly calculates that seriously confronting the United States poses grave dangers for the PRC regime.[28]

The foreign policies of the George W. Bush administration were very unpopular with regional elites and public opinion, weakening the U.S. position in the Asia-Pacific region. As the Obama administration has refocused U.S. attention positively on the region, regional concerns shifted to worry that U.S. budget difficulties and political gridlock in Washington seemed to undermine the ability of the United States to sustain support for regional responsibilities.

The following factors provide the main U.S. strengths in the Asia-Pacific region:[29]

- Governments are strong and viable in most of Asia; they make the decisions that determine direction in foreign affairs. In general, the officials see their governments' legitimacy and success resting on nation-building and economic development, which require a stable and secure international environment. Unfortunately, Asia is not particularly stable, and most regional governments privately are wary of and tend not to trust each other. As a result, they look to the United States to provide the security they need. They recognize that the U.S. security role is very expensive and involves great risk, including large scale casualties if necessary. They also recognize that neither China, nor any other Asian power or coalition of powers, is able or willing to undertake even a fraction of these risks, costs, and responsibilities.

- Support for the nation-building priority of most Asian governments involves export-oriented growth. The United States has run a massive trade deficit with China, and a total annual trade deficit with Asia valued at over $350 billion. Asian government officials recognize that China, which runs an overall trade surplus, and other trading partners of Asia are unwilling and unable to bear even a fraction of the cost of such large trade deficits, that nonetheless are very important for Asia governments.
- Effective in interaction with Asia's powers was a notable achievement of the Bush administration. The Obama administration has built on these strengths. Its emphasis on consultation and inclusion of international stakeholders before coming to policy decisions on issues of importance to Asia and the Pacific has been broadly welcomed. Meanwhile, U.S. military security and intelligence organizations have grown uniquely influential, with wide ranging webs of security and intelligence relationships.
- Reinforcing overall U.S. influence are uniquely powerful and long-standing American business, religious, educational, media, and other nongovernment interactions. Almost 50 years

351

of generally color-blind U.S. immigration policy since the ending of discriminatory U.S. restrictions on Asian immigration in 1965 has resulted in the influx of millions of Asia-Pacific migrants who call America home and who interact with their countries of origin in ways that undergird and reflect well on the American position in the region.

- The success of U.S. efforts to build webs of security-related and other relationships with Asia-Pacific countries has to do in part with active contingency planning by many Asia-Pacific governments. As power relations change in the region, notably on account of China's rise, regional governments generally seek to work positively and pragmatically with rising China on the one hand; but on the other, they seek the reassurance of close security, intelligence, and other ties with the United States amid evidence that rising China shifts to more assertiveness. The U.S. concern to keep stability while fostering economic growth overlaps constructively with the priorities of the vast majority of regional governments.

A CLOSER LOOK AT CHINA'S CURRENT CHALLENGE TO THE UNITED STATES

The Obama administration has more than 5 years of experience dealing with rising China. The experience shows that U.S. expectations of significant breakthroughs in the relations are justifiably low. The Chinese have proven to be difficult partners. Worst case thinking about U.S. intentions is married with media-propaganda campaigns establishing China's identity as resisting many aspects of American leadership. The government-sponsored outlets provide an array of information that demonizes American intentions while reinforcing Chinese self-righteousness.[30]

As Chinese capabilities grow, Beijing is likely to take actions that will further challenge the international order supported by the United States.[31] The challenges to the security and stability in the Asia-Pacific have been clear and seem primed to continue and perhaps advance. China's erosion of international economic norms is more hidden. China seems to support free trade by the United States and others in its ongoing efforts to exploit this open environment with state-directed means, widespread theft, intimidation, and coercion of companies and governments in a wholesale grasp of technology, know-how, capital, and competitive advantage in a head long drive for economic development at the expense of others.

Americans will face continuing impediments from China in dealing with nuclear proliferation by North Korea and Iran; China was of little help in dealing with Syria's use of chemical weapons or Russia's annexation of Crimea and coercion of Ukraine. Chinese leaders remain determined to support the Leninist one-party system in China that treats human rights selectively and capriciously, with eyes focused on sustaining the Communist state.

Taken together, these issues represent the focus of the China challenge for the United States in the immediate period ahead. They promise numerous headaches and problems for U.S. policymakers; American officials may grow somewhat weary in efforts to deal with various Chinese probes and machinations. However, the previously mentioned assessment shows that the China challenge is not a fundamental one, at least not yet. The United States can have some confidence that prevailing circumstances and constraints seem to preclude China seeking confrontation or power shift in Asia. Some aver that China has adopted a slow and steady pace as it seeks to spread its influence and undermine that of the United States, especially in the all important Asia-Pacific region.[32] Maybe so, but the record of Chinese advances over the past 25 years shows such mediocre results and conflicted approaches that the prospect of Chinese leadership in the Asia-Pacific region seems remote. More likely, China will continue to rise in the shadow of a United States increasingly integrated among a wide range of independent-minded Asian-Pacific governments viewing the United States as critically important to their stability, growth, and independence.

IMPLICATIONS OF THE SCENARIOS FOR U.S.-CHINESE RELATIONS

The three scenarios or "alternative futures" that provide a focus for this book rightly concentrate on Chinese military power and activity, which represents an important determinant in U.S.-Chinese relations. Of course, the U.S.-Chinese relationship has been and will continue to be influenced by several determinants on the Chinese and U.S. sides. For example, the 2012 U.S. presidential campaign showed that Chinese economic practices were no longer the positive force of the past in promoting convergence between Washington and Beijing. They topped the list of American criticisms of China—a trend likely to continue along with Beijing's continued exploitation of the international free market system in ways that disadvantage the United States.[33] Meanwhile, American ideological antipathy regarding China's Communist system reached extraordinary height in the decade after the Tiananmen crackdown — driving an enormous wedge between the United States and China that explains to a considerable degree the distrust prevailing in the current relationship over 20 years later.

Against that background, this section addresses the implications for future U.S.-Chinese relations of the three scenarios. It does so with the understanding that the military scenarios reflect elements important in determining the degree of convergence or divergence between the United States and China, but other factors not considered in these scenarios also may be important in influencing the degree of convergence and divergence in the relationship. Where appropriate, I will note such factors in the discussion.

As seen in the discussion, I find the first alternative future more clearly defined and more realistic than the other two. It provides an opportunity for some detailed forecasting. The other two scenarios are plausible. They depart greatly from the current context and are broadly defined. As such, they allow for general considerations but less detailed forecasting.

Alternative Future 1: A PLA Focused on Regional Issues.

The People's Liberation Army (PLA) buildup is an obvious challenge to the United States. As in the recent past, an effective U.S. response can help to keep tensions manageable.

This scenario seems to imply that China remains encumbered in its protracted rise in Asia. It shows no substantial change in China's overall approach to the region, including the strong self-righteousness and narrow win-win mindset seen in the recent past. As in the recent past, the U.S.-China tensions over the Obama administration's rebalancing policies and over economic, political, nonproliferation, and other differences probably will not reach the point of conflict. If Chinese and U.S. leaders remain preoccupied with other issues at home and abroad, and as expected interdependence and possibly cooperation grow between the two sides, tensions over differences can be managed effectively.

If the United States somehow has rebounded from its recent problems and resumes the kind of highly competitive activist international role seen at times after the Cold War, there is a danger of confrontation and crisis caused by greater U.S. pressure on areas of difference with China. More likely on the U.S. side is the kind of engagement policy toward both the Asia-Pacific region and China seen in the Obama administration's rebalancing policy initiatives. The reasons seem obvious and strong:

- The region is an area of ever greater strategic and economic importance for the United States;
- The United States remains strongly committed to long-standing U.S. goals of supporting stability and balance of power; sustaining smooth economic access; and promoting U.S. values in this increasingly important world area.

Future dynamics in Asia are seen as determined by five sets of factors:[34]

1. The changing power relationships among Asia's leading countries (e.g., the rise of China and India; changes in Japan; rising or reviving middle powers — South Korea, Indonesia, and Australia).

2. The growing impact of economic globalization and related international information interchange.

3. The ebb and flow of tensions in the Korean peninsula, southwestern Asia, and the broader U.S.-backed efforts against terrorism and proliferation of weapons of mass destruction.

4. The rise of Asian multilateralism.

5. The changing extent of U.S. engagement with and withdrawal from involvement with Asian matters.

In addition, a survey of leadership debates over foreign policy among Asian-Pacific leaders[35] shows movement toward perspectives of realism in international relations theory in the United States, China, Japan, Russia, India, and several middle and smaller powers including Indonesia, Australia, South Korea, Vietnam, Malaysia, and Singapore.[36] Such perspectives are important in how these leaders view the changing power dynamics and security issues seen notably in factors 1, 3, and 5. At bottom, the United States can best understand Chinese actions by using a realist perspective.

While vigilant regarding changing circumstances that could have an impact on their security, sovereignty, and other important interests, the Chinese government leaders also clearly recognize the importance of economic development, the lynchpin of their political legitimacy. Thus, they endeavor to use the liberal international economic order in ways that benefit them and their countries, and in so doing, they subscribe in various ways and to varying degrees to aspects of liberalism in international relations theory. As noted earlier, such Chinese use of liberalism is best seen as serving the realist approaches of Beijing's leaders to build Chinese wealth and power in world affairs.

Asian-Pacific leaders also show support for aspects of the international relations theory of constructivism. Such support is manifest in their ongoing efforts to build regional and international organizations and to support international norms as effective means to manage interstate tensions and differences and to promote greater interstate cooperation. Domestically, most Asian-Pacific governments also foster a strong identity for their nation as an independent actor in regional and global affairs representing the interests and qualities of the peoples of their respective countries. Supporting such an identity is an important element in their continued political legitimacy.[37] Again, the Chinese practice is to use stronger identity and involvement in international organizations in large measure to support along the lines of realist thinking regime goals of preservation and developing wealth and power.

A continuation of the type of U.S. engagement policy seen in the Obama administration's rebalancing initiatives fits well with most of these regional dynamics. The U.S. strengths look even stronger when compared with China's recent and likely future approaches.

Like China and other Asian governments, the United States also relies heavily on a realist perspective in its involvement in the Asia-Pacific. America has a proven record of bearing the costs and risks of sustaining regional stability that is essential for the development and nation-building sought by the regional government leaders. The United States takes these actions not so much because of liberal or constructivist beliefs, but rather out of a broad sense of American national interest tied to the ever more important regional order in the Asia-Pacific.

At present and for the foreseeable future, there is little perceived danger of offensive U.S. military, economic, or other policy actions amid repeated stress by American leaders against unilateral change in the status quo. By contrast, China has accompanied its rise in regional prominence with a conflicted message of closer economic cooperation on a mutually beneficial (win-win) basis and often strident Chinese threats and coercive actions backed by civilian and military government power against neighbors that disagree with China, especially on issues of sovereignty and security. The fact that China's stridency on these matters has grown with the expansion of coercive civilian and military power alarms many Asian neighbors who seek reassurance from closer relations with the United States in a variety of forms, thereby deepening and strengthening the American integration with the region.

Meanwhile, Chinese leaders continue focus on a narrow win-set of Chinese interests. They avoid the kinds of costs and risks borne by the United States in support of perceived American interests in the broader regional order that are well recognized by regional governments, reinforcing the regional governments' support for closer American involvement in regional affairs. Asian leaders watch closely for signs of U.S. military withdrawal or flagging American interest in sustaining regional stability. The Obama administration has affirmed its commitment to sustain the robust American security presence involving close military cooperation with the vast majority of Asian-Pacific governments built during the post-Cold War period. This engagement builds on the strong engagement efforts of the Bill Clinton and George W. Bush administrations, enjoys bipartisan political support in

Congress and seems likely to continue for the reasons noted earlier.

China's role as a trader, site for investment, and increasing important foreign investor will continue to grow in regional affairs. Unlike the United States, China has a great deal of money that could be used to the benefit of its neighbors. The governments engage in sometimes protracted talks with Chinese counterparts to find ways to use the money consistent with China's ubiquitous win-win formula. In general, China will part with its money only if there is assurance that it will be paid back, and the endeavor will support China's narrow win-set. China's location and advancing infrastructure connecting China to its neighbors are major positive attributes supporting closer Chinese relations with neighboring states.

Of course, much of the trade remains dependent on foreign investment and access to markets in the United States in particular. The United States almost certainly will not quickly reverse the large trade deficit that undergirds the export-oriented economies of the region. Asian leaders are watchful for signs of American protectionism, but the continued American economic recovery reinforces support for enhanced free trade initiatives from the United States.

By contrast, China's commitment to free trade remains selective and narrow. Beijing's tendency to go well beyond international norms in retaliating against others over trade and other issues has grown with the advance of China's economic size and influence. Its cyber theft of trade and economic information and property is enormous. Its currency manipulation and other neo-mercantilist practices are used deliberately to advance China's economy without much consideration of how they disadvantage neighboring economies along with the United States. China's recent extraordinary pressure on Japan for the sake of territorial claims risks enormous negative consequences for the regional economic growth. In contrast, the United States probably will see its interests best served in endeavoring to calm the tensions and play a role of stabilizer highly valued by most regional governments.

The growing U.S. security, economic, and political relationships with the wide range of Asian-Pacific governments built by the Clinton, Bush and Obama administrations have the effect of strengthening these governments and countries, reinforcing their independence and identity. While many of these governments continue to disagree with U.S. policies regarding the Middle East Peace process, electronic spying, and other issues, American interest in preserving a favorable balance of power in the region is supported by the prevalence of such stronger independent actors. By contrast, China's assertiveness shows its neighbors that Beijing expects them to accommodate a growing range of Chinese concerns, even to the point of sacrificing territory.

The range of Chinese demands probably will broaden with the growth of Chinese military, economic, and other coercive power. Strengthening those in the region that resist China's pressure is seen in Beijing as a hostile act. The recent willingness of the Obama administration to strengthen security and other ties with Japan, the Philippines, and other countries facing Chinese coercion and intimidation shows the kinds of actions that can be taken effectively by the United States to demonstrate to Beijing the significant downsides of its assertive "nibbling" of territory also claimed by China's neighbors. Overtime, effective U.S. reassurance and resolve can shape and direct Chinese assertiveness along less disruptive paths.

It is important to reiterate here that most Asian-Pacific governments probably will expect the U.S. Government to carry out its improvement of relations in the region in ways that do not seriously exacerbate China-U.S. tensions and thereby disrupt the Asia-Pacific region. The Obama administration has used the positive incentives of top-level engagement efforts with China along with the negative incentives of firm support of allies facing Chinese pressure and has a variety of other such carrots and sticks in its foreign policy tool box.

The Obama administration has also advanced markedly U.S. relations with the various regional organizations valued by Asian governments as part of their "constructivist" efforts to create norms and build institutions to ease interstate rivalries and promote cooperative relations. While U.S. orientation tends to follow more realist lines to advance American influence, the Obama administration seems sincere in pursuing interchange that is respectful of the regional bodies. These initiatives enjoy broad bipartisan support in the Congress and are likely to continue. China also depicts close alignment with these groups, though Chinese more assertive ambitions regarding disputed territories have seen Chinese leaders grossly manipulate these bodies or resort to coercion and intimidation.

Bottom Line.

This scenario suggests a continuation of trends seen in recent years in China's rise in Asia and the broader American leadership role in the Asian-Pacific region that have been examined here. I assess that those circumstances will continue to encumber China and preoccupy Chinese leaders who will remain cautious and unwilling to engage in serious military confrontation with the United States. The circumstances also are seen to support a stronger American leadership position increasingly well integrated with regional governments and organizations.

Wild Cards.

Heading the long list of variables that could disrupt the previously mentioned assessment are the actions of third parties and their impact on U.S.-Chinese relations. These include new leaders in Taiwan, Japan, India, and Southeast Asian states who may take actions that could provoke confrontation with China. In response to repeated challenges posed by leaders in Taiwan and Japan in the recent past, U.S. and Chinese maneuvers have sometimes raised tensions but have avoided confrontation. There is no guarantee that future challenges will be dealt with in this way, but the ability of the big powers to influence the lesser powers and the desire to avoid disastrous Sino-American war support a more optimistic than pessimistic outlook on these possible problems. More worrisome and uncertain is the situation in North Korea. The North Korean leaders are capable of wide swings in behavior and the underlying stability of the regime remains in doubt. The collapse of the North Korea state would pose an enormous challenge to American and Chinese policymakers seemingly well beyond the scope and intensity of past crises during the post-Cold War period.

Alternative Future 2: A Global Expeditionary PLA.

The implications of this scenario depend greatly on how and why the PLA shifted to power projection beyond China's periphery. There are a wide range of possibilities ranging from those with very positive implications for U.S.-Chinese relations to those with very negative implications for U.S.-Chinese relations.

At one end of the spectrum, the global expeditionary PLA could be the result of a peaceful and mutually agreeable understanding over Taiwan that was welcomed by such concerned powers as the United States and Japan. It could be accompanied by effective Chinese reassurance of its neighbors and the United States that their interests would remain secure. Against that background, the PLA activism could be seen as part of greater international cooperation by a confident China ready and willing to work closely with the United States and others in fostering international peace and stability. The distrust that has prevailed in Sino-American relations for so long would dissipate with ever greater U.S.-Chinese coordination on peace building and stabilization in troubled regions of the world.

At the other end of the spectrum, a globally expeditionary PLA could be the result of successful Chinese coercion and intimidation of Taiwan, and perhaps Japan and other neighbors, in the context of weakening American leadership in the Asia-Pacific. In effect, China will have used coercion, intimidation, and other manifestations of growing power to break through the encumbrances to China's sovereignty and security ambitions in the Asia-Pacific region. Against that background, the globally expeditionary PLA would signal great expansion of Chinese scope and activism as China endeavors to alter the world order in its favor after having successfully consolidated dominance in the Asia-Pacific, pushing out the United States.

The implications of this outcome for American interests in the Asia-Pacific and the world seem quite negative, but the outcome for U.S.-Chinese relations could vary. In particular, America may give way to Chinese ambitions and seek agreement with Beijing on divided world leadership that may satisfy China, perhaps for some time. There presumably will be a variety of international, economic and other areas where the United States and China could deepen cooperation. A key obstacle would be the need to overcome long-standing American prejudice against appeasement as a tool of statecraft, but the circumstances could support an appeasement of rising China. A more contentious outcome would result if the United States fell back from China's periphery but continued to resist Chinese expansion from off-shore in the Asia-Pacific and elsewhere. The success of this approach would require overcoming international skepticism of American power that failed to thwart the advance of coercive Chinese power in the Asia-Pacific.

A development to consider in any scenario of a globally engaged PLA is how such a new presence, whether the result of benign or adverse circumstances for America, will affect U.S. interests. Even under the optimistic possibility noted here, China's presence will compel a reduction of U.S. international security leadership in the face of an expeditionary PLA. Whether or not U.S. leaders will make the adjustment smoothly remains uncertain, though the optimistic possibility shows circumstances that would support pragmatic adjustment and accommodation in the face of new power realities.

Alternative Future 3: A Weakened PLA.

This scenario could arise because of pressure from the United States. It also could arise mainly because of domestic and other external factors undermining the Chinese Communist Party (CCP) regime. In both cases, it is logical to expect more U.S. interference and pressure, so long as the CCP regime persists. The continuation of the CCP regime matters greatly in future U.S.-Chinese relations. Broad American antipathy to China's authoritarian Communist system has remained strong for decades and is likely to continue to drive American policy. At the same time, it is not in American interests that regime change in China comes with major disruption to regional and global peace and prosperity. At bottom, in this scenario, continuing U.S. practices that weakened the PLA and other security bulwarks of the Communist government without causing governance collapse leading to widespread chaos seem in line with American objectives. Finding this proper balance will be difficult.

These scenarios of weakened and preoccupied Chinese Communist leaders probably mean greater American involvement in the Asia-Pacific. Chinese domestic concerns probably will open the way to expanding American engagement, while concerns of regional governments with China's uncertain future will likely prompt ever closer consultations among them and the United States.

A non-Communist China moving toward political pluralism and democracy probably will be much better treated by the United States than the current CCP regime. Such a non-Communist regime in China probably could expect strong U.S. support to deal with internal problems and less, if any, U.S. pressure.

The United States also could be expected to use its enhanced involvement in the Asia-Pacific to work closely with concerned regional powers to stabilize and support such a non-Communist Chinese government.

ENDNOTES - CHAPTER 11

1. This section summarizes findings in Robert Sutter, *U.S.-Chinese Relations*, Lanham MD: Rowman and Littlefield, 2013. For other perspectives, see, among others, David Shambaugh, ed., *Tangled Titans*, Lanham, MD: Rowman and Littlefield, 2012.

2. Don Keyser "President Obama's Re-election: Outlook for U.S. China Relations in the Second Term," Nottingham, UK: Nottingham University, China Policy Institute, November 7, 2012.

3. *Balancing Acts*, Washington, DC: Elliott School of International Affairs, 2013, p. 39, available from *www2.gwu.edu/~sigur/assets/docs/BalancingActs_Compiled1.pdf*.

4. Kenneth Lieberthal and Wang Jisi, *Addressing U.S.-China Strategic Distrust*, Washington, DC: The Brookings Institution, March 2012.

5. David Shambaugh, "The Rocky Road Ahead in U.S.-China Relations," *China-U.S. Focus*, October 23, 2012, available from *www.chinausfocus.com/print/?id=20902*.

6. This author participated in consultations in Washington, DC, involving groups of visiting Chinese specialists assessing U.S.-China relations after the U.S. elections and groups of concerned American specialists, November 8, 15, and 16, 2012.

7. *Balancing Acts*, pp. 7-10.

8. Among treatments of this subject, see Timothy Adamson "China's Response to the U.S. Rebalance," in *Balancing Acts*, pp. 39-43. See also tri-annual coverage of these issues in articles in *Comparative Connections*, available from *www.csis.org/pacfor*.

9. Aaron L. Friedberg, *Contest for Supremacy. China, America and the Struggle for Mastery in Asia*, New York: W. W. Norton and Company, 2011; Hugh White, "The China Choice" book review by Andrew Nathan, *Foreign Affairs* January-February 2013, available from *www.foreignaffairs.com/articles/138661/hugh-white/the-china-choice-why-america-should-share-power*.

10. See the treatment, among others, in Andrew J. Nathan and Andrew Scobell, *China's Search for Security*, New York: Columbia University Press, 2012. See also treatment of Chinese constraints in Sutter, *U.S.-Chinese Relations*, pp. 275-286; and Robert Sutter, "China and America: The Great Divergence?" *Orbis*, Vol. 58, No. 3, Summer 2014, pp. 1-18.

11. Stephen Roach, "China's Policy Disharmony," *Project Syndicate*, December 31, 2013, available from *www.project-syndicate.org*.

12. Robert Sutter, "China and U.S. Security and Economic Interests: Opportunities and Challenges," Robert Ross and Oystein Tunsjo, eds., *U.S.-China-EU Relations: Managing The New World Order*, London, UK: Routledge, 2010, pp. 143-163; James Shinn, *Weaving the Net*, New York, Council on Foreign Relations, 1996.

13. Phillip Saunders, *China's Global Activism: Strategy, Drivers, and Tools*, Institute for National Strategic Studies Occasional Paper, Washington, DC: National Defense University Press, June 4, 2006, pp. 8–9.

14. This section summarizes findings in Robert Sutter, *Foreign Relations of the PRC*, Lanham, MD: Rowman and Littlefield, 2013, pp. 1-26, 311-327.

15. *Ibid.*, p. 315.

16. John Garver, *Foreign Relations of the People's Republic of China*, Englewood Cliff, NJ: Prentice Hall, 1993.

17. Gilbert Rozman, *East Asian National Identities: Common Roots and Chinese Exceptionalism*, Stanford, CA: Stanford University Press, 2013.

18. James Przystup, "Japan-China Relations," *Comparative Connections*, Vol. 14, No. 3, January 2013, pp. 109-117.

19. Lawrence Saez and Crystal Chang, "China and South Asia: Strategic Implications and Economic Imperatives," Lowell Dittmer and George Yu. eds., *China, The Developing World, and the New Global Dynamic*, Boulder CO: Lynne Rienner, 2010, pp. 83-108; John Garver and Fei-ling Wang, "China's Anti-Encirclement Struggle," *Asian Security*, Vol. 6, No. 3, 2010, pp. 238-263; Satu Limaye, "India-US Relations," *Comparative Connections*, Vol. 15, No. 3, January 2014, pp 137-143.

20. Yu Bin, "China-Russia Relations: Guns and Games of August: Tales of Two Strategic Partners," *Comparative Connections*, Vol. 10, No. 3, October 2008, pp. 131–38; Yu Bin, "China-Russia Relations," *Comparative Connections*, Vol. 15, No. 3, January 2014, pp. 121–133.

21. Richard Bush, *Unchartered Strait*, Washington, DC: The Brookings Institution, 2013.

22. Scott Snyder, "China-Korea Relations," *Comparative Connections*, Vol. 15, No. 3, January 2014, pp. 87-94.

23. Linda Jacobson, "Australia-China Ties: In Search of Political Trust," *Policy Brief*, Lowy Institute, June 2012.

24. Sutter, *Foreign Relations of the PRC*, p. 319.

25. Yu Yongding, "A Different Road Forward," *China Daily*, December 23, 2010, p. 9.

26. Pu Zhendong, "Singapore Supports Strengthened Free-Trade Agreement with Beijing," *China Daily*, August 30, 2013, available from *usa.chinadaily.com.cn/epaper/2013-08/30/content_16932418.htm*.

27. Jonathan Pollack, "Why Does China Coddle North Korea? *The New York Times*, January 12, 2014, available from *www.nytimes. org*; Scott Snyder, "China's Post-Kim Jong Il Debate," *Comparative Connections*, Vol. 14, No. 1, 2012, pp. 107-114.

28. Robert Sutter, "Assessing China's Rise and U.S. Influence in Asia—Growing Maturity and Balance," *Journal of Contemporary China*, Vol. 19, No. 65, June 2010, pp. 591-604.

29. Author's findings based on interviews with more than 200 officials from 10 Asian-Pacific countries discussed most recently in Sutter, *Foreign Relations of the PRC*, pp. 321-326.

30. Gilbert Rozman, "Chinese National Identity and Foreign Policy," Gilbert Rozman, ed., *China's Foreign Policy*, Seoul, South Korea: The Asan Institute for Policy Studies, 2012, pp. 151-182.

31. For a review of the issues and disputes, see Susan Lawrence, *U.S.-China Relations: An Overview of Policy Issues*, Report R41108, Washington, DC: Congressional Research Service of the Library of Congress, August 1, 2013.

32. Friedberg, *Contest for Supremacy*.

33. Richard Wike, "Americans and Chinese Grow More Wary of Each Other," Washington, DC: Pew Research Center, June 13, 2013, available from *www.pewresearch.org/fact-tank/2013/06/05/americans-and-chinese-grow-more-wary-of-each-other/*.

34. Robert Sutter, *The United States in Asia*, Lanham, MD: Rowman and Littlefield, 2009, pp. 154-166; Suisheng Zhao, "Shaping the Regional Context of China's Rise: How the Obama Administration Brought Back Hedge in its Engagement with China," *Journal of Contemporary China*, Vol. 21, No. 75, May 2012, pp. 369-390; Robert Sutter, "Rebalancing, China and Asian Dynamics—Obama's Good Fit," *Pacnet #1*, Washington, DC: Center for Strategic and International Studies, January 5, 2014, available from *www.csis.org/pacfor*.

35. Henry Nau and Deepa Ollapally, *World Views of Aspiring Powers*, New York: Oxford, 2012.

36. Author interviews in *Foreign Relations of the PRC*.

37. Rozman, *East Asian National Identities*.

ABOUT THE CONTRIBUTORS

RICHARD A. BITZINGER is senior fellow and coordinator of the Military Transformations Program at the S. Rajaratnam School of International Studies. His work focuses on security and defense issues relating to the Asia-Pacific region, including military modernization and force transformation, regional defense industries and local armaments production, and weapons proliferation. Mr. Bitzinger was previously an Associate Professor with the Asia-Pacific Center for Security Studies (APCSS), Honolulu, HI, and has also worked for the RAND Corporation, the Center for Strategic and Budgetary Affairs, and the U.S. Government. In 1999-2000, he was a senior fellow with the Atlantic Council of the United States. Mr. Bitzinger has written several monographs and book chapters, and his articles have appeared in such journals as *International Security*, *The Journal of Strategic Studies*, *Orbits*, *China Quarterly*, and *Survival*. He is the author of *Towards a Brave New Arms Industry?* (Oxford University Press, 2003), "Come the Revolution: Transforming the Asia-Pacific's Militaries," *Naval War College Review* (Fall 2005), and "Military Modernization in the Asia-Pacific: Assessing New Capabilities," *Asia's Rising Power* (National Bureau of Asian Research, 2010). He is also the editor of *The Modern Defense Industry: Political, Economic and Technological Issues* (Praeger, 2009). Mr. Bitzinger holds a master's degree from the Monterey Institute of International Affairs and has pursued additional postgraduate studies at the University of California, Los Angeles, CA.

BERNARD D. COLE is Professor of Maritime Strategy at the National War College, Washington, DC. He served 30 years in the U.S. Navy, retiring as a Captain; commanded USS *Rathburne* (FF1057) and Destroyer Squadron 35; served with the Third Marine Division in Vietnam from 1967 to 1968. He is the author of many articles, book chapters, and seven books, the most recent of which is *Asian Maritime Strategies: Navigating Troubled Waters*, published in 2013. Dr. Cole holds an A.B. in history from the University of North Carolina, an M.A. in national security affairs from the University of Washington, and a Ph.D. in history from Auburn University.

JOSEPH FEWSMITH is Professor of International Relations and Political Science at Boston University's Pardee School for Global Studies. He is an associate of the John King Fairbank Center for East Asian Studies at Harvard University and the Pardee Center for the Study of the Longer Range Future at Boston University. Dr. Fewsmith is the author or editor of seven books, including, most recently *The Logic and Limits of Political Reform in China* (Cambridge University Press, January 2013). Other works include *China since Tiananmen* (2nd Ed., 2008) and *China Today, China Tomorrow* (2010). Other books include *Elite Politics in Contemporary China* (Armonk, NY: M. E. Sharpe, 2001), *The Dilemmas of Reform in China: Political Conflict and Economic Debate* (Armonk, NY: M. E. Sharpe, 1994), and *Party, State, and Local Elites in Republican China: Merchant Organizations and Politics in Shanghai, 1890-1930* (Honolulu, HI: University of Hawaii Press, 1985). His articles have appeared in such journals as *Asian Survey*, *Comparative Studies in Society and History*, *The China Journal*, *The China Quarterly*, *Current History*, *The Journal of Contemporary China*, *Problems of Communism*, and *Modern China*.

DANIEL GEARIN is a China military capabilities analyst with the Department of Defense (DoD). Prior to joining DoD, he completed internships with the Center for a New American Security, National Defense University, the U.S.-China Economic and Security Commission, and the Brookings Institution. Mr. Gearin holds a bachelor's degree from Northeastern University in international affairs with a focus on China and a master's degree from George Washington University.

ERIC HEGINBOTHAM is a senior political scientist at the RAND Corporation specializing in East Asian security issues. At RAND, he has led projects examining Chinese nuclear strategy, Chinese and U.S. Military capabilities, and regional dynamics in Northeast and Southeast Asia. Before coming to RAND in 2005, he was a senior fellow of Asia studies at the Council on Foreign Relations. He taught as a visiting faculty member of Boston College's Political Science Department and served for 16 years in the U.S. Army Reserves and National Guard. Dr. Heginbotham has co-authored or edited several books, including *Chinese and Indian Strategic Behavior: Growing Power and Alarm* (2012), and has published articles on Japanese and Chinese foreign policy and strategic issues in *Foreign Affairs, International Security, The Washington Quarterly, Current History*, and *The National Interest*. Dr. Heginbotham holds a B.A. from Swarthmore College and a Ph.D. from the Massachusetts Institute of Technology.

JACOB HEIM is an associate policy analyst with the RAND Corporation, specializing in strategic assessment and defense analysis with a background in international relations and mathematics. His research areas include the military balance in the Western Pacific, U.S. overseas force posture, and the challenge posed by anti-access/area-denial capabilities. Previously, he was a senior operations research analyst with the MITRE Corporation. Mr. Heim holds an M.A. with honors from the Johns Hopkins University School of Advanced International Studies and a B.A. with distinction in mathematics from Amherst College.

LONNIE D. HENLEY is an employee of the Defense Intelligence Agency (DIA) on detail to the Office of the Director of National Intelligence. As National Intelligence Collection Officer for East Asia, he develops integrated intelligence collection strategies on high-priority East Asian issues across the United States Intelligence Community. Mr. Henley has been a China specialist for over 35 years, beginning with 22 years as a China foreign area officer and military intelligence officer in Korea, at the DIA, on Army Staff, and in the History Department at West Point, NY. Upon retiring from the U.S. Army, he joined the senior civil service as Defense Intelligence Officer for East Asia and then Senior Intelligence Expert for Strategic Warning at DIA. After leaving DIA in 2004, he worked 2 years as a senior analyst with CENTRA Technology, Inc., then returned to government service as Deputy National Intelligence Officer for East Asia in the Office of the Director of National Intelligence. He rejoined DIA in 2008, serving for 6 years as the agency's senior China analyst, overseeing intelligence assessments on Chinese military and strategic issues across DoD. In addition to his government duties, Mr. Henley is an adjunct professor in the Security Policy Studies Program at The George Washington University. Mr. Henley holds a bachelor's degree in engineering and Chinese from the U.S. Military Academy at West Point, and Masters' degrees in Chinese language from Oxford University, which he attended as a Rhodes Scholar; in Chinese history from Columbia University; and in strategic intelligence from the National Defense Intelligence College (now National Intelligence University).

R. LINCOLN HINES was a Bridge Award Fellow with the Political and Security Affairs Group at the National Bureau of Asian Research from 2013 to 2014. Prior to this position, he was a David L Boren National Security Fellow studying in Beijing, China. Mr. Hines earned his BA in foreign affairs and East Asian studies from the University of Virginia, and his M.A. in international affairs from the American University School of International Service. He will begin his Ph.D. in government at Cornell University in the fall of 2015.

ROY KAMPHAUSEN is a senior advisor at The National Bureau of Asian Research (NBR), an adjunct associate professor at Columbia University's School of International and Public Affairs, and a senior advisor to the University of Connecticut, Office of Global Affairs. Previously, he was senior vice president for Political and Security Affairs and Director of NBR's Washington, DC, office. Prior to joining NBR, Mr. Kamphausen served as a U.S. Army officer, a career that culminated in an assignment in the Office of the Secretary of Defense as Country Director for China-Taiwan-Mongolia Affairs. Previous assignments include the Joint Staff as an intelligence analyst and later as China Branch Chief in the Directorate for Strategic Plans and Policy (J5). A fluent Chinese (Mandarin) linguist and an Army China Foreign Area Officer, Mr.

Kamphausen served 2 tours at the Defense Attaché Office of the U.S. Embassy in the People's Republic of China. He is a member of the National Committee on U.S.-China Relations, the Asia Society, and the Council for Security and Cooperation in the Asia-Pacific. His areas of professional expertise include China's People's Liberation Army (PLA), U.S.-China defense relations, U.S. defense and security policy toward Asia, and East Asian security issues. Mr. Kamphausen has co-authored the last eight volumes from the Carlisle PLA Conference. Mr. Kamphausen holds a B.A. in political science from Wheaton College and an M.A. in international affairs from Columbia University.

DAVID LAI is Research Professor of Asian Security Affairs at the Strategic Studies Institute of the U.S. Army War College. Prior to this position, he was on the faculty of the U.S. Air War College in Montgomery, AL. Dr Lai's research and teaching cover U.S.-China and U.S.-Asian relations and Chinese strategic thinking and military operational art.

ORIANA SKYLAR MASTRO is an assistant professor of security studies at the Edmund A. Walsh School of Foreign Service at Georgetown University where her research focuses on Chinese military and security policy, Asia-Pacific security issues, war termination, and coercive diplomacy. She is also an officer in the U.S. Air Force Reserve, for which she works as a reserve air attaché for the Asia-Pacific region. Previously, Dr. Mastro was a fellow in the Asia-Pacific Security program at the Center for a New American Security (CNAS), a University of Virginia Miller Center National Fellow and a Center for Strategic and International Studies (CSIS) Pacific Forum Sasakawa Peace Fellow. Additionally, she has worked on China policy issues at the Carnegie Endowment for International Peace, RAND Corporation, U.S. Pacific Command, and Project 2049. Dr. Mastro holds a B.A. in East Asian studies from Stanford University and an M.A. and Ph.D. in politics from Princeton University.

MICHAEL MCDEVITT, Rear Admiral, U.S. Navy Ret., is a senior fellow associated with CNA Strategic Studies, a division of CNA, and a not-for-profit federally-funded research center in Washington, DC. During his Navy career, Rear Admiral McDevitt held four at-sea commands, including an aircraft carrier battle group. He was a CNO Strategic Studies Group Fellow and the Director of the East Asia Policy Office for the Secretary of Defense during the George H. W. Bush Administration. He also served for 2 years as the Director for Strategy, War Plans, and Policy (J-5) for the U.S. Pacific Command (USPACOM). Rear Admiral McDevitt concluded his 34-year active duty career as the Commandant of the National War College in Washington, DC. He is a graduate of the National War College and holds a B.A. in U.S. history from the University of Southern California and a master's degree in American diplomatic history from Georgetown University.

MICHAEL RASKA is a research fellow in the Military Transformations Program at the S. Rajaratnam School of International Studies, Nanyang Technological University in Singapore. His research interests focus on military innovation and force modernization trajectories in East Asia. Dr. Raska is the author of *Military Innovation in Small States — Creating a Reverse Asymmetry* (Routledge, 2015), and co-editor of *Security, Strategy* and Military Change in the 21st Century: Cross-Regional Perspectives (Routledge, 2015). He holds a Ph.D. from Lee Kuan Yew School of Public Policy at the National University of Singapore.

ERIN RICHTER is a senior intelligence analyst for the Defense Intelligence Agency where she has specialized in Chinese military capabilities and civil-military interdependencies for the last 10 years. She has served for the last 17 years in the U.S. Marine Corps as a logistics and intelligence officer, completing reserve and active duty assignments in Japan, the Middle East, Balkans, and within the continental United States. Ms. Richter is a graduate of the Marine Corps Command and Staff College and holds a B.A. in anthropology from the University of Maryland and an M.A. in international affairs from American University.

PHILLIP C. SAUNDERS is Director of the Center for the Study of Chinese Military Affairs and a Distinguished Research Fellow at the Center for Strategic Research, both part of National Defense University's Institute for National Strategic Studies. He previously worked at the Monterey Institute of International Studies as Director of the East Asia Nonproliferation Program from 1999 to 2003, and served as an officer in the U.S. Air Force from 1989 to 1994. Dr. Saunders is co-author of The Paradox of Power: Sino-American Strategic Restraint in an Era of Vulnerability (National Defense University Press, 2011) and co-editor of books on PLA influence on Chinese national security decisionmaking, China-Taiwan relations, the Chinese navy, and the Chinese air force. Dr. Saunders attended Harvard College and holds an M.P.A. and Ph.D. in international relations from the Woodrow Wilson School at Princeton University.

ROBERT SUTTER is Professor of Practice of International Affairs at the Elliott School of International Affairs (ESIA), George Washington University. He also directs the ESIA program of Bachelor of Arts in International Affairs, involving more than 1,000 students. He taught full-time at Georgetown University (2001-2011) and part-time for 30 years at Georgetown, George Washington, Johns Hopkins Universities, or the University of Virginia. Dr. Sutter's government career (1968-2001) involved work on Asian and Pacific affairs and U.S. foreign policy. He was the Senior Specialist and Director of the Foreign Affairs and National Defense Division of the Congressional Research Service. He also served as the National Intelligence Officer for East Asia and the Pacific at the U.S. Government's National Intelligence Council, the China Division Director at the Department of State's Bureau of Intelligence and Research, and a professional staff member of the Senate Foreign Relations Committee. In 2013, Dr. Sutter published his 20th book, *Foreign Relations of the PRC: The Legacies and Constraints of China's International Politics since 1949* (Rowman and Littlefield), and the 2nd edition of *U.S.-Chinese Relations: Perilous Past, Pragmatic Present* (Rowman and Littlefield).The 3rd edition of his award-winning survey, *Chinese Foreign Relations: Power and Policy since the Cold War* (Rowman and Littlefield), was published in 2012. Dr. Sutter holds a Ph.D. in history and East Asian languages from Harvard University.